Microeconomic Studies

Edited by W. Güth, J. McMillan and H.-W. Sinn

Microeconomic Studies

J.-M. von der Schulenburg (Ed.), Essays in Social Security Economics.
XII, 222 pages. 1986.

B. Gutting, Taxation, Housing Markets, and the Markets for Building Land.
VIII, 138 pages. 1987.

H. Verbon, The Evolution of Public Pension Schemes.
XII, 287 pages. 1988.

M. Funke (Ed.), Factors in Business Investment.
VIII, 263 pages. 1989.

K. F. Zimmermann (Ed.), Economic Theory of Optimal Population.
X, 182 pages. 1989.

R. Pethig (Ed.), Conflicts and Cooperation in Managing Environmental Resources.
XII, 338 pages. 1992.

S. Homburg, Efficient Economic Growth.
VIII, 106 pages. 1992.

Notburga Ott

Intrafamily Bargaining and Household Decisions

With 18 Figures

Springer-Verlag
Berlin Heidelberg New York
London Paris Tokyo
Hong Kong Barcelona
Budapest

Dr. Notburga Ott
Johann Wolfgang Goethe-Universität
Fachbereich Wirtschaftswissenschaften
Senckenberganlage 31
D-6000 Frankfurt 11, FRG

HB
820
.O88
1992

ISBN 3-540-55061-5 Springer-Verlag Berlin Heidelberg New York Tokyo
ISBN 0-387-55061-5 Springer-Verlag New York Berlin Heidelberg Tokyo

This work is subject to copyright. All rights are reserved, whether the whole or part of the material is concerned, specifically the rights of translation, reprinting, reuse of illustrations, recitation, broadcasting, reproduction on microfilms or in other ways, and storage in data banks. Duplication of this publication or parts thereof is only permitted under the provisions of the German Copyright Law of September 9, 1965, in its version of June 24, 1985, and a copyright fee must always be paid. Violations fall under the prosecution act of the German Copyright Law.

© Springer-Verlag Berlin · Heidelberg 1992
Printed in the United States of American

The use of registered names, trademarks, etc. in this publication does not imply, even in the absence of a specific statement, that such names are exempt from the relevant protective laws and regulations and therefore free for general use.

2142/7130-543210 - Printed on acid-free paper

Preface

Recent demographic changes and the developments in female labor force participation in industrialized countries have induced a wide scientific research on family behavior. In this discussion the economic approach fascinates by the prospect of giving some type of structure for the complex decision making process of households and families based on formal models. Nevertheless, it is to a certain extent unsatisfactory because some of its results are far from daily experience, especially from those of women. The high poverty risk for women after the end of a marriage, characterized by the phrase of a 'feminization of poverty', indicates asymmetries within marriages or asymmetrical effects of family decisions for the spouses. Those asymmetries cannot be explained by the microeconomic models of the family, since they proceed from a joint household utility function.

Developing a model that can describe just this type of intrafamily asymmetries was the intention of this study. Inspired by the work of Manser & Brown and McElroy & Horney, family decisions are modelled as the result of intrafamily negotiations. Of the assumptions made in the models of the 'new home economics', only the joint household utility function is abandoned in favor of supposing two utility maximizing individuals who find their compromise depending on their individual bargaining power. All other assumptions (budget restrictions, human capital accumulation) are preserved. This, of course, permits a direct comparison of the models.

In the model, any two rational individuals are assumed. They, however, are not necessarily a couple, even though they may have identical characteristics. Nevertheless, the notation in this book with the indices m and f suggests an analogy to male and female behavior, respectively. This is intended in order to sketch the political relevance of the findings. Without regress to cultural or biological differences - which are not denied in general - observed typical 'male' and 'female' behavior can be described as a rational reaction to different environmental factors. Analyses of this type are important for efficient policy.

This book is the revised and translated version of my dissertation thesis which was accepted in December 1989 by the Department of Economics at the University of Bielefeld. I am greatly indebted to my academic advisor Prof. Dr. Heinz P. Galler for many helpful discussions during the whole time of research. His criticism and encouragement were an essential support to my work. I am also grateful to Prof. Dr. G. Schwödiauer, my second advisor, and Prof. Dr. W. Güth for their important and fruitful suggestions. Many thanks go also to all other colleagues who gave me valuable comments. Last but not least, I would like to thank M.A. Randal Sivertson, Dipl. Volksw. Evelyn Riera and stud. rer. pol Andy Steiman for their help in translating and preparing the English version of the study. All remaining errors are, of course, my responsibility.

Contents

1	**Introduction**	**1**
2	**Models of the 'new home economics'**	**6**
2.1	Decisions in an existing family	7
2.1.1	Labor supply models	8
2.1.2	Simple time allocation models	9
2.1.3	Extensions of time allocation models	10
2.1.4	Models of fertility	12
2.1.5	Empirical evidence	13
2.1.6	Remarks on household utility function	14
2.2	Family formation and marital stability	15
2.2.1	Marriage models	15
2.2.2	Models of marriage stability	15
2.2.3	Empirical evidence	16
2.3	Problems and further questions	17
3	**Family decisions as a bargaining problem**	**19**
3.1	The family as an organization of exchange	19
3.2	Household decisions as a non-cooperative game	22
3.3	Household decisions as a cooperative game	27
4	**A Nash bargaining model for household decisions**	**33**
4.1	Comparison with traditional approaches	35
4.2	Comparative statics	40
5	**Time allocation in a static bargaining model with household production**	**46**
5.1	The model	47
5.2	Division of work within the household	53
5.2.1.	The case of a joint net-income function	53
5.2.2	The case of individual net-income functions	55
5.3	Effects of an exogenous change in wages	56
5.3.1	Effects when the conflict point is held constant	57
5.3.2	The bargaining effect	63
5.3.3	The total effect	64
6	**A dynamic model with accumulation of human capital**	**68**
6.1	Intrafamily division of work and accumulation of human capital	69
6.2	The dynamic approach	72
6.2.1	Game with binding long-term contracts	74
6.2.2	Game without binding long-term contracts	75
6.2.3	The two-period model	77
6.3	Time allocation depending on individual bargaining power	80
6.3.1	Labor supply	82
6.3.2	Intrafamily division of work	96

7	**Pareto efficiency of family decisions**	**98**
7.1	Binding force of contracts and efficiency	98
7.2	Discrete choices	103
7.3	Fertility as a prisoner's dilemma	105
8	**The binding force of intrafamily contracts**	**110**
8.1	Self-enforcing contracts	111
8.1.1	Threat by future non-cooperative behavior	113
8.1.2	Reputation	115
8.1.3	Loyalty	117
8.2	Enforcement by institutions	120
8.2.1	The formal marriage contract	120
8.2.2	Divorce law	121
8.2.3	Social norms	123
8.3	Remarks on policy options	125
9	**Introducing uncertainty: the possibility of conflict**	**127**
9.1	Exogenous probability of conflict	128
9.2	Causes of conflict and negotiation strategies	131
9.3	Endogenous probability of conflict	137
9.3.1	Conflict probability and wage changes	138
9.3.2	Time allocation and conflict probability	141
10	**Empirical tests of the bargaining approach**	**144**
10.1	Tests based on the Slutsky restrictions	144
10.1.1	Derivation of testable hypotheses	145
10.1.2	Empirical results of Manser/Brown and Horney/McElroy	147
10.1.3	Some critical remarks	149
10.2	Test of Pareto efficiency	157
10.2.1	The parametric approach	157
10.2.2	The non-parametric approach	159
11	**Survey of empirical bargaining models**	**161**
11.1	Household labor supply: a model with fixed bargaining power	161
11.2	Household labor supply: a game theoretic model in a discrete choice setting	165
11.3	The distribution of welfare in the household: measuring the bargaining power	170
11.4	Marriage and divorce: estimates with explicit threat point	173
12	**Empirical evidence of the bargaining approach - first findings with German data**	**177**
12.1	Balance of power within marriages	177
12.2	Fertility decision	182
12.3	Divorce behavior	191
13	**Concluding remarks**	**196**
Appendix		199
Bibliography		227
Index		238

1 Introduction

Demographic changes and an increasing female labor force participation have been observed in nearly all industrialized countries in the last decades. Therefore, female employment behavior as well as family decisions have received an increasing attention in economic research. Today, analyses of female labor supply belong to the standard inquires made in economics. However, this research has been dominated by partial, static approaches which provide only a monocausal explanation of the observed behavior. Characteristics of the family are used in explaining female labor supply, but mostly they are treated as given for the actual decision. But, at least some of these characteristics, such as family composition, depend on prior family decisions and therefore are endogenous variables. In this sense, traditional economic household models are of a partial nature and neglect important aspects of the problem.

Interdependencies among family decisions have been emphasized by the 'new home economics' since the mid 60's. The traditional view of the household as the place for consumption and as the decision unit for factor supply was abandoned in favor of considering the household as the production place of the basic commodities. Today, female labor supply is no longer seen as an isolated decision, but as result of an optimal time allocation within the household utilizing comparative advantages in production of all family members. In this context fertility decisions are also analyzed. Based on these approaches the increased female labor force participations as well as the decline in the birthrates are explained by increased female wages, from which higher opportunity costs for household production and especially for child caring result.

Empirical research appears to confirm this relationship. Nevertheless, there are some empirical phenomena which cannot be explained by the 'new home economics'. For example, there is no consistent theoretical approach to explain the relationship between female labor force participation and divorce rates. Why both female labor force participation and birth rates are higher in some countries than in others, also has remained unexplained.

Usually, in the 'new home economics' models concerning time allocation or fertility operate with a household utility function which describes the joint interests of all household members. An intrafamily consensus is assumed, and the internal structure of the household is neglected. Such an approach is not unproblematical. The increase of divorce rates shows the relevance of intrafamily conflicts. Both, the formation as well as the dissolution of a partnership usually require decisions of the individuals involved. Therefore, since family decisions always contain the possibility of conflict, it should be assumed that in an existing family decisions are also based on individual interests.

Game theoretic bargaining models provide an appropriate way to consider interactions within the family in a formal model of household decisions. In these models a bargaining process for finding the internal compromise is assumed and the final outcome is determined depending on the rules of the game. Using such an approach, in the following household decisions are modelled as the result of an intrafamily bargaining process.

Treating the family as an economic organization, household behavior is explained by cooperation of utility maximizing individuals. If the individual bargaining power of the family members depends on the environmental factors in a different way, we should expect solutions different from those of traditional models. Especially this is true if the individual bargaining power is affected by the household decisions themselves. Then, individual behavior gain a strategic aspect.

Such a bargaining model should explain past developments better than traditional economic approaches. For this reason, the empirical evidence of the bargaining model and the possibilities of its practical use in empirical research also are investigated.

The book is organized as follows. First, in *chapter 2*, the models of the 'new home economics' are briefly discussed in order to point out their deficiencies in explaining family behavior. In *chapter 3*, the family is described as a community of individuals who can gain extra profits by pooling resources and by division of work in conjunction with intrafamily trade. Treating the family as such an organization of exchange, several approaches - non-cooperative as well as cooperative models - are discussed in view of their appropriateness to describe household behavior. Especially the impact of the alternatives to living in the family on the outcome of the bargaining process are discussed. It is concluded that axiomatic cooperative solution concepts appear as suitable instruments to model family decisions, if the main interest is in studying reactions of the bargaining outcome on changes in the environment.

In *chapter 4* the cooperative Nash solution is introduced for modelling household behavior as a two-person game. The comparison with the traditional approach shows that the model with a household utility function can be seen as a special case of the bargaining model - one with fixed bargaining power of the individuals. On the other hand, changing bargaining positions due to changes in the environment can be interpreted in the context of the traditional approach as changes in the preferences of the household and therefore as exogenous. In the bargaining model such changes can be analyzed as a systematic change in the preference order of the household, whereas the individual preferences remain constant.

The properties of a static household bargaining model with household production are examined in *chapter 5*. The conditions for the cooperative equilibrium as well as the comparative statics effects of wage changes are derived. The results regarding the optimal time allocation correspond to that of the traditional model: given different productivities of the family members, maximum specialization is optimal. On the other hand, wage rate changes affect the optimal time allocation not only as decribed by the known income and substitution effects but also through their influence on the external alternatives of the spouses which lead to an internal reallocation of the welfare distribution.

In *chapter 6* the model is extended to a dynamic approach. Intertemporal dependencies of household decisions are analyzed in a two-period model. In particular, the effects of intrafamily specialization are investigated. Because different activities - work at home or in the market - affect due to the accumulation of human capital the future wages in different ways, the future bargaining power and in turn the future welfare distribution depend on the time allocation in the first period. From the perspective of a utility maximizing individual the decision may then achieve a strategic character.

This problem is discussed for two extreme cases. If binding long-term contracts can be made, the spouses will agree at the beginning on maximum specialization and on a fixed welfare distribution for the whole future. Then, a later change in bargaining positions is irrelevant. But, if contracts are not binding for the whole future, individuals who take long-term effects into account will not accept decisions which deteriorate their future bargaining power. This has effects on the time allocation in the household. Because market work improves the external alternatives and therefore the intrafamily bargaining power there is an incentive to increase market time. In comparison to traditional approaches a lower reservation wage for the spouse specialized in household work results. Also a maximum specialization may not always result in the household optimum.

In such a solution, as shown in *chapter 7*, the allocation of household resources may be Pareto inferior because not all possible welfare gains are realized. In particular, this may be true for discrete choices like the decision on fertility. If the decision for a child is linked with a great change in the bargaining positions due to an interruption of the working life, a situation like a prisoner's dilemma may result. Without the possibility of making binding long-term contracts, no cooperative, Pareto efficient solution can be expected.

Regarding the great importance of long-term contracts for family behavior, in *chapter 8* the binding force of intrafamily contracts is investigated. Both, endogenous enforcement mechanisms - like the interest in continuing the partnership or reputation - as well as enforcement by a third party - by law or through social norms - appear insufficient for enforcing very asymmetrical contracts.

In *chapter 9*, the model is extended by introducing uncertainty, which allows an endogenous modelling of intrafamily conflicts. Considering the conflict payments as random variables, the probability for a dissolution can be derived in dependence of the specific bargaining situation. This probability for a conflict increases with decreasing marriage gains and, in turn, the external alternatives gain in importance for the cooperative solution.

The *last three chapters 10, 11 and 12* deal with the empirical relevance of the bargaining approach. First, the tests based on the Slutsky decomposition proposed by Manser/Brown and McElroy/Horney and the tests of Pareto efficiency of Chiappori are discussed in respect to their appropriateness to discriminate empirically between the bargaining approach and the traditional model. After that, a short survey of empirical bargaining models is presented. Finally, three estimates with German data are presented: a model for the intrafamily balance of power, a fertility model and a divorce model. The main problem in testing the bargaining model results from the fact that most variables which influence the bargaining power also affect the welfare production of the joint household. Variables which influence only the conflict point are in most cases not available. Although, a strong statistical test of the bargaining model against the traditional one is still outstanding, the empirical results of the estimates support the bargaining approach.

2 Models of the 'new home economics'

Microeconomic household theory traditionally deals with questions of labor supply and consumer behavior. No distinction is made between an individual or a household of several members. New concepts in the mid 60's however, such as the formalization of the human capital concept (e.g. Schultz 1959, Becker 1964), the consideration of consumption technology (e.g. Lancaster 1966, Muth 1966) and of time costs (e.g. Becker 1965) have led to a new approach on household behavior: the analysis of optimal time allocation was extended to include household production. Earlier theories have considered the 'household' as synonymous with the 'individual'. But in the meantime, the question of different time allocation patterns of individual household members - especially female labor supply - moved into focus (see Killingsworth/Heckman 1986). In most cases however, the household is still considered as a unique decision unit, and interactions between household members are neglected. This approach is often vindicated by the argumentation of Samuelson (1956) who discusses the existence of a family utility function.

With the development of the 'new home economics', economists now pay more attention to family decisions that go beyond traditional economic questions. Instead of being treated as a black box, the household is increasingly regarded as the production place of basic commodities, and interaction between family members has become an object of analysis. Modern microeconomic theory of the family is based particularly on the work of Gary S. Becker, who prominently applies microeconomic thought in explaining human behavior in general (Becker 1976). Assuming utility maximizing individuals, Becker models family decisions like marriage, divorce or fertility behavior. This approach was taken up and further developed by various authors.

As the large amount of new publications demonstrates, the approach of the 'new home economics' is applicable to nearly all household decisions. The household is regarded as a 'small factory' (Becker 1965, p. 496) in which the basic commodities are produced for the household members using market goods and time as inputs. "These commodities cannot be purchased in the marketplace but are produced as well as consumed by households using market purchases, own time, and various environmental inputs. These commodities include children, prestige and esteem, health, altruism, envy, and are much smaller in number than goods consumed" (Becker 1981, p. 7 f.). Such a notion of household production, introduced into microeconomic household models, allows for an explanation of household behavior as simultaneous decisions concerning consumption, labor supply and other household activities. Despite this homogeneous point of view of the household, a range of different explanatory approaches exist that do not form a closed theoretical framework on household decisions. Depending on the object at issue, different assumptions are encountered as to the impact and importance of interests of each family member.

2.1 Decisions in an existing family

Traditional models of time allocation suppose a joint utility function for the household as a unit. The income of all family members is pooled and all produced goods are used jointly or distributed 'fairly' within the family. According to Becker (1981) this distribution corresponds to the utility function of an altruistic head of the family, or is determined by the search in the marriage market (see Becker 1973). Other authors suppose a consensus in the family, from which a common household utility function is derived (e.g. Samuelson 1956).

These assumptions are fundamental for traditional models of labor supply and time allocation. Given that all income is pooled and all commodities are jointly consumed or fairly divided, a household utility function will be maximized. The various approaches differ only in the assumptions concerning the different ways of using time.

2.1.1 Labor supply models

In the models of labor supply[1] the total amount of time available is divided into work in the market[2] and leisure time. Leisure is treated as a consumption good. The time used in household production is either not considered at all or a fixed portion of total time is assumed for work at home. Household decisions concerning labor supply and consumption are viewed as the result of the maximization of the household utility function U subject to budget and time constraints:

$$\max_{L^i, M^i} U(X, L^m, L^f) \qquad (2.1)$$

$$\text{s. t.} \quad T = L^i + M^i \qquad i = m, f \qquad (2.2)$$

$$pX = w^m M^m + w^f M^f + I \qquad (2.3)$$

where X: composite market good,
L^i: leisure of individual i,
M^i: market work time of individual i,
w^i: wage rate of individual i,
I: non wage income,
p: price of the composite market good,
T: total amount of time available for each person.

Applying such labor supply models[3] to a multi-person household raises problems because the intrafamily division of work is not explained. Non-participation in the labor force of a family member results in these models only if his or her leisure time is highly valued in the household utility

---

[1] For an overview see Killingsworth (1983) or Killingsworth/Heckman (1986).

[2] The term 'work' will be used in the following for all activities comprising time spent in production of goods, either in the market or at home. 'Labor' will be used as synonymously to market work.

[3] Some earlier approaches (e.g. Bowen/Finegan 1969 and Parker/Shaw 1968) model the labor decisions of the family members as a sequential decision. The husbands labor supply is treated as being independent of the wife's decision, but the wife's labor force participation depends on the husband's income:

1. $\max \ U^m(L^m, Y^m)$
   s.t. $Y^m = Y^0 + w^m(T-L^m)$

2. $\max \ U^f(L^f, Y^f)$
   s.t. $Y = Y^m + w^f(T-L^f)$

Thus, a joint household utility function is assumed implicitly. Although two individual utility functions are introduced, the labor supply of both spouses is treated as a two-step decision in the decision-making process of the household. In proper, it is a matter of an optimal choice of the joint income (Y).

function - a quite unrealistic assumption. However, a high value for the non-market time of one family member may result from the assumption that non-market time is profitable for the entire family as a unit. Non-market time is not treated then as leisure, which is of direct utility to the individual, but rather as time spent in household production. This concept of 'leisure' implicitly assumes a household production function. This is taken explicitly into account in models of time allocation.

2.1.2 Simple time allocation models

Time allocation models basically assume that market goods are not directly utility-bearing and that consumption requires additional time input (e.g. Becker 1965). Production of basic commodities is seen as the result of market goods combined with housework time. Total time may be divided between work in the market (for earning income) and work at home. Leisure is not dealt with explicitly, but is considered as a commodity that is produced only with housework time and without input of market goods:

$$\max_{H^i, M^i} U(C) \tag{2.4}$$

$$\text{s. t.} \quad C = Z(X, H^m, H^f) \tag{2.5}$$

$$T = M^i + H^i \qquad i = m, f \tag{2.6}$$

$$pX = w^m M^m + w^f M^f + I \tag{2.7}$$

where   Z: household production function,
H^i: time of individual i spent in household production,
C: total consumption.

In such a model, comparative advantages in household or market work result in full specialization of the spouses depending on the individual wage rates. The spouse that is more productive in the market will specialize in market work, leaving household work to the other spouse. Assuming that individual productivity is changed by the accumulation of human capital, comparative production advantages between the spouses will result in the long run even if they have identical resources in the beginning. Thus, specialization is optimal in any case. The intrafamily division of work is characterized by the fact that no more than one family member will spend time on work at home and also in the market, while all other members specialize exclusively in one of the activities (see Becker 1981 and 1985, Cigno 1988).

2.1.3 Extensions of time allocation models

Extensions of these simple time allocation models (e.g. Graham/Green 1984, Gronau 1973 and 1977) suggest three different types of using time. The decision on time allocation includes a decision on how much time is to be spent for work in the market, for work at home and for leisure. Leisure and time for household production is explicitly distinguished by the character of the goods produced respectively. Leisure can be interpreted as a good in itself because it generates utility directly. The time spent in household production however is a factor in producing household goods. This leads to the following maximization problem:

$$\max_{L^i, H^i, M^i} U(C, L^m, L^f) \qquad (2.8)$$

$$\text{s. t.} \quad C = Z(X, H^m, H^f) \qquad (2.9)$$
$$T = L^i + M^i + H^i \qquad i = m, f \qquad (2.10)$$
$$pX = w^m M^m + w^f M^f + I \qquad (2.11)$$

With such a model, an explicit household production function can be estimated for measuring the value of housework[4]. With respect to the intra-family division of work these models yield the same results as the simple time allocation models (see Gronau 1973).

Based on this approach, several models have been developed in which the structure of household production is differentiated even further. However, most models were formulated only for single-person households.

- Gronau (1986) assumes that it is the activity itself, i.e. working in the market or at home, which generates direct utility:

    max   U(C, L, H, M)
    s. t.   (2.9) - (2.11)

---

[4] As will be shown later, empirical research based on these models might underestimate the actual value (see chapter 6.3).

- In another model Gronau (1986) abandons the assumption that home-produced and market-produced goods are perfect substitutes :

    max U(X_M, X_H, L)
    s. t. X_H = Z(H) X_H: home-produced goods
           X_M = X X_M: market-produced goods
           (2.10) and (2.11)

- A joint production of leisure and household goods is assumed by Graham and Green (1984)[5]:

    max U(C, F^m, F^f)
    s. t. (2.9) - (2.11)   with $F^i = L^i + g^i(H^i)$.

These recent time allocation models show the possibility of fruitful developments when the restrictive assumptions are replaced by more realistic hypotheses. However, considerable problems occur in empirical testing. Kooreman/Kapteyn (1987) point out that models with joint production cannot be distinguished from models without joint production, because they lead to the same first-order conditions.

Labor supply models and simple time allocation models consider only two ways of using time. As a consequence, they cannot be distinguished from one another empirically because the household production function Z is not observable (see Killingsworth/Heckman 1986, p. 139). This causes no problem in analyzing labor supply decisions of individuals in single-person households[6]. In such a case leisure can be treated as a good produced only with time spent at home. However, this is no longer appropriate for the multi-person household with an intrafamily division of work. In contrast to other goods produced in the household, 'leisure' or 'consumption time' requires a time input of the individual itself. Leisure is a commodity that cannot be transferred from one person to another. This means that the person specializing in work at home cannot produce leisure for other household members by her or his time input. As a consequence, it is necessary to distinguish between three types of using time in a multi-person

---

[5] The argument that household production contains aspects of leisure is also applicable to market work. Then the model would coincide with Gronau's model in which the activities themselves generate direct utility.

[6] Originally simple labor supply and time allocation models were developed for such analyses.

household. Models that account for only two types are therefore not appropriate for the analysis of the division of work in the family because they imply very rigid assumptions about household production (see also Gronau 1973). Either a fixed amount of time at home, a constant individual need for leisure, or a household production function with a Leontief technology is assumed.

The lack of interpersonal transferability is an argument which does not only apply for leisure but also for other home-produced commodities. This holds especially for immaterial goods which generate direct utility, e.g. psychic income resulting from activities such as child caring. By the same token, a psychic income may also result from work in the market and cannot be transferred between individuals either (see Gronau 1986). But, neglecting the possibility of a joint production of transferable and non-transferable goods, the necessary individual time inputs in household production can be subsumed under the good 'leisure'. 'Leisure' then means all the time spent in the production of non-transferable goods.

2.1.4 Models of fertility

Models of fertility[7] are time allocation models in which children are treated as 'consumer durables' (Becker 1960). In industrial societies the utility of having children is predominantly of an immaterial nature. However, the costs for children consist on a large scale of material expenses: the expenditures for market goods and the opportunity costs of the time spent for child care. The 'quality' of children is seen as the result of the time and money invested per child, and child care is regarded as time intensive. The time allocation problem and its solution then consists of two components: the optimal number of children and the time spent in other activities, particularly the labor supply of the wife. Assuming children are non-inferior goods, the demand for 'quantity' as well as 'quality' of children increases with rising household income. This however does not hold for the income of the wife because it is she who usually spends her time in child caring, so her potential income represents the opportunity costs. With increasing time costs however, time intensive activities become unprofitable. This implies

---

[7] For an overview, see Montgomery/Trussell (1986).

that increasing wage rates for women lead to increasing labor force participation and, at the same time, to decreasing birth rates.

2.1.5 Empirical evidence

Most of the econometric studies in this field[8] indicate the empirical evidence of the last thesis. For almost all industrialized countries a rise of female labor force participation and a decline in birth rates were observed in the last decades, simultaneously with increasing female wages. In international comparisons however, differences in this pattern appear which cannot be explained easily by Becker's approach. There are countries with a high female labor force participation and nonetheless a comparably high fertility. In other countries, low fertility is observed together with a low labor force participation, for example in the Federal Republic of Germany (see Ott/Rolf 1987).

Empirical research on the micro level (see von Zameck-Glyscinski 1985, p. 268) also do not show unambiguous results. Generally, there is a negative correlation between the current market wage and the number of children being born, but the causal relationship is not clear. Several studies using the labor force participation of the woman or her education level as an indicator for the opportunity costs of child caring show differing results due perhaps to inappropriate indicators. But regarding the influence of household income, empirical research also does not always coincide with the theoretical predictions. The expected positive correlation is shown based on time series, but a negative correlation is observed in cross-sectional analyses (see von Zameck-Glyscinski 1085, p. 251). This unexpected sign may be explained in part by the quantity-quality-trade off: families with higher income also have higher expenditures for their children (Becker/Lewis 1973). Even considering these influences, Beckers hypothesis cannot be confirmed (see von Zameck-Glyscinski 1985, p. 267f.).

With the models for the intrafamily division of work, the 'new home economics' offer an essential contribution in explaining division of work by gender. In most families, specialization is established to some degree. But, as time budget studies show, this specialization is not as strict as the theory

---

[8] For an overview, see e.g. Zimmermann (1985), pp. 132ff.

predicts. In most households both partners do market work as well as housework. Of course, labor market restrictions, especially regarding hours of work, may prevent a solution predicted by an unrestricted model. But this fact cannot explain the results of time budget studies which show that the participation of men in housework depends on their power within the family and control over its economic resources (e.g. Ross 1987, Berger-Schmidt 1986). A theory using models with a household utility function apparently is not fully appropriate to analyze such phenomena.

2.1.6 Remarks on household utility function

Traditional models of household decisions are often criticized because of their assumption of a common household utility function[9]. Up till now it has not been possible to derive a conclusive foundation for the existence of a household utility function. It is doubtful if an intrafamily consensus always exists as postulated by Samuelson (1956); several empirical studies in fact contradict this point (see von Zameck-Glyscinski 1985, p. 324ff.). Furthermore, there often is less actual consensus than the partners themselves assume (see e.g. Hahn 1983). There is also no substantial empirical evidence supporting Becker's (1981) description of household behavior with a household utility function based on the altruistic behavior of one family member. Becker's result depends on the power of the altruistic family head to carry out his decisions (see Hirshleifer 1977). Thus, the existence of a household utility function depends on additional conditions. These should be discussed because their validity cannot be assumed a priori.

In addition to these theoretical problems, there also is a methodical one. A common household utility function of all members can only be deduced for an existing family with a fixed composition. Questions arising from a change in the household composition therefore cannot be analyzed (see Nerlove 1974, p. 530f. and Grichiles 1974, p. 546f.). In particular, neither the formation of families nor their dissolution can be explained by such a model (see Becker/Landes/Michael 1977, p. 1144f.).

---

[9] See e.g. Manser/Brown (1979,1980), Berk/Berk (1983), Schilp (1984), p. 205ff., von Zameck-Glyscinski (1985), p. 318ff., Cameron (1985).

2.2 Family formation and marital stability

As for the most part in industrialized countries, formation and dissolution of families are based on individual decisions, in the 'new home economics' models with individual utilities are used for analyzing these occurences.

2.2.1 Marriage models

In his theory of marriage Becker assumes that marriage occurs only if both partners gain a higher utility than by staying single (see Becker 1973, 1974 and 1981). This is possible if the joint welfare production after marriage is higher than that of two single households. This surplus - usually called the 'marriage gain' - results from economies of scale, from specialization and from marriage-specific commodities like children or emotional security. The level of marriage gain depends on the attributes of the partners - their compatibility in the joint production of goods and their comparative advantages in division of work. Choosing a partner with the best attributes takes place during the search process in the marriage market[10]. This search process also determines the internal distribution of welfare in the family because the spouse with the most favorable payoff is chosen.

2.2.2 Models of marriage stability

By analogy to the assumptions in marriage models, it is supposed that a partnership will be dissolved if one partner can expect a higher utility from the situation after divorce than from continuation of marriage. But if the external option appears to be more attractive for only one spouse, the other one can offer a compensation in order to persuade the former to remain married (see Becker/Landes/Michael 1977, p. 1144). Therefore, a divorce results only if the joint welfare in the marriage does not exceed the sum of individual welfare of both partners in their best alternative outside the family (see Becker 1981, p. 226ff.). This may result from new information about external alternatives, uncertainty or incomplete information about the

---

[10] Keely (1977) describes an explicit search model of behavior in the marriage market. Lam (1988) investigates how the selection of the partner depends on different sources of the marriage gain (public goods or gains from specialization)

attributes of the partner and the possibilities of joint production (see Becker/Landes/Michael 1977). Viewed in this light, a divorce represents the revision of a miscalculation if the expected advantages are not realized by marriage. Becker (1981) also mentions changes in the attributes of the partners and in the possibilities of joint production that can diminish the surplus in the long run and makes the marriage advantageous only for a limited amount of time. On the other hand, marriage-specific capital increases the gain from marriage compared to the external options, thereby reducing the risk of divorce. Of course the high costs of divorce and high search costs for new partnerships also reduce the risk of divorce.

2.2.3 Empirical evidence

Empirical studies on marriage and divorce however sketch a contradictory picture although they generally confirm the theses of Becker's theory of marriage. Several analyses with U.S. Data show that the marriage quotas of women decline with higher income or higher earning power. Correspondingly, their age at first marriage increases, whereas the age at first marriage of men drops with increasing income (see Preston/Richards 1975, Havens 1973, Freiden 1974, McDonald/Rindfuss 1981, Boulier/Rosenzweig 1984, Keely 1977). Similar results are shown also for Germany, at least as far as the marriage behavior of women is concerned (see Galler 1979, Tölke 1985, Diekmann 1987). Regarding remarriages Hutchens (1979) shows that the time after divorce until remarriage depends upon the amount of welfare support.

The empirical results regarding divorce behavior are not clear (see e.g Diekmann 1987, p. 32ff.). Some of the studies confirm the theses of the theoretical models. Michael (1979), D'Amicio (1983) and Sander (1985) show that the probability of divorce rises with increasing (potential) wage rates of women compared to that of men. Houseknecht/Vaughan/Macke (1984) and Michael (1979) observe an increasing risk of divorce due to an increasing level of womens' education, whereas Mott/Moore (1979) and Ermish (1986) find this due to increasing professional experience. In opposition to such observations, Smith/Meitz (1983a) find that female employment has a stabilizing influence on marriage, and Mott/Moore (1979) and Bumpass/Sweet (1972) find the same for the education of women. South/Spitze (1986) and Cherlin (1977) show an educational effect that is sometimes positive and sometimes negative. For the Federal Republic of Germany Diekmann (1987) also finds no unambiguous influence.

Some empirical research supports Becker's thesis of a reduced risk of divorce due to marriage-specific capital. While the results of South/Spitze (1986) show that owning a house reduces the risk of divorce, other studies indicate that marriages with children reveal a lower proportion of divorces (Cherlin 1977, Smith/Meitz 1983b, Höhn 1980, Diekmann 1987). As Becker/Michael/Landes (1977) and Thornton (1977) demonstrate, this is true only for marriages with small children. But even this influence cannot always be shown (South/Spitze 1986 and Mott/Moore 1979). The results of Huber/Spitze (1980) that the risk of divorce drops with a more equal distribution of housework contradicts Becker's hypothesis that intrafamily specialization increases the marriage gain and as a consequence the stability of the marriage.

Although Becker, Landes and Michael (1977) discuss the ambivalent impact of education on the risk of divorce, the different results in several studies indicate that the model of divorce behavior is insufficiently specified. Education, labor force participation and the income of women show a differing impact depending on the constellation of other variables. This ought to be considered in the theoretical models. With regard to the effect of women's income, some researchers speak of an 'income effect' and an 'independence effect' (see Diekmann 1987, p. 35ff). However, these arguments are not integrated into a theory of divorce.

2.3 Problems and further questions

This short synopsis on the approaches of the 'new home economics' demonstrates some fundamental problems. Several models with different assumptions are used for different questions. Some models assume a common household utility function while others assume an individual one for each household member. We therefore have many theoretical models with a similar view of the household in principle, but together they do not constitute a consistent theory of household decisions. This is also emphasized by the insufficient empirical results.

Among the several approaches the arguments about the impact of individual interests are inconsistent. The theories of marriage and divorce assume individual utility fuctions. Therefore, the solution depends on the external options of the partners. On the other hand, a fixed internal distribution of welfare is supposed implicitly for an existing family by the joint household utility function which is independent from the outside options of the members. But for the case of varying external alternatives during the marriage, Becker's arguments about compensation payments in his theory of divorce seem plausible for an existing family as well. If the compensation is high enough to persuade the spouse with the better outside option to remain married, instead of divorce a new internal distribution will occur. This phenomenon cannot be analyzed using a household utility function. Thus, the explanation of household decisions using models with a common household utility function contradicts the arguments of the 'new home economics' in other areas.

3 Family decisions as a bargaining problem

Following the arguments of the 'new home economics', the household is regarded as the production place of basic commodities and the family is modelled as a community of individuals who can gain extra profits through joint production in the same household. We cannot assume realistically, then, that all members are in total agreement a priori about all relevant decisions. Instead, we should assume that the family members negotiate with each other in order to reach an agreement compromising the different individual interests. Here, however, it seems too rigid to assume a priori that the result of such negotiations can always be adequately described by a household utility function with neoclassical characteristics. By giving up the assumption of a joint household utility function and by proceeding from individual utility maximization, game theoretic bargaining models seem to be more appropriate for the analysis of intrafamily decisions. These models focus on the allocation within the household assuming that cooperative behavior enables an increased welfare production.

3.1 The family as an organization of exchange

Household specific commodities, economies of scale and gains by intrafamily division of work are the main aspects that Becker (1973) lists as elements of the marriage gain. He describes marriage as a long-term contract between a man and a woman (1981, p. 14f.). However, the negotiations that proceed the contract and the final contractual conditions themselves are not further investigated. The transaction cost approach, originally developed for the analysis of the internal structure of enterprises where similar phenomena occur, can be applied here. This approach considers that the exchange of many goods or services is not free of costs (see e.g. Williamson 1986 (part 2), Ouchi 1980), mostly because of the following reasons:

- Information on the characteristics of the good or the exchange partner is incomplete.

- Exchange takes place over a long period of time (e.g. employment relationships or insurances).

- Production depends on specific human capital, which requires investments that are profitable only through long-term guaranteed returns.

The exchange of many commodities thus creates transaction costs - information costs, negotiation costs, and costs of enforcement - which can be reduced by long-term contracts. These cost reductions can be reached through the formation of cooperative associations, resulting in a surplus compared to the next best alternatives.

The family can be described in this way as well: as an organization of exchange which can reduce transaction costs. Ben-Porath (1980) distinguishes between three types of family transactions which generate a surplus when compared to single-person households (see also Pollack 1985):

- As a *production company*, the family members can make use of comparative advantages by specializing in market work and work at home in conjunction with intrafamily trade. The family enables the exchange of home produced goods (e.g. cooking, shopping) for which usually no external exchange market exists.

- As a *consumer cooperative*, the family permits the joint use of indivisible goods (e.g. dwelling, car) and provides declining costs by economies of scale.

- As an *insurance coalition*, the family produces security through an exchange of mutual promises for aid. This includes material security for risks such as illness or unemployment as well as for old age.

Often the surplus resulting from cooperation will increase with the duration of the association. This is due to a learning process of the involved members concerning the characteristics of their partners. So over time, the need for information is reduced, enabling a reduction in information and negotiation costs. By the same token however, the learning process may disclose errors in regard to the characteristics of the partner which may lead to conflict.

Beside these considerations, the welfare of family members may increase in many ways due to affections that exist between them. First and foremost, family or marriage specific commodities like emotional security are obtained which cannot be produced outside of the family[11]. Secondly, affections lead to a certain degree of altruistic behavior. As Spiegel/Templeman (1985) show for the case of interdependent utility functions, a gain for both partners can be attained through redistribution. Thirdly, affections increase the partners' trust in each other as well as the willingness to keep contracts. Hence, affections can reduce costs of information and control.

Emotional relationships can also exist of course without a joint household, as well as in the reverse case, an economic surplus can result without the existence of a marriage or a partnership. This is shown by the existence of housing communities on the one hand and of 'living apart together' partnerships on the other hand. The latter are mostly persons with comparatively high income[12] who cannot find economic advantages in the establishment of a marriage or a common household. Therefore, the essential reason for joint housekeeping may lie in the economic advantages. Both aspects however, economic advantages as well as affection, probably play a role in the majority of marriages.

Because of these material and immaterial advantages, a welfare production within the family is possible which guarantees each family member a higher utility level than if he or she lived outside of the family. The total welfare production of the household forms the *payoff space*, which is the set of all possible combinations of the family members' welfare level. The solution finally realized depends on the behavior within the family. In principle, cooperative or non-cooperative behavior are both possible.

These internal behavior patterns will be analyzed more closely in the following. The family will be considered primarily as a production and consumption community. Intrafamily insurance and the affections are given less

---

[11] The production of these commodities is often inseparably linked with the production of other household goods, for which a market substitute exists. But, since the personal or family oriented aspects are missing, they have different qualities (e.g. a homemade cake vs. a purchased one). Therefore, only a restricted external market is to be found for these household commodities, even if they are marketable in principle.

[12] Simm (1989) shows, that cohabitations seldom lead to a marriage when both partners are highly qualified and especially when the woman has a higher status than the man.

weight, but will be also discussed to some extent. As in traditional approaches the term *family* or (family-)*household* stands for the nucleus family. In principle, this approach is also applicable for a larger family network (in which long-term relationships with relatives and social norms regarding the family reduce information costs and increase the reliability of long-term agreements) or for households without family ties (where the joint household is based solely on material cost advantages). In the following however, the nucleus family and especially the bilateral negotiation situation of the married couple will be considered. In industrialized societies this is the typical setting for decisions on resource allocation and about questions of family formation.

For analyzing interactions between family members, game theoretic approaches are appropriate instruments. They allow a modelling of both cooperative and non-cooperative behavior within the family. Up to now, there have been few attempts to model household decisions as a game. Some of them use a static non-cooperative concept. We will first investigate the ability of these approaches to analyze household behavior.

3.2 Household decisions as a non-cooperative game

A game is called *non-cooperative* when the players are unable to make binding contracts and credible promises because the commitments involved are not enforceable (see e.g. Schotter/Schwödiauer 1980, p. 486, Harsanyi 1977, p. 111). The players choose their strategies independently of each other but not necessarily simultaneous. A strategy which maximizes one's own payoff, given the strategy of the other player, is called a *best reply strategy*. An *equilibrium point* of the game is defined by a combination of mutual best replies, because in this case none of the players has an incentive to deviate. If the game has exactly one equilibrium point, rational players will choose their corresponding strategies and the equilibrium solution will be realized. But if there are multiple equilibrium points, the solution is not unique. However, an additional property of 'perfectness' (see Selten 1975) and the theory of equilibrium selection (see Harsanyi/Selten 1988) allows the elimination of inplausible equilibrium points.

If the players do not choose their strategies simultaneously and at least one of them is allowed to use a strategy that depends on previous actions, the game is called *dynamic*. The property of 'subgame perfectness' is then required. Only a dynamic non-cooperative model can describe the negotiation process itself because action, reaction and learning processes must be considered. Nevertheless, if the solution of a static game is identical with the final outcome of a dynamic approach, the static model is sufficient for many questions.

Up to now, only static non-cooperative games with a unique solution have been used in modelling household decisions[13]. In most cases, the Cournot-Nash equilibrium is assumed[14]. A basic problem arises nonetheless in all these models. It is not clear what 'non-cooperative behavior' in the family means. Producing a surplus in the family normally requires long-term contracts, i.e. cooperative behavior[15]. The family makes no gain if its members act non-cooperatively. In this case, there is no distinction between a family household and separate single-person households. For this reason the models suppose a non-cooperative behavior only for some decisions. For all other decisions a consensus is assumed. However, which decisions the partners agree upon appears to arbitrary.

An early non-cooperative model of household decisions is the labor supply model of Leuthold (1968). Each spouse maximizes his or her own utility function given the worktime of the other. The total income of the household is utilized for joint consumption but the allocation of time is an individual decision. Household production is not considered in the model. The system of simultaneous equations is:

---

[13] Fethke (1984) uses a two period model for analyzing the dependency of family savings and the division of assets in the case of divorce. But, because she supposes an exogenous income stream, which means that the allocation of resources is exogenously given, the model shall not be discussed further in the present context.

[14] Woolley (1988) also uses a 'rational conjectures' approach.

[15] Even the consumption of those commodities which are usually treated as public goods requires cooperative behavior, because with appropriate strategies one partner can withhold them from the other partner and declare them to private goods. This can be done with jointly used goods like a kitchen or a television, and with immaterial public goods like the cleanliness of the house or being together with the children.

$$\max_{L^m, M^m, X} U^m(X, L^m) \qquad (3.1)$$

$$\max_{L^f, M^f, X} U^f(X, L^f) \qquad (3.2)$$

subject to

$$X = w^m(T - L^m) + w^f(T - L^f) + I \qquad (3.3)$$

This approach differs from models with a household utility function only in determining labor supply. For all other decisions an intrafamily consensus is assumed implicitly.

Woolley (1988) introduces additional strategic parameters. In her model, spouses consume not only household public goods but private goods, too, and individual budget restrictions are used instead of a joint budget restriction. Household production is not considered in this model either. Therefore, the joint family household differs from two separate households only in the matter of public goods. Essential aspects of the family household may then be neglected[16].

Ulph (1988) avoids this problem by introducing individual utility functions which may be interdependent. This means that the spouses may care for each other. Ulph also suggests individual budget restrictions. He analyzes the consumption of the household including both private and household public goods. However, neither market work nor household production is considered. It is not clear therefore, how the total income of the household is obtained and how it is divided between the spouses. Furthermore, Ulph assumes explicitly that the spouses agree on a part of the consumption expenditures. They only decide individually on the remaining demand. Certainly, this pattern may often be realized in families, but this approach is hardly appropriate for empirical analysis because the agreements usually cannot be observed. The theoretical model does not yield any explanation of

---

[16] Woolley's approach seems to be more appropriate for modelling a 'housing community' than for modelling family interactions. Certainly, Woolley argues that the non-cooperative approach should be used to determine the threat point for cooperative bargaining. But, it is doubtful wether a 'housing community' is an adequate status quo for families without cooperation. Furthermore, if the non-cooperative solution only forms the threat point in the cooperative bargaining process, the model is not useful for empirical analysis, because the non-cooperative behavior would not be realized.

the agreement process or its consequences on the demand for goods. This, however, is necessary in order to use the model for empirical analysis.

Despite the different assumptions on individual decisions in these non-cooperative models, a common advantage over traditional household models becomes apparent through empirical research. Models with individual utility functions can explain the observed behavior better than traditional approaches based on a household utility function[17]. But the question arises whether the non-cooperative model is an appropriate approach to family behavior.

Woolley (1988) and Ulph (1988) argue that a failure to reach an agreement on resource allocation does not lead directly to a divorce or a dissolution of the family but to individual decisions on the controversal points instead. This seems intuitively plausible. Nevertheless, it is questionable whether the resulting situation can be described with the solution of a static non-cooperative game. If the information on the possible strategies of each partner is incomplete, a consistent solution is not assured in the short run. On the other hand, the solution is not unique if there are multiple equilibrium points in the game. A simple example is a setting like the well-known 'battle of sexes'. Decisions on resource allocation in the household can also cause such a situation. If there are restrictions for hours of work in the labor market and the individuals can only choose between full time house work and full time market work, the problem has two equilibrium points: the wife works in the market and the husband at home or vice versa. Both spouses would deteriorate their own situation if they did the same activity. But if they cannot communicate with each other and there are no additional rules for choosing strategies, the household may be in disequilibrium because of a failure in coordination.

Equilibrium points of non-cooperative games in general are not Pareto optimal and both players can gain by agreements (see e.g. Shubik 1984b, p. 172 or Kooreman/Kapteyn 1985, p. 7f.)[18]. As discussed above, most of the additional gains in the family require such agreements. Possible gains there-

---

[17] For an explicit test of traditional neoclassical approaches and the Leuthold model see Ashworth/Ulph (1981).

[18] This effect is well known from the analysis of the dyopol.

fore would not be realized in a non-cooperative solution. To establish a Pareto optimal solution it is necessary that the partners be able to communicate and to make binding contracts. Both is true for the family[19]. We therefore should expect cooperative behavior within the family because it seems implausible that the members will forgo or forfeit possible gains.

The non-cooperative models of household decisions also show a further principle theoretical problem. As in the traditional models, the existence of the family is assumed. Neither the formation of the joint household nor its dissolution can be explained with these approaches. If all decisions are made individually, the family household does not differ from two separate single households. An exception would be if merely the fact of living together increases the welfare of at least one spouse - even in the case of fully non-cooperative behavior. This cannot be assumed in general and it is not assumed in the models described. Rather the assumption is made - often implicitly - that the spouses agree on most decisions and act non-cooperatively only in part. How this consensus is reached and how the agreement affects the allocation of resources is not explained. In this point the non-cooperative models are less precise than traditional models, and a fundamental premise for family formation may be violated.

In traditional models a household utility function is maximized and all members participate in family gains per definition. This does not hold in non-cooperative models. The non-cooperative solution does not guarantee an internal distribution from which both partners gain in comparison to their best external alternatives, except that these outside options are evaluated in their utility functions. In this case, the individual preferences would change along with changes in the outside options. This is not considered in the models described, and the utility functions do not depend on the external alternatives. The non-cooperative solution then may possibly result in a less favorable situation for one spouse compared to his or her outside option. Should this be the case, the existence of the family requires internal compensations. This implies that cooperative decisions which are not considered in the models may include such compensations. But then, these

---

[19] This assumption does not hold for all cases and especially for some very long-term contracts as we will see later. But we can certainly assume that binding contracts are possible in the short and the medium term.

agreements with respect to the outside options are the essential decision problems which are neglected in the non-cooperative models.

3.3 Household decisions as a cooperative game

For analyzing cooperative agreements in the family game theoretic models of bargaining appear to be more appropriate. They offer solutions which are Pareto optimal and provide an internal distribution which depends on the bargaining power of the family members. Usually games are called cooperative if the players are able to communicate and - this is the essential condition - to make binding agreements (see e.g. Harsanyi 1977, p. 110ff.)[20]. We can assume both to be given in the family at least in the short and medium term. If agreements are not enforceable in the long run and a renegotiation is expected after a limited time interval, a dynamic model with subgame consistency can be used in which the cooperative bargaining theory is applied locally[21].

A bargaining game is described by the set of players, by the set of all feasible payoffs - called the *payoff space* or *feasible set* -, and by the outcome in the case of disagreement - called the *conflict point* - which is an element of the payoff space (see e.g. Roth 1979, p. 5). Further it is assumed that there is at least one feasible payoff vector with a better outcome for each player than in the case of disagreement, that can be reached by cooperative behavior. If there are more such payoff vectors for which all players are better off in comparison to their conflict payoff, the conflict point plays an essential role in selecting the optimal solution. Because the player who would lose more in the case of disagreement is more likely to make concessions, disagreement can be used as a 'threat' in the bargaining process in order to gain the most favorable distribution. Therefore, this point is also called the *threat point*.

---

[20] Harsanyi (1979) even postulates, that only the criterium of enforceable commitments should be used for the distinction between cooperative and non-cooperative games, because communication alone does not guarantee cooperative behavior, if at least one player can gain from violating the agreement. However, communication is in general necessary for making agreements.

[21] This concept was introduced by Güth (1978) and Selten/Güth (1982).

Classical game theory offers quite a number of different cooperative solution concepts which are classed with the static axiomatic approach. The solution of such an axiomatic bargaining model is a rule which assigns one Pareto-optimal feasible utility vector as the outcome of the game, and it can be interpreted as a simple model of the bargaining process (Roth 1979, p. 8). The solution characterizes the properties of the bargaining outcome for both players in accordance with some axioms that represent the assumptions about a 'fair division'. The bargaining process itself is disregarded. Harsanyi (1979), therefore, postulates to model the bargaining process as a non-cooperative game in extensive form, i.e. as a sequential strategic model involving all moves and countermoves of the players. Nevertheless, if the axiomatic solution gives a good approximation of the bargaining outcome, the explicit formulation of the bargaining process is unnecessary for many questions[22]. This is the case, for example, if the reaction of the bargaining outcome on changes in the environment is in the main interest of the analysis.

Up to now bargaining approaches have not often been used to model intra-family decision making. Several authors describe family decisions as a bargaining problem in a general way in order to explain societal developments (see Stark 1984, Moreh 1986, Sen 1985 and 1987). Weiss and Willis (1985) analyze divorce behavior and divorce settlements by using a model with intrafamily bargaining. But, they only investigated the property of Pareto efficiency and choose no specific bargaining solution concept. If the outcome of the game is to be analyzed explicitly, a problem in using cooperative game theory becomes obvious. Out of the number of different solution concepts there is no dominating one, which can be considered as the appropriate approach to analyze specific real-life situations (see e.g. Harsanyi 1979). Regarding household models sometimes the sum of the individual utilities is used as household welfare function, and a 'fair distribution' of the joint utility is assumed implicitly (see Lam 1988, Lommerud 1989). Then, given any distribution, the maximization of the household utility function would also maximize the individual utilities. This can be described as a game with side payments[23] for which transferable utility is required, which implies that

---

[22] See also the discussion to Harsanyi (1979).
[23] See e.g. Shubik (1984b), p. 81ff.

utility units can be transferred at a one to one rate between the spouses. However, the utility functions must have a very specific form in this case. Usually, quasi-linear utility functions are assumed (see Kaneko 1976). Bergstrom and Varian (1985) show that an indirect utility function in Gorman polar form is a sufficient but also necessary condition for transferable utility. However, this cannot be assumed in general in the family. As Lam (1988) shows, this assumption is not valid if the individual utility functions depend on both household public goods and at least one private good with a different price for each spouse, as is usually the case for the good 'leisure'. Therefore, no transferable utility can be assumed in general. But then, maximizing the joint utility does not lead to maximum individual utilities (Lam 1988, p. 471). Consequently, a model without side payments should be applied.

Bargaining models without side payments are used by Manser and Brown (1979 and 1980) and McElroy and Horney (1981). Both approaches analyse household labor supply in the context of a static bargaining model. The individual utility functions are formed in analogy to labor supply models. A dictatorial model, the Kalai-Smorodinsky solution and the Nash solution are chosen as solution concepts. From the Nash model theoretical implications are derived which can be used for empirical tests[24].

One crucial point in using cooperative bargaining theory for modelling household decisions is the definition of the threat point. In all previously developed bargaining approaches for family decisions the outside options play an important role for the internal distribution. Stark (1984), Moreh (1986) and Sen (1987) argue in a rather general way that the possibilities outside the family influence the bargaining power of the spouses. Individual control of economic resources is important because of the improved possibilities to arrange the outside option[25]. Manser/Brown (1979 and 1980)

---

[24] Further implications and empirical tests of the models of Manser/Brown and McElroy/Horney are to be found in Horney/McElroy (1988), Carlin (1985), Kooreman (1988), Kooreman/Kapteyn (1985) and Lundberg (1988).

[25] The importance of the available economic resources correspond with the results of the sociological exchange and resource theories. For an overview see Gelles (1979) or Gelles/Straus (1979). On the background of these theories Scanzoni/Polonko (1980) describe an explicit bargaining model.

and McElroy/Horney (1981) define the threat point explicitly as the utility vector if both partners would be single.

Such an approach is not uncontested. For instance Ulph (1989) and Woolley (1988) argue, that the occasional lack of consensus in general does not immediately lead to a separation, but - at least in the short run - the partners will threat with partial non-cooperative behavior. Already Schelling (1960) has pointed out, that a threat has to be credible to influence the bargaining process effectively, i.e. the partner must be convinced that the threat will be realized in the case of disagreement. Now it is intuitively plausible that a threat to leave the family is not credible in many particular bargaining situations like the day to day allocation of income, because the loss of the surplus which is produced within the family would be much higher than the gain from a small change in its distribution. Threatening with partial non-cooperative behavior is much more credible[26]. Then, a non-cooperative equilibrium in a continued marriage may be an appropriate status quo point for failing the agreement[27]. However, this non-cooperative status quo must be defined.

If there is no unique, well-defined disagreement outcome then the players can choose between different strategies, and the bargaining problem can be described as a general cooperative game (see e.g. Harsanyi 1977, p. 167ff.). The threat point in the cooperative subgame then results from an antecedent threat game. The threat strategies chosen in this game determine both the payoffs in the case of disagreement as well as the outcome in the subsequent

---

[26] Because there are many different actions in the family with different involvement of the members, there exists a large number of strategies for each individual to refuse cooperation partially. For example, if the family gain results from using comparative advantages in production by specialization, each partner can threat with a reduction of his performance. The partner specialized in market work may threat to reduce his hours of work in favor of individual leisure, while the other partner may withhold a portion of household production. Even the consumption of typical household public goods can be limited or denied. For example the utility of an appartment, which is at least partly a household public good, depends on the linked homeproduced goods like cleanness or homeliness. Therefore, many different threat points with partial non-cooperative behavior are possible.

[27] Surely, in reality not always an equilibrium point will be chosen as threat point for the cooperative game, because the moves and countermoves of the threat game are a real turning out process which requires time. But in the same time the partner bargain also about a cooperative outcome. Therefore, in the short run suboptimal threats may be chosen. But in the long run we should expect that the threats are mutually best replies.

bargaining game. Because both players rely on reaching a cooperative agreement, they expect the cooperative solution as the final outcome rather than their disagreement payoffs and will act accordingly. Then, an equilibrium point in the threat game is formed by a pair of threat strategies which are mutually best replies regarding the subsequent cooperative game. Given the partner's threat strategy each player will choose his own threat strategy which maximizes his own final outcome. Because the final outcome results from the subsequent cooperative game, with a well-defined feasible set, all solutions corresponding to any possible threat point lie on the Pareto frontier of this feasible set. There is no solution which is Pareto superior to any other, and therefore no pair of threat strategies is strictly dominated by another.

Regarding the family bargaining game this implies, that the mutual threats with dissolution are not dominated by another strategy pair. Moreover, they are also mutually best replies. Because the dissolution realized by one partner yields always the same payoffs for both spouses regardless of the strategy of the other, there is no better reply on the threat with dissolution than to do the same. Therefore, the dissolution point is an equilibrium point in the threat game.

The question here is, are there other equilibrium points with different final outcomes. Given the assumption that the members are free to leave the family[28] the threat with dissolution can always be chosen. Therefore, if one player cannot improve his final outcome by another threat strategy, but by threatening with dissolution, a rational player will do so. Given any strategy pair which yields a better payoff for one partner than his dissolution payoff and therefore a worse for the other one (because all final outcomes are Pareto efficient), the latter can improve his position at least by threatening with dissolution. But then, no pair of threat strategies which yield another final outcome than the dissolution point can be an equilibrium point

---

[28] This is a crucial assumption for choosing the dissolution point as threat point, because only then the conflict payoffs are exogenously given. As we will see later in chapter 11, under a divorce law where both spouses have to agree in divorce, the dissolution point cannot determine the intrafamily distribution, because the dissolution payoffs themselves are determined in the bargaining process. However, in the past many industrialized countries have changed their law to unilateral no-fault divorces. Therefore, the assumption of a free and unilateral decision on leaving the family is quite realistic.

because one partner has an incentive to deviate. This means, that all equilibrium points of the threat game result in the same final outcome[29].

Concluding, the mutual threat with dissolution is an equilibrium point in the threat game. Furthermore, because all other mutually best replies result always in the same final outcome as the threat with dissolution, this threat strategies determine all other equilibrium points. In particular, any change in the external alternatives will change all equilibrium points of the threat game. But, then in a simple model for the cooperative outcome the dissolution point should be used as threat point, especially if the reaction of the cooperative solution on changes in the environment are of interest.

---

[29] If a pair of threat strategies satisfies this condition, these strategies are also mutually best replies. A deviation does not improve the cooperative outcome but is more risky because the losses are bigger if the cooperative solution fails. Because the process of moves and countermoves in the threat game starts with less risky strategies it is likely that such an equilibrium point with partial non-coopertive behavior is chosen. Faced with the lot of strategies available for each partner we can assume that in most families such equilibrium points exist. Nevertheless, all these equilibrium points lead to the same cooperative solution as the threat to leave the family.

4 A Nash bargaining model for household decisions

Based on the work of Manser/Brown (1979 and 1980) and McElroy/Horney (1981) the cooperative Nash solution is used for further analysis. Out of the multitude of cooperative solution concepts[30] the Nash solution is one that can be derived from a formal model of the bargaining process. Based on Zeuthen's (1930) principle a model of the bargaining process in extensive form which yields the Nash solution was developed by Harsanyi (1956 and 1977, p. 153ff.). Other models which can be seen as a rationalization of the Nash solution are the model of Anbar/Kalei (1978) based on convergent expectations, the compressed Harsanyi-Zeuthen game (Harsanyi 1977, p. 162ff.) and the Rubinstein (1982) game. Binmore et al. (1986) and Krelle (1976, p. 629ff.) describe further dynamic non-cooperative games for which the cooperative Nash solution represents a good approximation of their equilibrium points. Therefore, the Nash solution seems to be an appropriate model for analyzing the bargaining outcome within the family, and its reactions on changes in the environment. In the following the distinctive features of the Nash bargaining solution for household decisions in comparison to traditional approaches shall be shown with a simple household consumption model.

The Nash solution is characterized by a division of the cooperation gain so that the product of the individual gains is maximized:

$$\max N = (U^m - D^m) * (U^f - D^f) \qquad (4.1)$$

$$\text{s. t.} \quad (U^m, U^f) \in P$$

$$U^i \geq D^i \qquad\qquad i = m, f$$

---

[30] For an overview see e.g. Shubik (1984a, p. 179ff.). The Nash solution is developed by Nash (1950, 1953). For a textbook representation see e.g. Harsanyi (1977), p. 143ff.

where   P: payoff space or feasible set, i.e. all feasible utility pairs,
   U^i: payoff (=utility level) of individual i if an agreement is reached,
   D^i: conflict payoff of individual i (=utility level at the best outside option).

Consider a household in which the couple decides on the allocation of their resources. The set of all utility pairs that the two spouses can reach with their joint resources build the payoff space or feasible set. If the individual utility functions are continuous and globally concave and the constraints form a convex set in the commodity space, then a convex feasible set results. If egoistic agents are assumed, the individual utility functions depend only on the spouses' own consumption $U^i(X^i)$. Neither the leisure and work time nor household public goods are considered in this simple model, and the total household income is assumed to be given. Then the Nash bargaining model is described as follows:

$$\max_{X^m, X^f} N = (U^m(X^m) - D^m) * (U^f(X^f) - D^f) \qquad (4.2)$$

subject to

the budget constraint[31]:

$$(X^m + X^f)' p = Y \qquad (4.3)$$

and

$$U^i \geq D^i, \qquad i = m, f$$

where X^i: vector of goods of individual i,
   p: price vector,
   Y: total household income.

Figure 4.1 gives a graphic representation of the solution. The axes represent the individual utility levels of the spouses. The locus of all Pareto efficient points, the utility frontier F, is the upper right boundary of the feasible set. If gains of marriage exist, the pair of outcomes in the case of disagreement (D^m, D^f), the 'conflict point', lies inside the utility frontier. Because none of the partners would accept an outcome lower than his conflict payoff, the *negotiation set* is that part of the utility frontier between the points A and B. Geometrically, the Nash solution results as the tangential point C of the

---

[31] In proper, the budget restriction implies an inequality $(X^m+X^f)'p \geq Y$. However, in combination with the the assumption of local nonsatiation the restriction is binding.

utility frontier F and of the hyperbola $(U^m-D^m)*(U^f-D^f)=$const. farthest away from the conflict point (D^m,D^f).

Figure 4.1

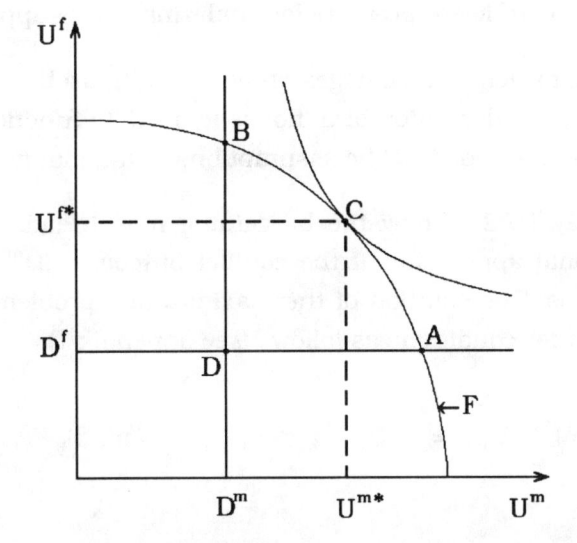

Hence the conflict point plays a dual role in the bargaining game. It determines the outcomes in the case of conflict and therefore, according to the rules of the game, the distribution within the household.

4.1 Comparison with traditional approaches

In comparison to traditional household models the bargaining model differs only in the objective function, whereas the budget and time constraints are identical. If the goods of the husband and the wife are separate arguments in the household utility function of the traditional model

$$U(X^m, X^f), \tag{4.4}$$

then the Nash function of the bargaining model

$$N = (U^m(X^m) - D^m) * (U^f(X^f) - D^f) \tag{4.5}$$

is formally a specific function in this function class. Up to this point, it seems unnecessary to give up the more general household utility function, because only a very specific type of intrafamily distribution is determined through the solution of a bargaining game. Furthermore, Kooreman/Kapteyn

(1985) and Chiappori (1988a) show that an explicit rule for distribution is not necessary for analyzing household decisions on the basis of individual utility functions. Chiappori (1988a) describes the conditions under which Pareto efficiency is a sufficient property for analyzing labor supply[32].

However, there are principle advantages of modelling household decisions as a bargaining game: the derivation of a 'household utility function' is not left to a black box, but is founded by the assumptions of rational negotiation.

As McElroy/Horney (1981) show the bargaining model leads to the same results as traditional approaches if the conflict outcomes (D^m and D^f) are fixed and exogenous. The solution of the maximization problem (4.2) - (4.3) leads to the first-order conditions as follows (see appendix 1):

$$\frac{\partial U^i}{\partial x_k^i} (U^j - D^j) - \lambda p_k = 0 \qquad i = m, f \qquad (4.6)$$

and

$$Y - (X^m + X^f)' p = 0 \qquad (4.7)$$

From this, the well-known result, that in the optimum for each partner the marginal rate of substitution between two goods is equal to the inverse ratio of the prices, follows:

$$\frac{\frac{\partial U^i}{\partial x_k^i}}{\frac{\partial U^i}{\partial x_l^i}} = \frac{p_k}{p_l} \qquad (4.8)$$

In addition, the division of the cooperation surplus dependent on the conflict outcomes can be derived. In the optimum, the net gain of cooperation is divided between the spouses in proportion to the rate of substitution of one (and therefore of every) good:

---

[32] As will be shown later, this requires very restrictive assumptions.

$$\frac{\frac{\partial U^f}{\partial x_k^f}}{\frac{\partial U^m}{\partial x_k^m}} = \frac{U^f - D^f}{U^m - D^m} = -\frac{\partial U^f}{\partial U^m} \qquad (4.9)$$

If the spouses do not consume the same good, as it is true for the good 'leisure' which is different for the partners at least in price, the division of the surplus from cooperation is proportional to the rate of substitution between two individual goods of the partners weighted by the price ratio:

$$\frac{\frac{\partial U^f}{\partial x_k^f}}{\frac{\partial U^m}{\partial x_l^m}} \frac{p_1}{p_k} = \frac{U^f - D^f}{U^m - D^m} = -\frac{\partial U^f}{\partial U^m} \qquad (4.10)$$

The value of this ratio represents the 'marginal rate of the utility transfer' (see Harsanyi 1977, p. 179), which is equal to the slope of the utility frontier in the optimum. This slope becomes smaller the higher the conflict outcome of the partner is whose utility forms the numerator. Therefore, this value represents a measure for the relative bargaining power of the partners.

Figure 4.2

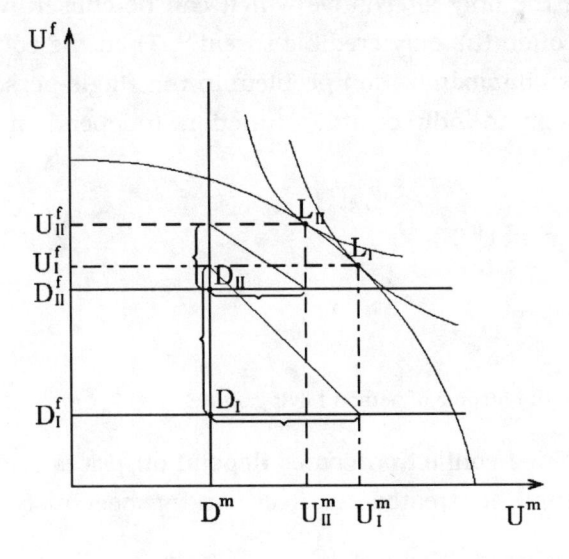

In figure 4.2. person f has a higher conflict outcome at conflict point D_{II} than at conflict point D_I. Therefore, she has a relatively better bargaining position in situation II and her resulting cooperative payoff is greater than in situation I (see also Thomson 1987). Under the usual assumption of decreasing marginal utility the slope of the utility frontier is steeper in situation I, which means that in situation I the utility can be transferred more easily from m to f than in situation II. Therefore, the relative share of the cooperation surplus decreases with increasing conflict outcomes:

$$\frac{U_{II}^f - D_{II}^f}{U_{II}^m - D_{II}^m} < \frac{U_I^f - D_I^f}{U_I^m - D_I^m} \tag{4.11}$$

So far, by assuming a fixed and exogenously given conflict point, the bargaining model brings about no additional findings for questions concerning resource allocation. Certainly, the division of the cooperation surplus is theoretically interesting, but it is not useful for empirical analyses since the individual utilities cannot be observed.

The real advantages of the bargaining model become apparent when the assumption of a fixed conflict points is abandoned. Let us assume that for both spouses the best alternative outside the family is to live alone in a one-person household. This is a rather conservative assumption, one that represents the minimal threat potential. At the time of the negotiation, living alone is in general the only alternative which can be chosen with certainty, and therefore it is often the only credible threat[33]. Then the conflict outcome results from the usual maximization problem in the single-person-household and can be written as an indirect utility function, independent of prices and income:

$$D^i(p, Y^i) = \max_X U^i(X) \tag{4.12}$$

s.t. $\quad X'p = Y^i$

where Y^i is the income of person i living alone.

Because the so defined conflict outcomes depend on prices and income, the conflict point cannot be treated as fixed and exogenously given. First,

---

[33] Options to build new partnerships can influence the negotiations also, but this is very different for each individual case.

changes in the environment do not only affect the household production but also the conflict points: exogenous changes of prices or wages as well as institutional changes, e.g. of public transfers or the child care system, have consequences for the individual conflict outcomes. Second, the conflict point depends on the household decisions themselves, because savings or losses in earning capacity during the interruption of employment also influence the outside options. Therefore, exogenous as well as endogenous changes in the conflict outcomes should be considered in the formal model.

Manser/Brown (1979 and 1980) and McElroy/Horney (1981) investigate the case of price dependent conflict points in their models, i.e. the dependency of the cooperative solution on exogenous changes of prices and wages. Their results show that the relationship between the traditional approach and the bargaining model can be seen also as a reverse ranking. Because a bargaining model with a fixed conflict point leads to the same results as the traditional model, the latter can be regarded as a special case of the bargaining model: one with a fixed conflict point.

However, in order to investigate situations with variable conflict points a model with individual utility functions is required. Chiappori (1988a) showed that the property of Pareto efficiency is sufficient for analyzing the influence of exogenous price changes on the resource allocation within the household[34]. In this case, an explicit rule of distribution is not necessary. If, however, changes in the conflict outcome depend on the household decisions themselves, it is necessary to specify an explicit negotiation rule that describes a single-valued mapping of the set of conflict points in the feasible set. Only then is it possible, to model endogenous changes in conflict points[35].

---

[34] Kooreman/Kapteyn (1985) and Spiegel/Templeman (1985) also use only the property of Pareto efficiency in their models.

[35] This puts limits to an approach like that of Chiappori (1988a and 1988b). Also this approach can be used only for a static analysis, because no feedback of the household decision on the conflict outcome can be considered.

4.2 Comparative statics

First of all, the effects of exogenous price changes in the Nash bargaining model are discussed in comparison to traditional approaches (see also McElroy and Horney 1981). The fundamental results are not limited to the Nash solution but are valid for all cooperative solutions because they only depend on the property of Pareto efficiency. However, the derivation on the basis of the Nash solution is more illustrative, especially since the subsequent analyses are based on the Nash solution.

In order to analyse the effects of exogenous changes in prices or income in a bargaining model the usual instruments of comparative statics can be applied. If a hypothetical 'household utility function' is used to compare the results with a traditional approach, this function must reach its maximum for exactly the same allocation which maximizes the Nash function[36]. Then the hyperbolas $(U^m-D^m)*(U^f-D^f)$=const. can be treated as 'indifference curves of the household'. The product of the individual gains remains constant along this curve. If one interprets this product as a 'household utility', then the 'household' regards the different points on the hyperbola to be equivalent: what the one spouse loses in utility is compensated through the utility gain of the other spouse.

Figure 4.3 shows the effects of a change in prices in favor of person f. Because the solution depends on the distribution of the individual utilities, but the adjustments are made by reallocation of real goods, we should look at the movements in the utility space as well as in the commodity space. If we only consider one aggregate consumption commodity for each person, the effect can be illustrated by a four quadrant diagram with connected coordinate systems. In figure 4.3 the first quadrant, i.e. the upper right one, represents the utility space and the third quadrant the commodity space. The corresponding axes symbolize the individual utilities U^m and U^f and the individual consumption goods X^m and X^f. The two spaces are connected by the individual utility functions depending on the individual commodity. These functions are shown in the second and fourth quadrants. Any budget constraint in the commodity space defines a utility frontier in the utility

---

[36] Such a household utility function could be, for example, $U^H=D^f+D^m+(U^m-D^m)*(U^f-D^f)$.

space, and any hyperbola corresponding to a given conflict point defines an indifference curve in the commodity space.

Figure 4.3

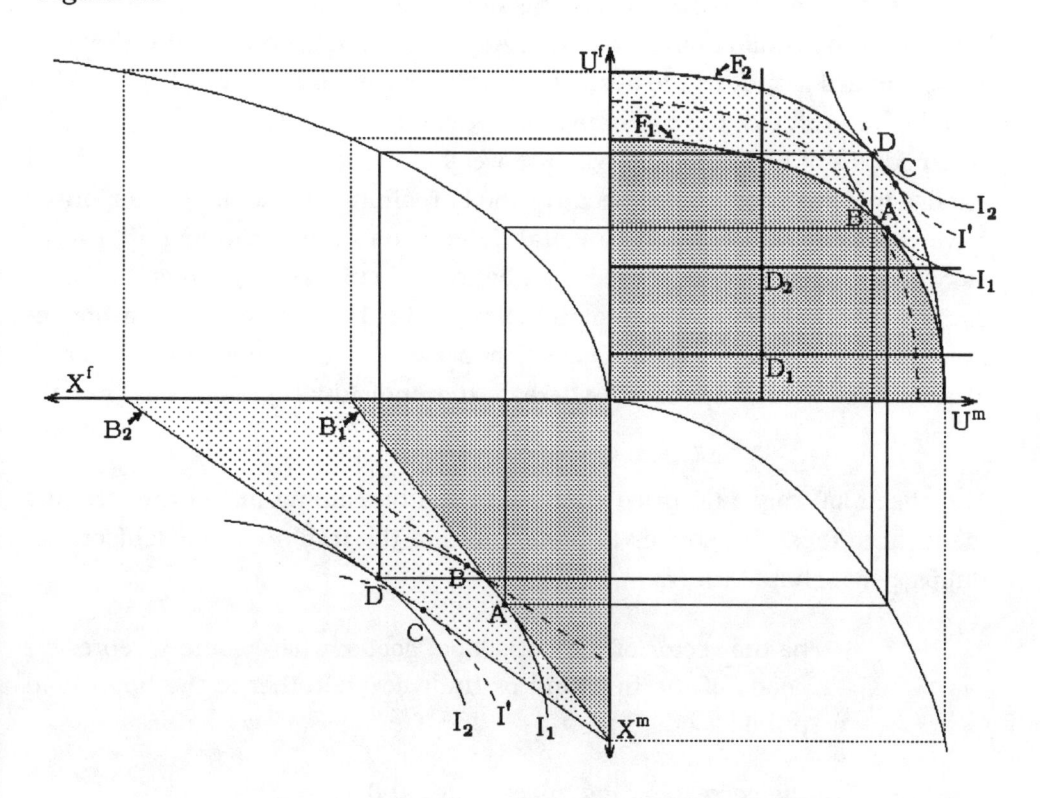

Let us start with the initial solution point A on the utility frontier F_1 which is generated by the initial budget line B_1. If prices vary in favor of person f, the budget line will shift to the new one which is denoted by B_2. The corresponding utility frontier is denoted by F_2. Like in traditional models, the total effect can be decomposed in different effects. The movement from A to B represents the compensated *substitution effect*, i.e. the change in demand and the corresponding change in the resulting individual utilities keeping the 'household utility' (=Nash product) constant. Graphically, this means a rotation of the budget line and therefore of the utility frontier along the 'indifference curve' (see the dotted lines in the figure). The *income effect* leads to a shift to another 'household utility level' and is represented by the movement from B to C. So far, the results coincide with those of traditional approaches.

In addition to this, there is a third effect in the bargaining model (the movement from C to D). Given the definition (4.12), a change in prices influences the conflict outcomes, too. A change of the conflict point (from D_1 to D_2) implies a shift in the system of 'indifference curves' (from I' to I_2). This can be interpreted as a 'change in preferences' of the household. The commodities of husband and wife are weighted differently before and after a change in conflict outcomes because the bargaining positions of the spouses have changed. This is a fundamental difference to the traditional approaches, where changes in preferences can be treated only as exogenous. In a bargaining model, however, systematic changes in the preferences of a household can be analyzed, which arise solely because of a change in the external alternatives of the spouses, whereas the individual preferences remain constant.

The effects of wage and price changes in the bargaining model are formally identical to those of changes in preferences in the traditional model (see e.g. Phlips 1974, chap. VII). Let

- X   be the vector of the household goods, where some x_i represent goods of the husband or the wife and other x_i the household public goods,

- p   the corresponding price vector, and

- Y   the 'full' income of the household,

then the maximizing problem to be solved is

$$\max_{X} N = (U^m(X^m) - D^m) * (U^f(X^f) - D^f) \tag{4.13}$$

$$\text{s.t.} \quad X'p = Y$$

$$U^i \geq D^i, \qquad i = m, f$$

Then the fundamental matrix equation of this system with preference changes is (compare Phlips 1974, p. 181ff.):

$$\begin{bmatrix} X_Y & X_p^* & X_D \\ -\lambda_Y & -\lambda_p^{*'} & -\lambda_D^{*'} \end{bmatrix} = \begin{bmatrix} B & b \\ b' & c \end{bmatrix} \begin{bmatrix} 0 & \lambda I & -V \\ 1 & X' & 0 \end{bmatrix} \qquad (4.14)$$

where

$X_p^* = \left[\dfrac{\partial x_k^*}{\partial p_l} \right]$ the matrix of the changes in demand induced by price changes holding the nominal income and the conflict point constant,

$X_Y = \left[\dfrac{\partial x_k}{\partial Y} \right]$ the vector of the changes in demand induced by a change in nominal income holding prices and the conflict point constant,

$X_D = \left[\dfrac{\partial x_k}{\partial D^j} \right]$ the matrix of the changes in demand induced by changes in the conflict outcomes holding prices and the nominal income constant,

$\lambda_p^* = \left[\dfrac{\partial \lambda^*}{\partial p_l} \right], \quad \lambda_Y = \left[\dfrac{\partial \lambda}{\partial Y} \right], \quad \lambda_D = \left[\dfrac{\partial \lambda}{\partial D^i} \right]$

the vectors of the partial derivations of the Lagragne multiplier λ,

$V = \left[\dfrac{\partial^2 N}{\partial x_k \partial D^i} \right] = \left[\dfrac{\partial U^j}{\partial x_k} \right] = -U \qquad \begin{matrix} i \neq j \\ i,j = m, f \end{matrix}$

the matrix of the effects of a change in the conflict outcomes on the marginal Nash product with respect to good x_l

$H = \begin{bmatrix} B & b \\ b' & c \end{bmatrix}$ the inverse of the bordered Hessian matrix, where B is symmetric and semidefinite.

However, the change in the conflict point is not exogenously given, but also depends on changes in prices (see equation (4.12)). In addition, in the case of wage changes (the price of the good 'leisure'), the nominal income changes at the same time. The change of the entire demand may be decomposed as follows (for the detailed derivation see appendix 2):

$$\left[\frac{dx_k}{dp_l}\right] = \left[\frac{\partial x_k^*}{\partial p_l}\right] + \left[\frac{\partial x_k}{\partial Y}\right]\left[\frac{dY}{dp_l}\right] + \left[\frac{\partial x_k}{\partial D^i}\right]\left[\frac{dD^i}{dp_l}\right]$$

$$X_p = X_p^* + X_Y * Y_p + X_D * D_p$$

$$= \lambda B - bX' + b * Y_p + BU * D_p$$

$$= \lambda B - bq' + BUD_p$$

$$= K - bq' + \frac{1}{\lambda} KUD_p \qquad (4.15)$$

K - bq' is the effect if the conflict point remains unchanged and it corresponds to the results of the traditional model with constant preferences. In this, the term bq' represents the income effect and K the matrix of the compensated substitution effects. The remaining expression $\frac{1}{\lambda}$ KUD$_p$ results from the change of the conflict points and can be interpreted as a *bargaining effect*. A corresponding term results in a traditional model only from exogenous changes in preferences.

This bargaining effect becomes larger, the smaller the Lagrange multiplier λ is. This multiplier represents the marginal 'household utility' of the income. Because of the decreasing marginal utility of the income, households with high incomes have a small λ, and as a consequence the bargaining effect may be more important.

Changes of the individual utility levels can also be derived from the reactions of household demand on changes in prices. Again a decomposition into a part independent of the conflict point and into a bargaining effect is possible:

$$\frac{dU^i}{dp_l} = \sum_k \frac{\partial U^i}{\partial x_k} \frac{dx_k}{dp_l} \qquad (4.16)$$

$$= \sum_k \frac{\partial U^i}{\partial x_k} \left[\frac{\partial x_k^*}{\partial p_l} + \frac{\partial x_k}{\partial Y}\frac{dY}{dp_l} + \sum_j \frac{\partial x_k}{\partial D^j}\frac{dD^j}{dp_l}\right]$$

$$= \left.\frac{dU^i}{dp_l}\right|_{D_{fix}} + \frac{dU^i}{dD^i}\frac{dD^i}{dp_l} + \frac{dU^i}{dD^j}\frac{dD^j}{dp_l} \;.$$

The size and the sign of the effect are determined by the differences in the reaction of the welfare production to price changes between the joint household and the separated households. How large these differences are, depend on the technology available in the different households, and can be analyzed only with an explicit modelling of household production.

5 Time allocation in a static bargaining model with household production

The discussion of the intrafamily division of work in chapter 2 shows that three types of time use should be considered. The output of some activities can be transferred between family members, whereas the benefits from other activities are derived only by the individuals involved. Time spent on market work is used for earning income which is transferable. In economic literature, the term *market work* is usually used in this sense. On the other hand, the terms household production, housework, home production, homework, do-it-yourself work, consumption time and leisure time are used differently and are seldom clearly distinguished one from another. In the following, *household production* or *household work* is understood as the production of commodities in a household that can be transferred interpersonally. But, because of high transaction costs, normally these goods are exchanged only within the household. In opposition to this, *leisure* stands for all activities requiring a time input by the individual consumer.

Process benefits, i.e. direct utility generated by work at home or market work[37], are neglected in the following. It will be assumed that no joint production of interpersonally transferable goods and non-transferable goods takes place. To take all of this into account would overload a first model. Therefore, it is left to further research.

---

[37] For example, such process benefits arise in market work through social contacts and acceptance, or in household work through autonomous work and comprehensive production.

5.1 The model

In analogy with the approaches regarding household production (see Gronau 1986), it is assumed that market goods cannot be directly consumed. Market goods and time are the inputs in the production of basic commodities. The time input of different household members may not be equally efficient in this household production. The bundle of commodities is produced corresponding to the household production function Z, and it is regarded as a composite commodity:

$$C = Z(aH, X) \qquad (5.1)$$

where C: composite commodity
          H: time spent in household production
          a: parameter of efficiency in household production
          X: composite market good

Assuming that no saving takes place and that wages and income are measured in terms of the market good, the amount of market goods is subject to the budget constraint:

$$X = Y(wM + I) \qquad (5.2)$$

where w: wage rate in terms of the market good
          M: time spent in market work
          I: non-wage income in terms of the market good
          Y: net-income function.

Therefore, the disposable income can be used directly as an argument in the household production function. Consumption and leisure are the arguments of the individual utility functions $U^i(D^i, L^i)$, and are assumed to be greater than zero.

Now, the decision problem can be described by the following model[38]:

---

[38] Public household goods are not considered. Considering public goods C^h, the utility functions become $U^i(C^h, C^i, L^i)$ and the budget constraint (5.4) is $C^h + C^m + C^f = Z(a^m H^m + a^f H^f, Y(w^m M^m + w^f M^f + I^m + I^f))$. However, the principle statements with regard to the intrafamily division of work do not change.

$$\max_{L^i, H^i, M^i} N = (U^m(C^m, L^m) - D^m) * (U^f(C^f, L^f) - D^f) \qquad (5.3)$$

subject to

budget constraint:

$$C^m + C^f = Z(a^m H^m + a^f H^f, Y(w^m M^m + w^f M^f + I^m + I^f)) \qquad (5.4)$$

time constraints:

$$T = M^m + H^m + L^m \qquad (5.5)$$
$$T = M^f + H^f + L^f$$

non-negativity constraints:

$$C^m > 0, C^f > 0, L^m > 0, L^f > 0 \qquad (5.6)$$
$$H^m \geq 0, H^f \geq 0, M^m \geq 0, M^f \geq 0$$

conflict outcomes

$$D^i(w^i, a^i, I^i) \qquad i = m, f \qquad (5.7)$$

are the solutions of utility maximization in a single-person household[39]

$$\max_{L^i, H^i, M^i} U^i(\mathcal{C}^i, \mathcal{L}^i)$$
$$\text{s.t.} \quad \mathcal{C}^i = Z(a^i \mathcal{H}^i, Y(w^i \mathcal{M}^i + I^i))$$
$$T = \mathcal{M}^i + \mathcal{H}^i + \mathcal{L}^i$$

From the Kuhn-Tucker thoerem the Lagrangian follows

$$\begin{aligned}
\mathcal{L} = & (U^m - D^m) * (U^f - D^f) \\
& + \lambda \{ Z(a^m H^m + a^f H^f, Y(w^m M^m + w^f M^f + I^m + I^f)) - C^m - C^f \} \\
& + \mu^m (T - M^m - H^m - L^m) + \mu^f (T - M^f - H^f - L^f) \\
& + \nu^m H^m + \nu^f H^f + \sigma^m M^m + \sigma^f M^f
\end{aligned}$$

from which the first order conditions can be derived. Here the subscripts denote the partial derivatives:

---

[39] The optimal allocation in the alternative situation is denoted by italic letters.

(1) $\quad \dfrac{\partial \mathcal{l}}{\partial C^i} = U_C^i(U^j - D^j) - \lambda = 0 \qquad i = m, f \quad j \neq i$

(2) $\quad \dfrac{\partial \mathcal{l}}{\partial L^i} = U_L^i(U^j - D^j) - \mu^i = 0 \qquad i = m, f \quad j \neq i$

(3) $\quad \dfrac{\partial \mathcal{l}}{\partial H^i} = \lambda Z_H a^i - \mu^i + v^i = 0 \qquad i = m, f$

(4) $\quad \dfrac{\partial \mathcal{l}}{\partial M^i} = \lambda Z_Y Y_M w^i - \mu^i + \sigma^i = 0 \qquad i = m, f$

(5) $\quad \dfrac{\partial \mathcal{l}}{\partial \lambda} = Z(a^m H^m + a^f H^f, Y(w^m M^m + w^f M^f + I^m + I^f)) - C^m - C^f = 0$

(6) $\quad \dfrac{\partial \mathcal{l}}{\partial \mu^i} = T - M^i - H^i - L^i = 0 \qquad i = m, f$

(7) $\quad v^i H^i = 0 \qquad i = m, f$

(8) $\quad \sigma^i M^i = 0 \qquad i = m, f$

where

$U_C^i = \dfrac{\partial U^i}{\partial C^i}, \quad U_L^i = \dfrac{\partial U^i}{\partial L^i}$ are the first derivatives of the utility function with respect to consumption and leisure

$Z_H = \dfrac{\partial Z}{\partial \tilde{H}}, \quad Z_Y = \dfrac{\partial Z}{\partial Y}$ are the first derivates of the household production function with respect to household work and net income

with $\tilde{H} = a^m H^m + a^f H^f$

$Y_M = \dfrac{\partial Y}{\partial \tilde{M}}$ is the first derivative of the net-income function with respect to income from market work

with $\tilde{M} = w^m M^m + w^f M^f$

The first order conditions give the following relationships:

$$\frac{U_C^i}{U_C^j} = \frac{U^i - D^i}{U^j - D^j} \tag{5.8}$$

$$\frac{U_L^i}{U_L^j} = \frac{\mu^i(U^i - D^i)}{\mu^j(U^j - D^j)} \tag{5.9}$$

$$\frac{U_L^i}{U_C^i} = Z_H a^i + \frac{v^i}{U_C^i(U^j - D^j)} \tag{5.10}$$

$$\frac{U_L^i}{U_C^i} = Z_Y Y_M w^i + \frac{\sigma^i}{U_C^i(U^j - D^j)} \tag{5.11}$$

The conditions for allocating time in work at home and in the market can be derived from the equations (5.10) and (5.11). If individual i spends time in market work, then $\sigma^i = 0$ holds due to condition (8). On the other hand, if an individual works at home $v^i = 0$ results due to condition (7). Then, the following cases can be distinguished:

Case 1: Person i allocates time to the market as well as to the household: In this case, $H^i > 0$, $M^i > 0$, $v^i = 0$, $\sigma^i = 0$ and the following relationship results:

$$Y_M w^i = \frac{1}{Z_Y} \frac{U_L^i}{U_C^i} = \frac{Z_H a^i}{Z_Y}. \tag{5.12}$$

This condition implies a ratio of the marginal product of the housework ($Z_H a^i$) and the marginal product of the income (Z_Y) equal to the marginal return of market work (= marginal net wage rate). This is true if the marginal product of an additional hour of market work is equal to the marginal product of an additional hour of housework, and both, at the same time, are equal to the marginal rate of substitution between leisure and consumption:

$$Z_Y Y_M w^i = \frac{U_L^i}{U_C^i} = Z_H a^i. \tag{5.13}$$

If there are points in the relevant range of the household production function up to the optimum, for which this relationship is true, then the individual spends time in market work as well as in work at home.

In the case of a linear net-income function (Y) and a constant marginal product of the income in household production (Z_Y)[40] there exists exactly one point in the household production function for which (5.13) holds. At this point, a switch from household work to market work is profitable. This is point A in figure 5.1. Up to this point, an additional time unit spent in work at home increases the household production more than if it is spent in market work. Above that point the reverse holds. Therefore, the person will work only at home up to point A and then start to work in the market. If the optimal solution point B is above point A, then the individual works both at home and in the market. Because the net-income function is linear, the last time unit spent in work at home gives the same output as each one worked in the market.

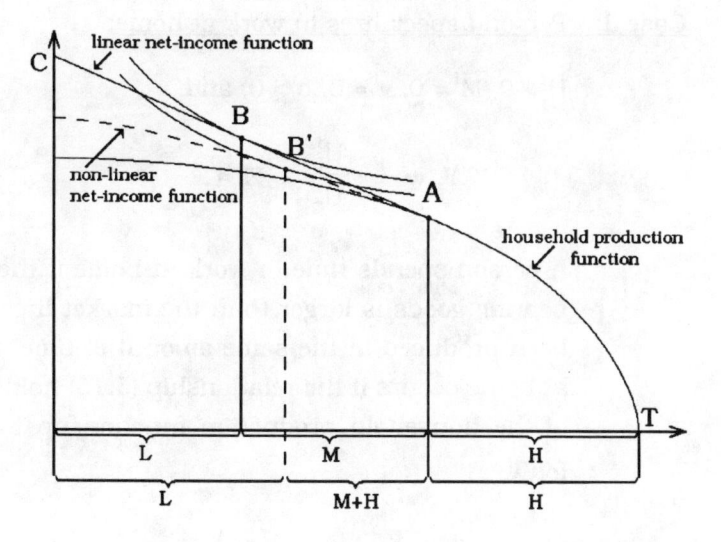

Figure 5.1

---

[40] This is true if home produced goods and market goods are perfect substitutes. Then Z_Y is equal 1, the price of the composite market good.

However, if the net-income function is non-linear due to progressive taxation, or the marginal returns of income to household production are not constant[41], then condition (5.13) may be fulfilled in a larger range of the household production function. In this range the time is divided between both activities corresponding to the relationship of the marginal productivities.

Case 2: Person i specializes in market work:

$H^i = 0$, $M^i > 0$, $v^i > 0$, $\sigma^i = 0$, and

$$Z_Y Y_M w^i = \frac{U_L^i}{U_C^i} > Z_H a^i. \qquad (5.14)$$

Thus, an individual uses the time exclusively for market work if the marginal product of time spent in market work is larger than that of time spent at home. If condition (5.14) holds for the entire range of the household production function up to the optimum, then the individual specializes in market work.

Case 3: Person i specializes in work at home:

$H^i > 0$, $M^i = 0$, $v^i = 0$, $\sigma^i > 0$, and

$$Z_Y Y_M w^i = \frac{U_L^i}{U_C^i} < Z_H a^i. \qquad (5.15)$$

A person spends time in work at home if the production of utility-bearing goods is larger than the market income which would have been produced in the same amount of time. Specialization in work at home occurs if the relationship (5.15) holds over the entire range of the household production function up to the optimal solution point.

---

[41] The latter is true, in general, in the case of limited substitutionability. Then equation (5.13) represents the least-cost combination in the household production at the optimum, and may hold over a larger range of the production function.

5.2 Division of work within the household

Considering the family as a production company, the surplus is realized by efficient allocation of the members' resources in the joint production of all the goods consumed by the household members. Then, the optimal intra-family division of work can be derived from the above conditions.

5.2.1. The case of a joint net-income function

In the case of a joint net-income function for the household members, for example due to a joint taxation of the spouses, each additional unit of gross income acquired through market work results in the same marginal net income, regardless of which spouse has earned it. If the spouses have different wages, then the marginal revenues of time spent in the market also differ between both partners within the entire range of the household production function:

$$w^i < w^j \qquad\qquad i \neq j$$

$$\Rightarrow \quad Y_M w^i < Y_M w^j$$

$$\Rightarrow \quad Z_Y Y_M w^i < Z_Y Y_M w^j.$$

Case 1: Productivity of the spouses in work at home is identical:

$$a^i = a^j = a$$

In this case, the condition (5.13) holds only for one partner, this means that one of the following relationships is true:

$Z_Y a = Z_Y Y_M w^i < Z_Y Y_M w^j$ — person j specializes on market work, whereas person i spends time in market work and work at home

or

$Z_Y Y_M w^i < Z_Y Y_M w^j = Z_Y a$ — person j spends time in market work and work at home, and person i specializes in household work.

Case 2: The partner with the lower wage is more productive in work at home:

$$a^i > a^j$$

The same division of work results as in case 1 because only one of the two conditions can be true:

or
$$Z_Y a^j < Z_Y a^i = Z_Y Y_M w^i < Z_Y Y_M w^j$$
$$Z_Y Y_M w^i < Z_Y Y_M w^j = Z_Y a^j < Z_Y a^i$$

In both cases the spouse with the higher wage works in the market, while the other works at home. Which of the two partners specializes exclusively on one activity depends on the household technology. An exclusive specialization of both partners in different activities only occurs if the optimal solution point lies exactly on the threshold for entering the market of the spouse with the lower wage (point A in figure 5.1). Due to the fact the inequalities are true for the entire range of the household production function, the case in which both partners allocate time to both activities cannot be an optimal solution.

Case 3: The partner with the higher wage is also more productive in household production:

$$a^j > a^i$$

In this case, the division of work depends on the comparative production advantages. Depending on whether

$$\frac{Y_M w^i}{a^i} < \frac{Y_M w^j}{a^j} \quad \text{or} \quad \frac{Y_M w^i}{a^i} > \frac{Y_M w^j}{a^j}$$

is true, the spouse with the higher ratio of the productivities works in the market, while the other works at home. A person spends time in both activities, if the following holds:

$$\frac{Y_M w^i}{a^i} > \frac{Z_H}{Z_Y}.$$

This result concerning the intrafamily division of work is known from traditional approaches (see Becker 1985, Gronau 1973, Cigno 1988). No more than one household member will participate in both market and household activities, whereas all other members specialize totally in one activity. This specialization of the members in their most productive activity leads to a welfare production in the joint household which is larger than the aggregate welfare production of the single-person households.

However, this result depends on the assumption of a joint net-income function, i.e. that the net marginal revenue of an earned unit of money is the same for each person. This is true if tax payments are based on the joint gross income of the household, as is the case in Germany. Because each additional unit of money is taxed by the same marginal rate, the marginal net income of an additional time unit spent in market work is higher for a higher gross wage rate.

5.2.2 The case of individual net-income functions

Another situation results, however, in the case of individual net-income functions which may result from individual taxation as is the case, for example in Sweden. With a progressive tax system, a higher individual gross income is taxed with a higher rate, and the marginal net income for an additional hour of work can be higher for a person with a lower gross wage than for a person with a higher gross wage.

This implies that ranges may exist in the household production function in which the marginal product of work time is equal for both partners even if the gross wages differ:

$$Z_Y Y_M^i w^i = Z_Y Y_M^j w^j.$$

Even if both spouses have different household skills, a range exists in which the following is true:

$$\frac{Y_M^i w^i}{a^i} = \frac{Y_M^j w^j}{a^j}.$$

If the optimal solution falls within this range, then also

$$\frac{Y_M^i w^i}{a^i} = \frac{Y_M^j w^j}{a^j} = \frac{Z_H}{Z_Y}.$$

holds, and both spouses participate in market and household activities (see also Gustafsson/Ott 1987).

5.3 Effects of an exogenous change in wages

As we have seen, the static bargaining model yields the same result concerning the intrafamily division of work as traditional model approaches do. Therefore, the same effects of changes in wages on the production structure in the household result, i.e. which person increases (decreases) the hours of work or enters (leaves) the labor force. Nevertheless, another amount of time may be spend in the activities due to a changed demand for the good leisure. As has been shown in chapter 4, this demand is also affected through the bargaining effect (equation (4.15)) resulting from a changed welfare distribution in the household. Any reallocation in the utility space implies a reallocation in the commodity space between the goods of the spouses and vice versa. But because each spouse may also substitute within his or her bundle of goods due to changed price ratios, the reallocation between the spouses will be analyzed by the effects on the individual utility level.

When analyzing the effects of an exogenous wage change the following points should be considered:

- If the person is employed, then a wage change varies the nominal income of the household and the price of the good 'leisure' for this person, which also means a change in real income.

- If the person does not work in the market before as well as after the wage change, then the price of leisure is determined by the value of household production and is not affected by a change in the potential wage. Also the nominal income of the household does not change.

- In addition, the external alternatives of a person outside of the family are affected by a wage change. Assuming that both household production and income are necessary for an efficient welfare production in the household, specialization in work at home in a single-person household is only possible, if a sufficient non-wage income is available. However, this is not true for the majority of individuals. In general, if a person is living alone, the optimal time allocation includes market work, and consequently, a wage change will influence the utility level. This means, that normally a wage change affects the conflict outcome of a person, even if this person is not employed in the joint household.

These different influences of a wage change on the individual utility levels of the spouses shall be analyzed in the following. As has been shown with relation (4.16) the effects of a wage change can be decomposed into an effect independent of the conflict outcome and into the bargaining effect. First, these two effects will be analyzed separately before the total effect will be discussed.

5.3.1 Effects when the conflict point is held constant

As was shown in chapter 4, the results when the conflict point is held constant correspond with those of the traditional model. But in the traditional approach, only the change in demand at the household level is analyzed, and the individual utility positions are not considered. Using the bargaining model, the effects on the individual utility levels can be derived by the differentiating equations (5.3) and (5.9) holding the conflict point unchanged:

$$\left.\frac{dN}{dw^i}\right|_{D_{fix}} = (U^j - D^j) \left.\frac{dU^i}{dw^i}\right|_{D_{fix}} + (U^i - D^i) \left.\frac{dU^j}{dw^j}\right|_{D_{fix}} \quad (5.16)$$

$$\frac{\partial U_L^i}{\partial w^i}(U^j - D^j)\mu^i + U_L^i \frac{dU^j}{dw^i}\mu^i + U_L^i(U^j - D^j)\frac{\partial \mu^j}{\partial w^i} = \quad (5.17)$$

$$= \frac{\partial U_L^j}{\partial w^i}(U^i - D^i)\mu^j + U_L^j \frac{dU^i}{dw^i}\mu^j + U_L^j(U^i - D^i)\frac{\partial \mu^i}{\partial w^i}$$

From these relations the individual marginal utilities can be derived:

$$\left.\frac{dU^i}{dw^i}\right|_{D_{fix}} = \frac{1}{2(U^j - D^j)} \left.\frac{dN}{dw^i}\right|_{D_{fix}} + \qquad (5.18)$$

$$+ \frac{(U^i - D^i)}{2} \left[\frac{1}{U^i_L} \frac{\partial U^i_L}{\partial w^i} - \frac{1}{U^j_L} \frac{\partial U^j_L}{\partial w^i} \right]$$

$$+ \frac{(U^i - D^i)}{2} \left[\frac{1}{\mu^j} \frac{\partial \mu^j}{\partial w^i} - \frac{1}{\mu^i} \frac{\partial \mu^i}{\partial w^i} \right]$$

and

$$\left.\frac{dU^j}{dw^i}\right|_{D_{fix}} = \frac{1}{2(U^i - D^i)} \left.\frac{dN}{dw^i}\right|_{D_{fix}} + \qquad (5.19)$$

$$+ \frac{(U^j - D^j)}{2} \left[\frac{1}{U^j_L} \frac{\partial U^j_L}{\partial w^i} - \frac{1}{U^i_L} \frac{\partial U^i_L}{\partial w^i} \right]$$

$$+ \frac{(U^j - D^j)}{2} \left[\frac{1}{\mu^i} \frac{\partial \mu^i}{\partial w^i} - \frac{1}{\mu^j} \frac{\partial \mu^j}{\partial w^i} \right].$$

Each of these two equations contains three terms which reflect the effects of the traditional Slutsky decomposition in the commodity space. In addition to this, they also describe corresponding effects in the utility space. This decomposition will be discussed in detail for equation (5.18):

$$\left.\frac{dU^i}{dw^i}\right|_{D_{fix}} = \frac{1}{2(U^j - D^j)} \left.\frac{dN}{dw^i}\right|_{D_{fix}} + \frac{(U^i - D^i)}{2} \left[\ \tilde{U}\ \right] + \frac{(U^i - D^i)}{2} \left[\ \tilde{\mu}\ \right]$$

COMMODITY SPACE — income effect — income compensated substitution effect

UTILITY SPACE — welfare effect — compensated substitution effect in utility space

In equation (5.18) the first two summands, taken together, represent the income effect at constant prices (see appendix 3), and the third summand represents the income compensated substitution effect. Here these effects refer to the individual utility positions, whereas in the traditional Slutsky decomposition, income and substitution effects are described referring to the objective function which is the household utility function. These effects are described in the commodity space, i.e. the effect of a wage change on the allocation of the commodities.

However, in the bargaining model two individual utility functions are assumed which together determine the objective function. The commodities are arguments of the individual utility functions and not directly of the objective function. Therefore, a substitution in the commodity space causes, in general, a substitution in the utility space, because the utility transfer rate between the partners changes due to the altered price relationship. But also an income change might induce different marginal utility changes and induce a substitution in the utility space[42]. Therefore, the conditions for the income compensated substitution effect in the commodity space contain a constant ratio of the individual marginal utilities.

In analogy to the Slutsky decomposition, in the utility space the effect of a change in prices or wages can be decomposed into two effects. These will be called *welfare* and *substitution effect*. In equation (5.18) the first summand represents the welfare effect with a constant utility transfer rate. The second and the third summand together represent the compensated substitution effect in the utility space given a constant Nash gain. The two terms of this substitution effect describe the substitution between the partners, which is caused by the change of the relative prices and by the change of the income. These three effects will be treated separately in the following.

Welfare effect

The first summand of the equation (5.18) represents the effect in the utility space resulting from the change in the real income if the utility transfer rate between the partners and the conflict outcomes are held constant. It is

---

[42] A graphical illustration of the relationship between commodity and utility space is given in figure 4.3 in chapter 4.2.

defined by the weighted reaction of the Nash gain on a change in income ignoring the change in conflict outcomes, and it describes the change in the 'utility of the household'. Therefore it is called the *welfare effect*. The reaction of the Nash gain on a wage change, given a fixed conflict point, results from the marginal contribution of market work to the Nash function, i.e. it is determined through the marginal product of the income in the household production, the marginal 'household utility' λ of the commodities, and the amount of time spent in market work (see appendix 3):

$$\left.\frac{dN}{dw^i}\right|_{D_{fix}} = \lambda Y_M Z_Y M^i \geq 0. \tag{5.20}$$

If the person does not participate in market work, then the term is equal to zero, because there are no changes in income.

In order to consider the pure welfare effect, i.e. the change in the 'household utility' level, no substitution between the partners should occur. Therefore, the marginal rate of substitution is held constant, which means that the additional Nash gain is divided between both partners by the previous distribution ratio. Then the share of person i is as follows (see appendix 3):

$$\frac{\partial U^i}{\partial N} = \frac{1}{2(U^j - D^j)} \tag{5.21}$$

and a change in the 'household utility' level leads to a corresponding proportional effect on the individual outcomes.

Graphically (see figure 5.2), the welfare effect implies a 'parallel' shift of the utility possibility frontier (from curve I to I') so that the slope in the solution point remains constant with respect to every possible conflict point. The new solution point (B) then lies on the connecting line of the conflict point and the old solution point (A).

Income induced substitution effect

In addition to this welfare effect, which leads to a proportional change in the utility level for both spouses, a substitution in utility outcomes between the spouses results from a change in the real income, because the individual marginal utilities of income are different for the spouses in general. This

Figure 5.2

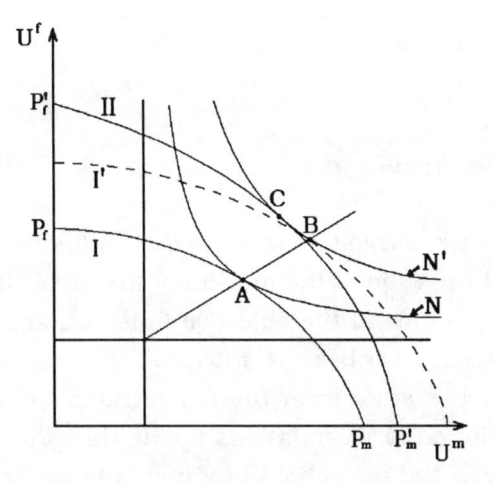

effect, the second summand of (5.18), is called in the following the *income induced substitution effect* and is calculated holding the Nash gain and prices constant (see appendix 3). The sign of this effect depends on the change in the marginal utility of the income of both partners. This is determined by the form of the utility functions and by the individual utility levels.

Assuming identical utility functions with decreasing marginal utilities for both partners, the income induced substitution effect works in favor of the person with the more expensive bundle of commodities.

In figure 5.2 higher prices are assumed for individual f, which lead to an asymmetrical utility possibility frontier I. Therefore, the angular point P_f lies on a lower utility level than P_m, and the marginal utility of the income is larger for individual f. Then, the increase in utility $P_f P_f'$ for a given increase in income is larger than $P_m P_m'$, and the new utility possibility frontier II is less asymmetrical. As already discussed above, the welfare effect represents the shift to the higher utility level N'. The income induced substitution effect, however, causes a rotation of the utility possibility frontier along the 'indifference curve' to a more symmetrical curve (movement from B to C)[43]. In contrast to this, an income reduction leads to a stronger asymmetry. If the potential wage varies for an individual who does not participate in the market before and after the change, then the income induced substitution

---

[43] Both effects together form the income effect in the commodity space which is represented by the shift from B to C in the figure 4.3 in chapter 4.2.

effect disappears because the household income does not change (see appendix 3).

Income compensated substitution effect

The third term in (5.18) - the *income compensated substitution effect* - results when the Nash gain and the ratio of the individual marginal utilities, i.e. the contribution of the commodities to the objective function, are held constant (see appendix 3). This effect describes the substitution between the partners in the utility space, which results from the substitution in the commodity space caused by the altered price relationship. If the price of leisure is determined by the value of the household production because the person is and continues to be specialized in household work, then no substitution takes place as a consequence of a wage change, and the effect is equal to zero. Otherwise, the price for leisure increases with a wage increase. If both spouses spend time in market work, the effect has a negative sign for that person whose wage varies. The bundle of commodities will be more expensive for this person in comparison to that of the partner. Therefore, a further rotation of the utility possibility frontier along the 'indifference curve' takes place in favor of the partner. With a wage reduction, the income compensated substitution effect works in favor of the person affected by the wage change. But, if the partner is specialized in household work, no income compensated substitution effect exists, because the price ratio does not change. In this case, the leisure price for the partner is determined also by the wage of the spouse who works in the market. Each additional unit of leisure for that person specialized in work at home reduces his or her time in household production, which has to be substituted by an additional time unit in household work of the other spouse. Because the latter spent time also in market work, the price for that unit of time is determined by his or her wage, and the price for leisure will change for both spouses in the same way.

Combining both substitution effects, the final sign cannot be determined without further assumptions about the utility functions. If both individuals have identical utility functions and the wage change affects the partner with the higher commodity prices, then both effects work in the same direction and are negative for the person with an increasing wage and are positive for the partner. Otherwise, the effects work in opposite directions, and the sign is undetermined, but the entire substitution effect might turn out to be relatively small.

5.3.2 The bargaining effect

In addition to these previously described effects at a constant conflict point, a wage change also affects the conflict outcome. But as discussed above, changes in the conflict point also have effects on the cooperative solution. The increase of the conflict outcome of a person has a positive effect on her cooperative outcome (see also Thomson 1987) and a correspondingly negative one for the partner. However, the changes in the cooperative solution with a convex negotiation set are smaller than the changes in the conflict outcome.

Differentiating equation (4.9) with respect to D^i gives the reaction of the cooperative outcome on a change of the conflict outcome (see appendix 3):

$$\frac{dU^i}{dD^i} = \frac{1}{2 - \frac{(U^i - D^i)^2}{U^j - D^j} \frac{d^2 U^j}{dU^{i2}}} < 1 \text{ and } > 0 \qquad (5.22)$$

and

$$\frac{dU^i}{dD^j} = \frac{dU^j}{dU^i} \frac{dU^i}{dD^j} = \frac{-\frac{U^j - D^j}{U^i - D^i}}{2 - \frac{(U^i - D^i)^2}{U^j - D^j} \frac{d^2 U^j}{dU^{i2}}} < 0 \qquad (5.23)$$

The size of the bargaining effect depends on the marginal rate of utility transfer and on the curvature of the utility possibility frontier. The more difficult it is to transfer the utility of the person with the changed conflict outcome to that of the partner, the smaller the bargaining effect. This means that a change in the conflict outcome has a larger effect on the cooperative outcome of the partner with the comparatively inferior bargaining position. Therefore, the effect becomes larger the more asymmetrical the bargaining situation is.

But, above all, the size of the bargaining effect depends on the reaction of the conflict point to a wage change. As discussed above, in general, a wage change affects the outside options, even if the person is not employed in the cooperative solution. The conflict outcome of the other spouse remains unchanged. Therefore, the relative bargaining position shifts with changes in the wage ratio.

Solving the maximization problem (5.7) for the single-person household, the change in the conflict outcome is given by (see appendix 3)

$$\frac{dD^i}{dw^i} = \lambda \mathcal{Y}_M Z_y \mathcal{M}^i \geq 0. \tag{5.24}$$

This expression disappears only if the non-wage income available is high enough so that no employment is necessary for the optimal resource allocation in the single-person household. Since this is only applicable in exceptional cases, a positive reaction of the conflict payment on a wage change is assumed for the following.

5.3.3 The total effect

Given the previous results, the total effect of a wage change on the individual outcome of the person affected can be decomposed into the following components:

(5.25)

$$\frac{dU^i}{dw^i} = \frac{1}{2 - \dfrac{(U^i - D^i)^2}{U^j - D^j} \dfrac{d^2 U^j}{dU^{j2}}} \lambda \mathcal{Y}_M Z_y \mathcal{M}^i \quad \Bigg\} > 0 \quad \text{bargaining effect}$$

$$+ \frac{1}{2(U^j - D^j)} \lambda Y_M Z_Y M^i \quad \Bigg\} \geq 0 \quad \begin{array}{l}\text{welfare effect} \\ \text{(0 for } M^i = 0\text{)}\end{array}$$

$$+ \frac{(U^i - D^i)}{2} \left[\frac{1}{U_L^i} \frac{\partial U_L^i}{\partial w^i} - \frac{1}{U_L^j} \frac{\partial U_L^j}{\partial w^i} \right] \quad \Bigg\} \begin{array}{l}>\\=\\<\end{array} 0 \quad \begin{array}{l}\text{income induced} \\ \text{substitution effect} \\ \text{(0 for } M^i = 0\text{)}\end{array}$$

$$+ \frac{(U^i - D^i)}{2} \left[\frac{1}{\mu^j} \frac{\partial \mu^j}{\partial w^i} - \frac{1}{\mu^i} \frac{\partial \mu^i}{\partial w^i} \right] \quad \Bigg\} \leq 0 \quad \begin{array}{l}\text{income compensated} \\ \text{substitution effect} \\ \text{(0 for } M^i = 0\text{)}\end{array}$$

If the person is not employed before as well as after the wage change, the last three terms disappear and the changes in the cooperative solution result only from the altered outside options. Except in the case discussed above, the bargaining effect has a positive sign. This implies that even in the case of an unchanged income and an unchanged production structure, a wage change results in an internal reallocation of the goods due to the bargaining effect. If the person is employed, additional effects result from changes in income and prices.

The sign of the total effect is not clearly predictable because the welfare effect is positive, but the income compensated effect and eventually the income induced substitution effect are negative. Nevertheless, the total effect of a wage increase on the individual outcome is more positive,

- the larger the bargaining effect is, i.e. the worse the bargaining position of the person in comparison to that of the partner and the larger the reaction of the conflict outcome is,

- the larger the welfare effect is, i.e. the larger the marginal contribution of the income is, which depends on both the level of income and the household technology,

- the larger the income induced substitution effect is, i.e. the more asymmetrical the situation is, and

- the smaller the income compensated substitution effect is, i.e. the less the ratio of the shadow prices of an additional time unit of both partners changes, which also depends on the household technology.

Altogether, a wage increase has, in general, a positive effect on the individual outcome for the affected person, especially if that person is in an inferior bargaining position in comparison to the partner. But, the effect may be small in households, in which the marginal contribution of income to the Nash gain is exceptionally small since the household production based on a very high income level cannot be increased sufficiently by additional earned income. In addition, if this is also true for the single-person household in the case of conflict and as a consequence the bargaining effect turns out relatively small, the negative substitution effects may compensate the positive welfare and bargaining effects. In particular, this might occur, if the affected person was in the superior bargaining situation, because then the income induced substitution effect is also negative. In this case the effect of a wage increase on the individual outcome is very small.

Regarding the income of men and women - with lower wages for women - the household technology in a single-person household might be more capital intensive for men than for women. Then, the bargaining effect and consequently the total effect of a wage increase should be smaller for men than for women. Therefore, we should expect a significant positive effect of a wage change on their individual utility level for women.

Corresponding to the change in the person's individual outcome, the outcome of the partner is also affected by a wage change. In analogy to (5.25) it can be decomposed as follows:

$$\frac{dU^j}{dw^i} = \frac{-\frac{U^j - D^j}{U^i - D^i}}{2 - \frac{(U^i - D^i)^2}{U^j - D^j}\frac{d^2U^j}{dU^{i2}}} \lambda \mathcal{Y}_M Z_y \mathcal{M}^i \quad \Bigg\} < 0 \quad \text{bargaining effect} \tag{5.26}$$

$$+ \frac{1}{2(U^i - D^i)} \lambda Y_M Z_Y M^i \quad \Bigg\} \geq 0 \quad \begin{array}{l}\text{welfare effect}\\ (0 \text{ for } M^i=0)\end{array}$$

$$+ \frac{(U^j - D^j)}{2}\left[\frac{1}{U_L^j}\frac{\partial U_L^j}{\partial w^i} - \frac{1}{U_L^i}\frac{\partial U_L^i}{\partial w^i}\right] \quad \Bigg\} \begin{array}{l}<\\=\\>\end{array} 0 \quad \begin{array}{l}\text{income induced}\\ \text{substitution effect}\\ (0 \text{ for } M^i=0)\end{array}$$

$$+ \frac{(U^j - D^j)}{2}\left[\frac{1}{\mu^i}\frac{\partial \mu^i}{\partial w^i} - \frac{1}{\mu^j}\frac{\partial \mu^j}{\partial w^i}\right] \quad \Bigg\} \geq 0 \quad \begin{array}{l}\text{income compensated}\\ \text{substitution effect}\\ (0 \text{ for } M^i=0)\end{array}$$

Here, analogous considerations apply. Three effects - the bargaining effect and the two substitution effects - affect the partner in the opposing direction. Only the welfare effect is always positive for both partners. Therefore, a wage increase, which leads to a positive change in the individual outcome of the affected person does not always have a negative effect for the partner. Particularly, in households with a low income, the welfare effect may be so important that the effect is positive for both partners. Certainly, the effect proves to be smaller for the partner than for the person who gets a higher wage. If the welfare effect is small, however, the effects on the cooperative outcomes of both partners have a different sign, with a positive sign for the affected person and a negative sign for the partner.

6 A dynamic model with accumulation of human capital

In the previous chapters the effects of wage and price changes were investigated in a static bargaining model. As we have seen, such changes result in systematic changes of the conflict outcomes. But up to now, only exogenous wage changes have been considered. If the changes of the conflict points have significant effects on the internal distribution within the family, the question arises whether such modifications depend only on exogenous factors, or whether the decisions made in the family also influence the external alternatives outside of the family.

Now, as is known from human capital theory, changes in wages are not only caused by exogenous factors, but they are determined also by investment in human capital. In particular, *on the job training* is an investment in human capital that results in higher wages. Thus, employment not only results in actual income, but it also increases the stock of human capital and hence earning power for the future. On the other hand, during non-employment, human capital is depreciated as market skills are forgotten or become obsolete, and as a consequence the potential wage rate is reduced.

A special characteristic of human capital is that the skills are inseparably bound to the individual. Therefore, investments in human capital during marriage only increase the earning capacity of the person. However, if the individual remains in the household, the potential household income is also increased. But, if the individual leaves the family, the investments in human capital now increase only the outcome for the individual. Therefore, the family members' participation in market work must not only be considered under the viewpoint of the actual and future household income but also with respect to the individual's outside options. This brings up the question of human capital accumulation by the family members in a household with specialization[44].

6.1 Intrafamily division of work and accumulation of human capital

Specialization on work at home implies a renouncement of investments in human capital which increases earning power. While the surplus produced by specialization is divided between both spouses, the renouncement of human capital accumulation by one of the partners means an individual loss in earning capacity.

On the other hand, through specialization in work at home additional skills in household production are acquired. Such skills that increase the productivity in the household production have been called household capital (Becker 1981) or marriage-specific capital (Pollak 1985). As Becker (1981, 1985) shows, the gains from specialization for the household exceed the pure effects resulting from differing wage rates due to such increases in household productivity. However, Becker does not examine the internal distribution of the produced commodities. If this distribution depends on the external alternatives, the question arises how specialization and the accumulation of different kinds of human capital affect the conflict outcomes.

The value of investments in human capital depends on the gains in productivity, and secondly, on the opportunities to utilize an additional productivity.

a) Productivity gains:
In general, specialization in market work means a specialization in very specific activities because production based on a strong division of labor is efficient for goods with a large exchange market. Therefore, persons who are active in the market, will specialize in only one activity in a wide variety of rather specific activities. Market work is remunerated monetarily, and the income can be used to purchase market goods. On the other

---

[44] Benham (1974) and Kenny (1983) investigate the accumulation of human capital by males during marriage.

hand, a characteristic of goods produced in the household is that an exchange on the market is difficult or impossible. The reduction in the transaction costs achieved by the 'exchange by identity' is a direct advantage of the family (see chapter 3). While goods with low transaction costs can be produced more efficiently in the market than in the household, this is not the case for many goods with high transaction costs. As a consequence, the production of heterogeneous commodities has remained in the households, and household production includes rather different activities. Therefore, assuming that the increases in productivity obtained by specialization are larger if the activity is more specific, the productivity gains that result from a specialization in work at home are smaller as compared to that from a specialization in market work.

Secondly, the productivity of the worker also depends on the technology being used. The productivity of market work is determined by characteristics of the workplace, but it is independent from the household composition. This is not the case for household production. Let us assume a s-shaped household production function satisfying the law of diminishing returns but with increasing marginal returns for low capital input. This appears to be realistic because the change from a time intensive to a time saving technology requires a basic capital endowment. Then, if the capital input is low, productivity may be increased more by additional capital than by additional skills. In comparison with the joint household, less capital is available for investments in household technology in two separate households. Then, it is more likely that in the case of conflict the capital endowment in the single-person household is low. In this case, additional income is more important for the welfare production in the single-person household than additional household skills. Therefore, compared to a multi-person household the the gains in productivity are smaller for the single-person household. Thus, investments in household specific human capital by specialization in work at home will increase household productivity more in the joint household than for the case of conflict.

b) Opportunities of utilization:

The possibility of exchanging the goods produced is essential for an efficient utilization of productivity advantages. In the case of specialization in market work a sufficiently large exchange market for the output is available. An exchange takes place by means of money paid for market work which can be used to purchase the market goods.

But for the most part, the goods produced in the household can only be used within the household because there is no external market or another quality or mode of production of these goods is required on the market[45]. As long as the joint household exists, an exchange market also exists, and the increased productivity can be efficiently utilized. However, in the case of conflict, the exchange market is withdrawn from the person specialized in work at home. If the person lives alone, the productivity advantages can only be utilized in production for him- or herself. In this case, the additional skills in household production will not compensate the losses in income due to the loss in earning capacity.

Therefore, in contrast to marketable human capital, household-specific capital is not only bound up with the person but also with the composition of the household. But then, a specialization in work at home or in the market contains different risks for the case of conflict. The spouse specialized in market work can utilize the increased productivity in the joint household as well as when living alone. But, the spouse specialized in work at home loses her exchange market in the case of conflict and as a consequence the possibility to utilize her productivity advantages efficiently.

Thus, the accumulation of different types of human capital has miscellaneous effects for the individuals. First, there result different gains of productivity which must be considered with regard to the long-term production of the household. Secondly, the external options of the individuals are influenced differently by the unequal increases in productivity and by their different utilization in separated households. In the case of conflict,

---

[45] This applies, above all, to immaterial, person-oriented commodities like the rearing of children. But, it also applies to many material goods that have immaterial aspects, e.g. cooking, shopping, etc. However, even if the goods or services are marketable, a different manner of production is required than usually used in the household. For instance, the clothes washed in the household washing machine or the food prepared in customary household portions might be difficult to market. This also applies to services like nursing care or cleaning. Hence, the human capital accumulated by working at home can be used in the market only in a limited way. Furthermore, the marketing of goods requires advertising capabilities and the ability to acquire customers which are not normally learned by specialization in work at home.

specialization in work at home leads to lower returns for the time invested. If the conflict outcomes determine the internal bargaining solution, then investments in different types of human capital will influence the future internal distribution. Rational individuals will take such intertemporal dependencies into account when making their decisions.

6.2 The dynamic approach

In order to take these intertemporal dependencies into consideration in the bargaining model individual life time utility functions will be used in the further analysis. The life time is separated in two periods, and the utility functions are assumed to be intertemporarily additive[46]:

$$U^i = U^{i1} + U^{i2} \tag{6.1}$$

where U^{it} represents the individual utility in period t.

The two periods are defined as follows:

- In period 1 the accumulation of human capital does not yet have any effects. The production in this period is determined only by the productivities at the beginning of the game.

- Period 2 contains the whole remaining time interval of the life cycle. Here, the returns depend on the investments in human capital of period 1. Thus, decisions in period 1 affect the outcomes of period 2.

In this case the spouses bargain in period 1 not only for the distribution of current welfare production of the household, but also with regard to the expected outcomes in period 2. Then, the objective function of the bargaining model is given by

---

[46] For the sake of simplicity no discounting factor is used, and U^{i2} represents the discounted utility. This has no effect on the results in principle, merely the influence of the individuals' time preference cannot be analyzed.

$$\max \quad N = (U^m - D^m) * (U^f - D^f) \tag{6.2}$$

$$= (U^{m1} + U^{m2} - D^m) * (U^{f1} + U^{f2} - D^f)$$

In each period, the decision parameters are the time allocation of the family members and the distribution of the produced goods. The time spent in period 1 in work at home and in the market determines the human capital stock of the individuals in period 2 and therefore the wage rates and household productivities. This means that both the negotiation set (= welfare production of the household) and the conflict outcomes in period 2 depend on the decision in period 1.

With these assumptions the selection of an appropriate solution concept is more difficult than in the static model. The Nash solution, like all other cooperative solution concepts, presumes that binding contracts can be made for all decisions at the time of the negotiation. In the two-period approach, the negotiation takes place at the beginning of period 1, but some activities are carried out later in period 2, which depend on decisions in period 1. In this case, it is important whether the decisions for these activities can be determined by the negotiation at the beginning or not. Is it possible to make contracts which are also binding for period 2, that means for the whole life time? Or is it more realistic to expect renegotiation after time, i.e. in period 2?

The binding force of contracts depends on the incentives to break them, i.e. on the individual gains resulting from the breach and also on the duration of the contract. Short-term contracts often enforce themselves because many decisions are irreversible in the short run. Consumption decisions, for example, are realized immediately and are scarcely revisable. Also decisions about market work are usually stable in the short run, because work contracts cannot be modified or canceled arbitrarily, and searching a job requires time. Flexibility may be greater for self-employed workers, but even here the necessary contact with clients requires a certain continuity. Therefore, decisions on the intrafamily division of work can only be changed over a longer time, and thus have a certain stability - at least for short time periods. Thus, the short term decisions within the family might be viewed as reliable agreements by all the participants. It will be assumed in the following that this holds for all decisions and contracts which are realized in period 1.

No such assumption can be made in general regarding long-term contracts, that are made in period 1, but finally fulfilled in period 2. Contracts about future cooperative payments and future time allocation are of this type. Indeed, the partners are free in period 1 to fix the future distribution, but the realization of this decision takes place later when the situation may have changed. Then an incentive may exist for one of the partners to break the agreement if his bargaining power has increased.

As has been argued above, a specialization in market work or work at home leads to different conflict outcomes and therefore to an asymmetric bargaining power of the spouses in period 2. If the distribution is separately negotiated in each period rather than in one decision at the beginning of the game, the partner with the better earning capacity receives a higher cooperative outcome in period 2. Therefore, an incentive exists for him to break agreements about the future distribution and to ask for renegotiations. Nevertheless, if there are additional factors like sanctions and costs of a breach, long-term contracts can also be enforceable.

6.2.1   Game with binding long-term contracts

Under the assumption that all long-term contracts are enforceable in the future, all decisions can be made at the beginning, and the distribution for period 2 can be fixed in period 1.

In this case the model can be formally written as follows

$$\max_{L^{it}, H^{it}, M^{it}} N = (U^m - D^m) * (U^f - D^f) \qquad (6.3)$$
$$= (U^{m1} + U^{m2} - D^m) * (U^{f1} + U^{f2} - D^f)$$

subject to
the usual budget and time constraints for each period.

The individual total utilities, i.e. the outcomes in period 1 and period 2, depend on the conflict point at the beginning of the negotiation process, but not on that of period 2. Changes in the productivities due to specialization affect only the potential future welfare production of the household, i.e. the model constraints, but not the objective function. Then, the model is equivalent to a dynamic traditional model because 'household preferences' will not change endogenously.

6.2.2 Game without binding long-term contracts

If contracts have no binding force for the future, such agreements will not be made by rational individuals. But, given rational expectations, the individuals will expect a new bargain with the same partner. Because every negotiation requires time, not all possible partnerships can be compared with each other at each point in time. On the other hand, the current partnership has the advantage of fewer information requirements and negotiation costs, because the bargaining partner is known. Therefore, if the gain in the current partnership is sufficiently large as compared to the known external alternatives, no extensive search for a better partnership is to be expected[47]. Additional costs may result from sanctions when social norms related to the exclusiveness of marriages are violated.

However, if the partners expect new negotiations in the future, the decision parameters which determine the distribution in period 2 get a strategic character. Then a special problem arises. Some decisions in period 1 affect the production in period 1, the possible production for period 2 and, simultaneously, the distribution in period 2. Especially, the decision concerning time allocation is an important one. With regard to a high welfare production of the household in both periods, the interests of the partners are identical, but regarding the effects on the bargaining power in period 2 the partners have opposite interests. Each partner is interested in the best possible relative bargaining position for period 2, which improves with an

---

[47] Nevertheless, in many cases the partners may search at any time in order to improve the information about external alternatives and to reinforce one's own threat position. But, usually this external search is not very extensive. First, given a fixed distribution of possible partners, the probability in finding a better partnership decreases with the duration of the current partnership due to the decreasing transaction costs while learning about the partner. Second, resources spent on an external search are lost for the joint production. Therefore, the mutual promise to cooperate without an external search is a rational agreement at the beginning. But, because better outside options would also increase the internal individual outcome, a breach of this agreement is to be expected and an external search will happen in a reduced extent, especially if the search costs are not large. In general, an external search is more likely to occur when the individual cooperative outcome is small (compare the arguments regarding search behavior in Becker/Landes/Michael 1977).

increasing own conflict outcome and a decreasing one for the partner. Hence, the decision about time allocation in period 1 has a cooperative as well as a strategic aspect.

Classical game theory offers no solution concept for such problems, like Harsanyi (1979) states: "Another difficulty lies in the fact that classical game theory is restricted to *fully cooperative* games, where all agreements are always fully enforceable, and to *fully noncooperative* games, where no agreements are ever enforceable at all. It does not cover *partially cooperative* games, where some types of agreements may be fully enforceable, while other types may be either unenforceable or enforceable with specified probabilities; ... Within the class of partially cooperative games, special importance attaches to cooperative games with a *sequential structure*. There are games involving two or more succesive stages, in which agreements among the players may be built up gradually in several consecutive steps. Unlike strictly cooperative games, in which any agreement is always final, such sequential games will often permit renegotiation and modification of earlier agreements under certain conditions in later stages of the game. In real life, games of this type are extremely important, yet they are altogether beyond the reach of classical game theory" (ibid. p. 9). One approach for modelling such situations was proposed by Selten and Güth (1982). They combine "the local application of the Nash's two-person bargaining theory with the idea of subgame consistency" (ibid., p. 178) in a dynamic model with repeated wage bargaining, in which commitments can be made only for one period.

For the purpose of the present analysis a comparable approach is used for the two-period model. It is assumed that in each period the cooperative Nash solution is reached, but that both the negotiation set and the conflict outcomes in period 2 depend on the solution in period 1. Then, the spouses bargain in period 1 not only for the distribution of current household production but also with regard to the expected outcomes in period 2. Given rational expectations[48], the partners will expect a cooperative solution in period 2 depending on the conflict point of this period. This assumption satisfies the condition of subgame perfectness.

---

[48] Rational expectations in bargaining games are characterized by expecting rational behavior from the other players (see Harsanyi 1977, p. 117-199).

Then the model can be written as follows:

$$\max_{L^{i1}, H^{i1}, M^{i1}} N = (U^m - D^m) * (U^f - D^f) \quad (6.4)$$
$$= (U^{m1} + U^{m2} - D^m) * (U^{f1} + U^{f2} - D^f)$$

$$\max_{L^{i2}, H^{i2}, M^{i2}} N_2 = (U^{m2} - D^{m2}) * (U^{f2} - D^{f2}) \quad (6.5)$$

subject to
the budget and time constraints for each period.

6.2.3 The two-period model

This two-period model can be solved recursively. First, the conditional solution for period 2, which depends on the wage rates and on the productivity in the household and thereby on the time use in period 1, is derived. The resulting indirect utility functions $U^{i2}(M^i, H^i, M^j, H^j)$ are then used to solve the maximization problem of period 1.

The decision problem with binding agreements for period 2 can also be described by an equivalent two-period model, in which the relative bargaining position and the utility transfer rate are held constant for both periods (see appendix 5). This model coincides with the model without binding agreements for period 2 with one exception: the expected value for the payment in period 2 results from a bargaining game based on the conflict point of the beginning. An interpretation of this setting is that the partners in period 1 agree to negotiate in period 2 with respect to a quasi-conflict point that leaves the relative bargaining position of the partners unchanged in both periods.

Thus, a unique model can be formulated, and the two cases represent two variants of this bargaining model with different assumptions regarding the basis of negotiation in period 2:

- Period 1 is the time period in which the accumulation of human capital does not yet have any effect on the production. It is assumed that binding agreements can be made for this time period. The distribution[49] of goods

---

[49] This short-term distribution can be observed empirically.

and time in period 1 results from a bargaining game, in which the individual utility functions depend on the expected outcomes of period 2. The conflict point in period 1 is exogenous, i.e. it depends only on decisions which were made previously.

- Period 2 extends over the total remaining life cycle. The expected individual outcome for this period encloses all expected future payoffs which again result from a cooperative bargaining game. The potential welfare production and, as a consequence, the negotiation set as well as the conflict point of the subgame in this period depend on the decisions in the first period. However, in the game with binding agreements, the partners do not bargain with respect to this conflict point, but to a quasi-conflict point which leaves the relative bargaining position unchanged.

Thus, the two-period model can be written as follows:

$$\max_{L^{i1},H^{i1},M^{i1}} N = (U^{m1} + U^{m2} - D^m) * (U^{f1} + U^{f2} - D^f) \qquad (6.6)$$

$$\max_{L^{i2},H^{i2},M^{i2}} N_2 = (U^{m2} - D^{m2}) * (U^{f2} - D^{f2}) \qquad (6.7)$$

subject to

household production in each period:

$$C^{mt} + C^{ft} = Z(a^{mt}H^{mt} + a^{ft}H^{ft}, X^t) \quad t = 1, 2 \qquad (6.8)$$

budget constraint in each period:

$$X^t = Y(w^{mt}M^{mt} + w^{ft}M^{ft} + I^{mt} + I^{ft}) \quad t = 1, 2 \qquad (6.9)$$

time constraints in each period:

$$T = M^{it} + H^{it} + L^{it} \qquad t = 1, 2 \quad i = m, f \qquad (6.10)$$

non-negativity constraints:

$$C^{mt} > 0, \ C^{ft} > 0, \ L^{mt} > 0, \ L^{ft} > 0 \qquad t = 1, 2 \qquad (6.11)$$
$$H^{mt} \geq 0, \ H^{ft} \geq 0, \ M^{mt} \geq 0, \ M^{ft} \geq 0$$

accumulation of human capital:

$$w^{i2} = f(w^{i1}, M^{i1})$$
$$a^{i2} = f(a^{i1}, H^{i1})$$
$$i = m, f \qquad (6.12)$$

conflict outcome in period 2:

$$K^{i2}(w^{i2}, a^{i2}, I^{i2}) \qquad i = m, f \qquad (6.13)$$

is the solution of the utility maximization in a single-person household

$$\max_{L^{i2}, H^{i2}, M^{i2}} U^i(C^{i2}, L^{i2})$$
$$\text{s.t. } C^{i2} = Z(a^{i2}H^{i2}, Y(w^{i2}M^{i2} + I^{i2}))$$
$$T = M^{i2} + H^{i2} + L^{i2}$$

in the game with binding agreements:

$$\frac{U^m - D^m}{U^f - D^f} = \frac{U^{m2} - D^{m2}}{U^{f2} - D^{f2}} \qquad (6.14a)$$

i.e. the threat point (D^{m2}, D^{f2}) is the quasi-conflict point

in the game without binding agreements for period 2:

$$(D^{m2}, D^{f2}) = (K^{m2}, K^{f2}) \qquad (6.14b)$$

i.e. the threat point (D^{m2}, D^{f2}) is the actual conflict point

where $U^{it} = U^i(C^{it}, L^{it})$
- D^i: conflict payoff for person i in period 1, i.e. total outcome if a conflict results in period 1
- C^{it}: consumption of person i in period t
- M^{it}: hours of market work of person i in period t
- H^{it}: hours of work at home of person i in period t
- L^{it}: leisure of person i in period t
- Z: household production function
- a^{it}: individual specific parameter of efficiency in household production
- X: market goods
- Y: netto income function
- I^{it}: non-wage income of person i in period t
- w^{it}: wage of person i in period t.

This model describes two extreme cases - the case with fully enforceable long-term contracts and the case without agreements for period 2. In reality, the bargaining process in the family probably will not coincide fully with one of the two cases. It is more likely that long-term contracts are made, but that they are enforceable only with a given probability. There is always a risk that the spouse with an improving bargaining position might later demand a revision of the agreement in his or her favor. Therefore, each of the two solutions in period 2 are realized with a certain probability p and (1-p), and the expected value of the individual outcome in period 2 results from

$$U^{i2} = pU_r^{i2} + (1-p)U_a^{i2}, \tag{6.15}$$

where U_a^{i2}: the outcome in the case of performed agreement (condition (6.14a))
U_r^{i2}: the outcome in the case of renegotiation (condition (6.14b))
p: the probability of renegotiation.

Then it is sufficient to analyse the reactions in the two extreme cases, because the specific effects determine the decisions of the family with different degrees of importance. How strong these individual influences are, depends on the probability of fulfilling the long-term contracts. This probability may also depend on the decisions in period 1. This will be discussed in the next chapter. First, the intrafamily division of work and the labor supply of the family members will be analysed more closely in the two extreme cases. Since the second period corresponds to the simple static model, the results obtained in chapter 4 can be used for the following analysis.

6.3 Time allocation depending on individual bargaining power

The solution of the model (6.6) to (6.14) gives the conditions for time allocation in the household. A person spends time in both the market and the household sector if the following equation holds (see appendix 6):

$$\frac{1}{U_C^{i1}}\frac{dU^{i2}}{dM^{i1}} + \frac{1}{U_C^{j1}}\frac{dU^{j2}}{dM^{i1}} + Z_Y Y_M w^{i1} = \frac{U_L^{i1}}{U_C^{i1}} = Z_H a^{i1} + \frac{1}{U_C^{i1}}\frac{dU^{i2}}{dH^{i1}} + \frac{1}{U_C^{j1}}\frac{dU^{j2}}{dH^{i1}} \tag{6.16}$$

or in a simplified notation

$$\Psi_M^i + Z_Y Y_M w^{i1} = \frac{U_L^{i1}}{U_C^{i1}} = Z_H a^{i1} + \Psi_H^i \qquad (6.17)$$

This equation differs from the condition (5.13) of the static model by the terms Ψ_M^i and Ψ_H^i, which represent the effects of the time use in period 1 on the outcomes in period 2. They include the change in the person's own future utility as well as that of the partner, if an additional unit of time is used for market work (respectively work at home) in period 1. The weighted sum of these marginal utilities of both spouses represents the 'marginal utility' on the household level. Condition (6.17) holds, if the marginal rate of substitution between leisure and consumption in period 1 is equal to both the 'marginal output' of market work, i.e. in both periods, and to the 'marginal output' of work at home.

The conditions for specialization in market work result similarly

$$\Psi_M^i + Z_Y Y_M w^{i1} = \frac{U_L^{i1}}{U_C^{i1}} > Z_H a^{i1} + \Psi_H^i \qquad (6.18)$$

and also that for specialization in housework:

$$\Psi_M^i + Z_Y Y_M w^{i1} < \frac{U_L^{i1}}{U_C^{i1}} = Z_H a^{i1} + \Psi_H^i \qquad (6.19)$$

Given a linear net-income function, different wages for husband and wife result in specialization of the spouses in market work and work at home in both the traditional model as well as in the static bargaining model (see chapter 5). This is no longer true in the dynamic model. If the effects of market work and work at home (Ψ_M^i and Ψ_H^i) are different for period 2, equation (6.17) may hold for both spouses. For this result, given different wages $w^{i1} < w^{j1}$, either $\Psi_M^i > \Psi_M^j$ or $\Psi_H^i < \Psi_H^j$ or both must hold. This implies that, for the partner with the higher wage rate, market work results in a smaller, or work at home in a higher marginal output for period 2. In this case, equation (6.17) holds for both partners, and the optimal time allocation in the household might not result from complete specialization.

6.3.1 Labor supply

Because in the optimum the marginal output of time is equal for all chosen activities, the decision to participate in market work depends on the wage rate. If the wage rate is so small that time spent in other activities results in a higher outcome, the person will not work in the market. This condition for labor force participation was given in the static model by equation (5.12), which determines the 'reservation wage'.

Reformulating equation (6.17) of the dynamic model, an additional term results in comparison to the static approach:

$$Z_H a^{i1} = Z_Y Y_M w^{i1} + \frac{1}{U_C^{i1}} \left[\frac{dU^{i2}}{dM^{i1}} - \frac{dU^{i2}}{dH^{i1}} \right] + \frac{1}{U_C^{j1}} \left[\frac{dU^{j2}}{dM^{i1}} - \frac{dU^{j2}}{dH^{i1}} \right] \quad (6.20)$$

$$= Z_Y Y_M w^{i1} + \Phi$$

The term denoted by Φ describes the effect on the decision to participate in the market, which results from the effect on the individual utilities in period 2 of both time spent in the market or at home. This term can be decomposed further by using equations (5.17), (5.18), (5.20) and (5.22):

$$Z_H a^{i1} = Z_Y Y_M w^{i1} + \quad (6.21)$$

$$+ \frac{1}{U_C^{i1}} \left[1 - \frac{U^i - D^i}{U^j - D^j} \frac{U^{j2} - D^{j2}}{U^{i2} - D^{i2}} \right] \frac{\partial U^{i2}}{\partial D^{i2}} \left(\frac{\partial D^{i2}}{\partial w^{i2}} \frac{dw^{i2}}{dM^{i1}} - \frac{\partial D^{i2}}{\partial a^{i2}} \frac{da^{i2}}{dH^{i1}} \right)$$

$$+ \frac{1}{U_C^{i1}} \left[1 + \frac{U^i - D^i}{U^j - D^j} \frac{U^{j2} - D^{j2}}{U^{i2} - D^{i2}} \right] \frac{\partial U^{i2}}{\partial N_2} \left(\frac{\partial N_2}{\partial w^{i2}} \frac{dw^{i2}}{dM^{i1}} - \frac{\partial N_2}{\partial a^{i2}} \frac{da^{i2}}{dH^{i1}} \right)$$

$$+ \frac{1}{U_C^{i1}} \left[1 - \frac{U^i - D^i}{U^j - D^j} \frac{U^{j2} - D^{j2}}{U^{i2} - D^{i2}} \right] \left(\left. \frac{\partial U^{i2}}{\partial w^{i2}} \right|_{D,N_{fix}} \frac{dw^{i2}}{dM^{i1}} - \left. \frac{\partial U^{i2}}{\partial a^{i2}} \right|_{D,N_{fix}} \frac{da^{i2}}{dH^{i1}} \right)$$

$$= Z_Y Y_M w^{i1} + \Phi_B + \Phi_W + \Phi_S$$

Time allocation in period 1 affects the wage rate as well as the productivity in household production in period 2. Because the subgame in period 2 is identical with the static model, effects result as they were described in chapter 4 for exogenous wage changes. In the same way the effects of changing household productivity can be derived (see appendix 4). These effects, derived from the marginal time use in period 1 and weighted by the change in the relative bargaining power, are given by the three additional summands in equation (6.21). The first term represents the effect that is caused by the change of the conflict point for alternative time use. In the following, it will be referred to as the *bargaining effect* (Φ_B). The second term is the *welfare effect* (Φ_W), which is caused by the change of the household gain in period 2. The third term results from substitutions between the partners and is called the *substitution effect* (Φ_S). These effects for period 2 affect the decision on time use in period 1. Since they must be considered by analyzing the decision of period 1.

Relative bargaining position

The weights of the different effects are determined by the change in the relative bargaining power between the spouses. The expression contained in each term

$$\frac{U^i - D^i}{U^j - D^j} \frac{U^{j2} - D^{j2}}{U^{i2} - D^{i2}} \qquad (6.22)$$

represents the change in the relative bargaining position of the spouses between the two periods and reflects the impact of the partner's future utility on the optimal decision. The term results if the representation with weights given by the marginal utilities of consumption of both spouses (U_C^{i1} and U_C^{j1}, see equation 6.20) is reformulated into a weighting by the marginal utility of the affected person (U_C^{i1}) only. After this reformulation, the effect on one's own future utility is compared with the marginal utility of the present consumption (U_C^{i1}) (weight = 1), while the effect on the future utility of the partner is weighted by the change in the relative bargaining positions. If the effects on the utility levels of the spouses are in the same direction, both weights are added, otherwise they are subtracted.

For the bargaining effect (Φ_B) and the substitution effect (Φ_S) the total weight results from the difference of both weights

$$1 - \frac{U^i - D^i}{U^j - D^j} \frac{U^{j2} - D^{j2}}{U^{i2} - D^{i2}} \tag{6.23}$$

because the effects on the partner's utility counteracts the impact on own utility. A time allocation changing the future conflict outcome and substitution rate in favor of one spouse has a negative effect on the utility of the other spouse. These opposing interests concerning the joint time allocation decision in period 1 result in a reduced propensity to choose a specific time use. Only the welfare effect works in the same direction for both partners, because an increase in the future welfare production benefits both partners. The weight for the welfare effect then results from

$$1 + \frac{U^i - D^i}{U^j - D^j} \frac{U^{j2} - D^{j2}}{U^{i2} - D^{i2}} \tag{6.24}$$

The term (6.22) is always positive. The first factor of (6.22) is the marginal rate of the utility transfer of the entire game, the second factor is that of period 2 (compare (4.9)). If the bargaining power of both partners remains unchanged - as this is assumed in a game with binding contracts for period 2 - then both marginal rates are equal, and the expression (6.22) has the value 1. In this case, both the bargaining effect and the substitution effect disappear ((6.23) becomes equal 0), and only the welfare effect has an impact on the time allocation in period 1. This means, that in the game with binding long-term contracts the decision on labor supply is determined by the actual productivities and by the accumulation of human capital, but only with respect to future possibilities for welfare production of the household. If this effect is positive, a higher propensity for participation in the market results.

On the other hand, if no long-term contracts can be made, the relative bargaining position between the spouses will normally change as a consequence of different individual time allocation. In the case of a deteriorating relative bargaining position in period 2 for person i the following inequality results (compare (4.11)):

$$\frac{U^i - D^i}{U^j - D^j} < \frac{U^{i2} - D^{i2}}{U^{j2} - D^{j2}} \tag{6.25}$$

In this case, the expression (6.22) becomes smaller than 1, and the individual influences (bargaining and substitution effect) gain importance. Then, person i will have a higher propensity for that time use, for which the bargaining and the substitution effects become positive.

In contrast to this, if the relative bargaining position for person i improves ceteris paribus, the following relation holds

$$\frac{U^i - D^i}{U^j - D^j} > \frac{U^{i2} - D^{i2}}{U^{j2} - D^{j2}} \qquad (6.26)$$

and expression (6.22) exceeds 1. This implies that the influences of the bargaining and the substitution effect work in the opposite direction. Because the decision is made jointly by the spouses, the propensity decreases for a time allocation in the household that results in a further increase in the bargaining position of person i. This can be interpreted as a compensation in advance for later changes in the bargaining position.

Productivity

In addition, all three effects of the equation (6.21) depend on the effect of a marginal change of market- or housework on the wage rate and efficiency parameter of the household production, respectively. These are determined by human capital accumulation. As has been already discussed at the beginning of this chapter, marketable human capital is in most cases specific, because an exchange market for the products exists which makes a strong division of work with high specialization profitable. In contrast to this, household work includes many different activities, and thus, productivity increases through specialization only to a limited extent. Therefore, one can assume that, in general,

$$\frac{dw^{i2}}{dM^{i1}} > \frac{da^{i2}}{dH^{i1}} \qquad (6.27)$$

is true. Moreover, it appears to be plausible that the change in the productivity as result of a marginal change in time use depends on the amount of time already used for the respective activity. Because the learning effects in general will be smaller if much time has already been spent in the activity, a negative relation between the amount of time spent and the productivity gains may be assumed. So, in general, taking up a job might cause a larger increase in productivity than the expansion of full-time work by overtime. Then the relationship (6.27) will be true if the market activity of a person is small. Regarding the question of entry into the market, i.e. in the case of non-employment of a person, (6.27) can be assumed as valid.

Bargaining effect

In order to determine the sign of the bargaining effect (Φ_B) in equation (6.21), the marginal utility of income and housework in a single-person household must be considered. For this purpose, the term in parentheses will be transformed further.

In the case without binding agreements for period 2, D^{i2} is identical with the conflict outcome in this period ($D^{i2} = K^{i2}$), and using equations (5.24) and (A4.2) the following equation results:

$$\frac{\partial D^{i2}}{\partial w^{i2}} \frac{dw^{i2}}{dM^{i1}} - \frac{\partial D^{i2}}{\partial a^{i2}} \frac{da^{i2}}{dH^{i1}} = \qquad (6.28)$$

$$\frac{\partial K^{i2}}{\partial w^{i2}} \frac{dw^{i2}}{dM^{i1}} - \frac{\partial K^{i2}}{\partial a^{i2}} \frac{da^{i2}}{dH^{i1}} = \lambda \mathcal{Y}_M Z_\mathcal{Y} \mathcal{M}^{i2} \frac{dw^{i2}}{dM^{i1}} - \lambda Z_\mathcal{H} \mathcal{H}^{i2} \frac{da^{i2}}{dH^{i1}}$$

$$= \frac{\partial K^{i2}}{\partial w^{i2}} \left[\frac{dw^{i2}}{dM^{i1}} - \frac{Z_\mathcal{H} \mathcal{H}^{i2}}{\mathcal{Y}_M Z_\mathcal{Y} \mathcal{M}^{i2}} \frac{da^{i2}}{dH^{i1}} \right].$$

The sign of this expression is determined by the marginal change in productivities discussed above and by the marginal utilities of increased market or household skills in the case of conflict in period 2 (terms in italics), that means by the ratio of the marginal products of housework time ($Z_\mathcal{H}$) and market time ($\mathcal{Y}_M Z_\mathcal{H}$) and by the ratio of time spent at home and in the market $\frac{\mathcal{H}^{i2}}{\mathcal{M}^{i2}}$ in the single-person household.

The marginal products of housework and market time depend on the household production technology. In a single-person household it is quite likely that an increased capital input allows the change from a time intensive to a time saving technology, and therefore the marginal productivity of time spent for earning income exceeds that of housework time[50].

The ratio of time spent at home and in the market $\frac{\mathcal{H}^{i2}}{\mathcal{M}^{i2}}$ is determined by the optimal time allocation in the case of conflict in period 2. Now, in the optimum the total time is divided up into the different activities in such a way that the marginal utility for each use of time is the same. As discussed above, the marginal utility of household production depends on the size of the household due to the lack of an external exchange market. In a single-person household the production of more household goods than required for the individual does not increase the utility substantially, because they cannot be easily exchanged for other utility-bearing goods. The marginal utility of housework, therefore, decreases significantly in a single-person household. On the other hand, the marginal utility of market work decreases more slowly, because the outcome from these activities, i.e. monetary income, is necessary for many utility-bearing goods and can be utilized for the acquisition or production of the goods with the highest marginal utility. Therefore, it is likely for most single-person households, that a larger part of the time is used for market work than for household production[51].

From both arguments it follows in general that

$$\frac{Z_{\mathcal{H}}\mathcal{H}^{i2}}{\mathcal{Y}_{\mathcal{M}}Z_{\mathcal{Y}}\mathcal{M}^{i2}} < 1. \tag{6.29}$$

Then with (6.27), a positive sign for the expression (6.28) results. This indicates that a marginal increase in the market work in period 1 leads to a stronger improvement of the conflict outcome in period 2 than a marginal increase in housework time.

These effects on the conflict outcome also result in the game with binding agreements and would be relevant in the case of conflict, if this could occur

---

[50] Exceptions are households with a high non-wage income which can use a capital intensive technology without earning income.

[51] Exceptions might be households with a high non-wage-income, so that if no or less additional income is necessary to buy the market goods. Then, a large part of time will be used as leisure. But time for one's own production is required to some extent in any case.

here at all[52]. Nevertheless, these effects do not determine the cooperative solution in period 2 ($K^{12} \neq D^{12}$), and therefore do not influence the decision in period 1 (term (6.23) disappears).

In the game without binding agreements for period 2, a change in the conflict point leads to a parallel change in the cooperative solution ($\frac{\partial U^{12}}{\partial D^{12}} > 0$, compare (5.22)). If expression (6.28) is positive, then the bargaining effect has a positive sign for persons whose relative bargaining position deteriorates, and a negative one for individuals with an improving relative bargaining position.

The change of the relative bargaining positions can be derived by considering the effects on the single-person household. Since for a single-person household the income capacity is more important than the productivity in the household production, the partner with the higher earning capacity has more bargaining power. Therefore, because the partner with higher earning capacity spends more time in market work in period 1, his or her earning capacity is further improved, so that a relatively better bargaining position in period 2 results.

In general, the relative bargaining position deteriorates for the partner with the smaller participation in the market, and expression (6.28) becomes positive for that person. Then in the decision on labor supply, the bargaining effect is positive, and it increases the propensity for market work. On the other hand, for the partner with the larger market participation, the bargaining effect is negative and works against a further expansion of market work.

---

[52] With the assumption of binding agreements a conflict cannot occur, because the contract must be enforced, even if the conflict outcome would be preferred individually. An exogenous dissolution of the partnership is also excluded with the assumption of complete information. However, in a model with incomplete information the conflict outcome is also relevant in the case of binding agreements in an existing partnership (see chapter 9).

Welfare effect

Using (5.20) and (A4.3) the second term in parenthesis of the welfare effect (Φ_W) in equation (6.21) can be transformed in the same way as the bargaining effect, but regarding the joint household:

$$\frac{\partial N_2}{\partial w^{i2}} \frac{dw^{i2}}{dM^{i1}} - \frac{\partial N_2}{\partial a^{i2}} \frac{da^{i2}}{dH^{i1}} = \lambda Y_M Z_Y M^{i2} \frac{dw^{i2}}{dM^{i1}} - \lambda Z_H H^{i2} \frac{da^{i2}}{dH^{i1}} \qquad (6.30)$$

$$= \frac{\partial N_2}{\partial w^{i2}} \left[\frac{dw^{i2}}{dM^{i1}} - \frac{Z_H H^{i2}}{Y_M Z_Y M^{i2}} \frac{da^{i2}}{dH^{i1}} \right].$$

However, the conclusions for the multi-person household are different. First, the total income of a multi-person household is larger or, at least it is not smaller than the incomes in each hypothetical single-person household of the individual household members. Thus, it is more likely that a capital intensive household technology is available. This means that increasing capital input does not lead to substantial additional time savings by changing the household technology, and the marginal products decrease for both income as well as housework time. Without further assumptions, the ratio of these marginal products is unknown. At least for households with a low income we may obtain the same results as in the single-person household whereas in households with higher income the opposite may be true.

Secondly, the 'marginal utilities' of the different kinds of time use are unlike those in a single-person household, because the 'marginal utility' on the household level, i.e. the marginal change of the Nash gain, must be considered. The larger number of household members implies a larger demand for time intensive household goods. Therefore, transaction costs can be reduced, which increases the 'marginal utility'. In the multi-person household the 'marginal utility' of housework is less decreasing than in a single-person household, and additional time spent in household production by some household members contributes more to the family surplus than market work. This may be the case, above all, if there are small children in the household, because in this case household production is very time intensive. Since, however, the second period in the model covers the remaining lifetime of a person, the question arises whether this relationship will be true for the whole future. Assuming that in a two-person household without children like in single-person households the optimal time allocation contains only a small part of the housework time, and that total specialization in housework is not efficient in those households, then beyond a period of child rearing market work will be taken up again. The average of the ratio of time spent in the market and at home during period 2 depends on the long-term biographical decisions. The shorter the period with higher household productivity in the life course is, the sooner the total amount of time spent in the market in period 2 will exceed the time spent at home. Then the development of the income capacity becomes more important for the decision in period 1.

Therefore, the sign of the welfare effect cannot be uniquely predicted, because depending on the household technology it may result in

$$\frac{Z_H H^{i2}}{Y_M Z_Y M^{i2}} > 1 \text{ or } < 1. \tag{6.31}$$

But, this expression is more likely to be less than 1 (and then the welfare effect is positive), the smaller the income of the household is and the shorter the time period with high productivity of housework time. In both cases an increasing income capacity may be more important in the long run than additional household skills. In this case the propensity for housework in period 1 is reduced. This result is independent of whether binding agreements can be made for period 2 or not.

Substitution effect

The third effect in equation (6.21), the substitution effect (Φ_S), can be decomposed into the income induced and the income compensated substitution effect (see chapter 5). Using equations (5.17) and (A4.1) the term in parenthesis can be transformed as follows:

$$\left.\frac{\partial U^{i2}}{\partial w^{i2}}\right|_{D,N_{fix}} \frac{dw^{i2}}{dM^{i1}} - \left.\frac{\partial U^{i2}}{\partial w^{i2}}\right|_{D,N_{fix}} \frac{da^{i2}}{dH^{i1}} = \quad (6.32)$$

$$= \frac{U^{i2} - D^{i2}}{2} \left[\frac{1}{U_L^{i2}} \frac{\partial U_L^{i2}}{\partial w^{i2}} - \frac{1}{U_L^{j2}} \frac{\partial U_L^{j2}}{\partial w^{i2}} \right] \frac{dw^{i2}}{dM^{i1}} \left.\vphantom{\frac{1}{1}}\right\}$$
$$- \frac{U^{i2} - D^{i2}}{2} \left[\frac{1}{U_L^{i2}} \frac{\partial U_L^{i2}}{\partial a^{i2}} - \frac{1}{U_L^{j2}} \frac{\partial U_L^{j2}}{\partial a^{i2}} \right] \frac{da^{i2}}{dH^{i1}} \left.\vphantom{\frac{1}{1}}\right\} \text{income induced substitution effect}$$

$$+ \frac{U^{i2} - D^{i2}}{2} \left[\frac{1}{\mu^{i2}} \frac{\partial \mu^{i2}}{\partial w^{i2}} - \frac{1}{\mu^{j2}} \frac{\partial \mu^{j2}}{\partial w^{i2}} \right] \frac{dw^{i2}}{dM^{i1}} \left.\vphantom{\frac{1}{1}}\right\}$$
$$- \frac{U^{i2} - D^{i2}}{2} \left[\frac{1}{\mu^{i2}} \frac{\partial \mu^{i2}}{\partial a^{i2}} - \frac{1}{\mu^{j2}} \frac{\partial \mu^{j2}}{\partial a^{i2}} \right] \frac{da^{i2}}{dH^{i1}} \left.\vphantom{\frac{1}{1}}\right\} \text{income compensated substitution effect}$$

The income induced substitution effect resulting from changes in the wage and the household productivity work in the same direction, i.e. towards more symmetry (see chapter 5). Therefore, in (6.32) they compensate each other in part, because the overall effect is the weighted difference of both and might be relatively small. The sign depends on which of the two changes has the larger income effect on the household level. As a consequence, the income induced substitution effect has the same sign as the welfare effect.

The income compensated substitution effect is negative if person i in period 2 specializes in market work (see appendix 7). In this case, the price of the good leisure is only determined by the wage rate. With an increasing wage rate, the consumption of person i becomes more expensive in comparison to the partner's consumption, from which substitution in favor of the partner results. That means, holding the level of welfare production in the household constant, an increase of income capacity through working in the market in period 1 has a negative effect on the outcome in period 2. Conversely, the effect is positive if person i specializes totally in housework in period 2. Then a change of the wage in period 2 does not produce a substitution in favor of the partner, because the price of leisure in period 2 is not affected by it. If person i in period 2 allocates time to both activities, then the sign results from the marginal products of housework time and income and the marginal returns in productivity from human capital accumulation (see apendix 7). If the marginal product of the income in period 2 is larger than that of the housework time and the increase of productivity between the two periods is higher for market work (relation (6.27) holds), then the income compensated substitution effect is negative. This implies that in general the income compensated effect is negative for the spouse with the larger amount of market work in period 2. Because the spouse with the larger income capacity will allocate more time in market work, the effect works against a further expansion of the market work time of this person in period 1. Therefore, in general, the income compensated substitution effect works in the same direction as the bargaining effect.

However, the substitution effect only appears in a game without binding agreements for period 2. In a game with binding long-term contracts, the same changes in prices and the marginal utilities occur, but because the utility distribution was fixed in period 1, corresponding compensation payments are necessary in period 2. The substitution effect, however, has no influence on the decision of time allocation in period 1.

Total effect

Summarizing the discussion of the separate effects of equation (6.21)

$$Z_H a^{i1} = Z_Y Y_M w^{i1} + \Phi_B + \Phi_W + \Phi_S$$
$$= Z_Y Y_M w^{i1} + \Phi,$$

the following conclusions can be drawn regarding the labor supply decision. The bargaining effect (Φ_B) has, in general, a positive sign for the person whose relative bargaining position worsens over the course of time. The signs of the welfare- and the substitution effects are indefinite. However, positive signs may be expected for households with low income and for households with few children, for which the period with high housework productivity is short. Then the total effect (Φ) is positive. In the model with binding long-term contracts, the bargaining- and the substitution effect disappear, and the time allocation in period 1 is influenced only by the welfare effect.

The counterpart for equation (6.21) in a traditional static model is

$$Z_H a^{i1} = Z_Y Y_M w^{i1} \qquad (6.33)$$

which is customarily used for determining the reservation wage. In comparison to this condition an additional term (Φ) results on the right hand side of (6.21), which has a positive sign under the assumptions just mentioned. Therefore, in general a lower reservation wage results than in the traditional model. This means that employment is taken up at a lower wage than is assumed in traditional labor supply models.

In principle, the effect on the household level - the welfare effect - can also be analyzed by a traditional model with a joint household utility function, if not the customary static approach is used but the human capital accumulation is considered explicitly. For example, Lehrer and Nerlove (1981) find "that a woman may supply labor to the market in any given period, even if her current wage is smaller then the price of her time at home, if the increase in future earnings that she would otherwise forego is large enough" (p. 131). In the dynamic model with a joint household utility function the same effects result as in a game with binding long-term contracts. Thus, the traditional model can also be regarded in the dynamic approach as a special case of the bargaining model.

In comparison to the static model, the dynamic approach predicts a lower reservation wage, since the future income losses due to reduced human capital accumulation are considered in the decision on labor supply. But these income losses do not only affect the future welfare production of the household. In the case of conflict the losses must be carried by the person who foregoes capital accumulation, and therefore that person's bargaining position worsens if long-term contracts are not enforceable. This effect is a further incentive to enter into the market even at a lower wage rate. This additional bargaining effect is positive for the person with the inferior bargaining position, and a reservation wage results in the dynamic bargaining model without binding long-term contracts, which is lower than that in a traditional dynamic model.

Therefore, a person will enter the labor market, even if the marginal productivity of housework surpasses that of income. As a result, analyses of household production based on traditional approaches underestimate household productivity, because for the same observed housework time, a traditional approach assumes a lower slope of the household production function.

Figure 6.1a

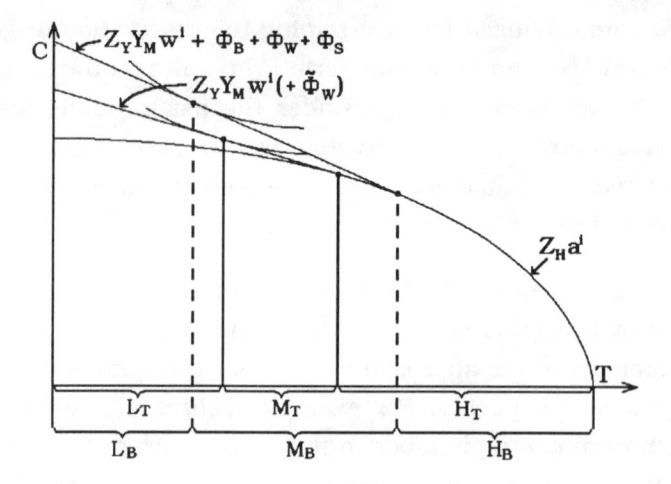

[Figure 6.1a: graph with axes C and T, showing curves labeled $Z_Y Y_M w^i + \Phi_B + \Phi_W + \Phi_S$, $Z_Y Y_M w^i(+ \tilde{\Phi}_W)$, and $Z_H a^i$; x-axis divided into regions L_T, M_T, H_T (upper labels) and L_B, M_B, H_B (lower labels).]

Figure 6.1b

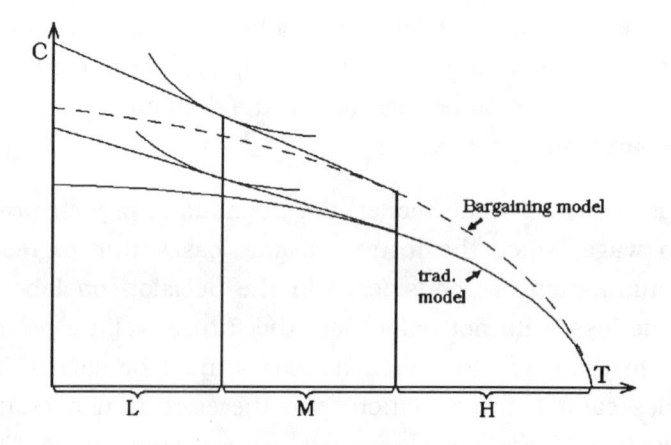

[Figure 6.1b: graph with axes C and T, showing "Bargaining model" (dashed) and "trad. model" curves; x-axis divided into L, M, H.]

This is illustrated in figure 6.1a, in which a linear income function is assumed. The lower curve in figure 6.1a is the household production function for pure housework and the upper that with efficient time use, i.e. with an entry into the market if the marginal products are equal ($Z_H a^{i1} = Z_Y Y_M w^{i1} + \Phi_B + \Phi_W + \Phi_S$). The line in the middle corresponds to the assumptions of the traditional model ($Z_H a^{i1} = Z_Y Y_M w^{i1} + \tilde{\Phi}_W$). Because the traditional model predicts a higher reservation wage, more hours spent in housework (H_T) than in the dynamic bargaining approach without binding long-term contracts (H_B) and less hours spent in market work ($M_T < M_B$) are expected. This is independent of whether a static or a dynamic traditional model approach is used. A steeper slope results from the bargaining effect.

However, for empirical analyses only the actual wage rate (slope of the curves) and the realized time allocation (L, M, H) can be observed. Estimating a household production function on the basis of such data, a traditional approach will underestimate the household production, as is illustrated in figure 6.1b.

The result that the bargaining effect is positive and the reservation wage is underestimated in the traditional approach, is true only for persons whose relative bargaining position worsens ceteris paribus. The signs of the bargaining and the income compensated substitution effect are inverted for people with an improvement in their relative bargaining position, and the bargaining effect, at least, turns out to be negative. That implies, that the propensity for market work is diminished by the bargaining effect for those persons, because the negative effect on the cooperative outcome of the partner predominates in the joint decision. However, questions of entering the market are irrelevant for these persons. As discussed above, the relative bargaining position of the partner with a larger market participation improves due to human capital accumulation. Therefore, except in households in which market work is not necessary due to a high non-wage income, the partner with the better bargaining position already works in the market. However, the effects also determine the decision to extend the working time. In the case of a negative bargaining effect the person will have a lesser propensity to work overtime than is predicted by traditional approaches.

Considering the participation in the labor market of men and women, then, in general, men are employed to a larger extent than their wives. Because of the differences in wages of men and women, this is an efficient allocation of the working time for a joint household. But then, it is mostly the women whose relative bargaining position worsens over the course of time, and it is important for them not to lose too much in their relative bargaining position in the long run (positive sign of the bargaining effect). In addition, with a diminishing number of children also on the household level a long-term specialization in housework may be suboptimal (positive welfare effect). Analyses of women's labor force participation based on traditional approaches, therefore, might overestimate the reservation wage of women, because they may already enter into the market when the household productivity still surpasses the market wage.

6.3.2 Intrafamily division of work

When, as a result of the bargaining model, the decision to enter the market is to be valued in a different way than in the traditional approach, one must ask whether the results concerning the intrafamily division of work also differ. Does the result of the static approach maintain, that no more than one household member will participate in both market and household activities, whereas all other members specialize totally in one activity? Or does specialization possibly lead to a suboptimal result?

A necessary condition for the participation of both spouses in market and in household activities is, that equation (6.21) holds simultaneously for both partners:

$$Z_H a^{i1} = Z_Y Y_M w^{i1} + \Phi_B^i + \Phi_W^i + \Phi_S^i = Z_Y Y_M w^{i1} + \Phi^i$$

$$Z_H a^{j1} = Z_Y Y_M w^{j1} + \Phi_B^j + \Phi_W^j + \Phi_S^j = Z_Y Y_M w^{j1} + \Phi^j$$

From this the following condition results:

$$\frac{Z_Y Y_M w^{i1} + \Phi^i}{a^{i1}} = Z_H = \frac{Z_Y Y_M w^{j1} + \Phi^j}{a^{j1}} \qquad (6.34)$$

Assuming $w^{i1} < w^{j1}$ und $a^{i1} > a^{j1}$ this equation can only be satisfied if $\Phi^i > \Phi^j$. Because with these assumptions the relative bargaining position of person i deteriorates, the bargaining effect of i (Φ_B^i) is positive and that of j (Φ_B^j) negative. If the welfare effect of j (Φ_W^j) does not strongly exceed that of i (Φ_W^i), then $\Phi^i > \Phi^j$ results. So far, in general, at least one point exists, in which equation (6.34) is satisfied. However, it is unlikely, that this point represents the optimal solution of the household.

But, if Φ^i and Φ^j are not fixed values, but monotonous decreasing functions in M^{i1} or M^{j1}, then equation (6.34) holds in a larger range of the household production function. Then it is more probable that the solution point of the household might lie within this range, and the optimal time allocation will not imply total specialization of the household members. Now, it is not implausible that a smaller marginal change of the wage rate in period 2 results for persons with a large amount of working time than for those with a shorter working time. If a person is either working part-time or not at all, then each additional hour of work brings about essential job experience, whereas the overtime of a full time worker hardly has any increasing effect on the future wage. With that, $\frac{dw^{i2}}{dM^{i1}}$ becomes smaller the larger M^{i1} is. In the case that the total effect is positive for both partners - which is probable for positive and sufficiently large welfare effects and, therefore, is true in the game with binding long-term contracts -, then Φ^i (or Φ^j) also becomes smaller the larger the amount of time spent in the market in period 1. Then, condition (6.34) holds in a larger range of the household production function. If the optimal solution point falls into this range, then both spouses will participate in both market and household activities.

7 Pareto efficiency of family decisions

In the previous chapter, intrafamily division of work was described as the solution of a two-period bargaining game. Such a model allows to analyze problems with as well as those without binding long-term contracts. Regarding intrafamily specialization the propensity to specialize is smaller when long-term contracts are not enforceable. If there are gains from specialization, then it is likely, that in the game without binding long-term contracts a non Pareto-optimal allocation of household resources results. Here the question arises, which conditions must be satisfied for a Pareto-efficient solution.

7.1 Binding force of contracts and efficiency

The two-period game falls into the class of the so-called composite games (see Harsanyi 1977, p. 188ff.), which are played as a sequence of subgames, in which the threat point of a subgame is determined by the solution of the previous subgame. Then in the subgames only such outcomes will be accepted from both players which do not change the relative bargaining power (see Harsanyi 1977, p. 181). An exception occurs when the solution space is restricted and does not contain a threat point for the next subgame which leaves the relative bargaining power unchanged.

This problem can be solved, if one player accepts his worsening bargaining position and both players agree to bargain in the next step as if the optimal threat point had been realized. This means they agree to choose the Nash solution corresponding a *quasi-threat point* in the next step. A necessary condition for this proceeding is the enforcement of this agreement. In the game with binding long-term contracts this condition is satisfied, and a Pareto-efficient solution is realized for the total game.

But, even without such agreements, it might be rational to accept a worsening bargaining position, if the cooperative solution of the total game results in a higher outcome for both players. This might occur if the negotiation set of the subsequent subgame depends on the decision of the previous step in such a way, that a changing relative bargaining power is combined with a higher total outcome. The two-period model of household decisions without binding long-term contracts is such a case. Intrafamily specialization leads to a higher welfare production of the household and, at the same time, to a change in the relative bargaining power of the spouses. If the increase in welfare production of the household is big enough, so that both spouses will gain even with a changed bargaining power, a Pareto-efficient allocation would be realized. But, if one partner would loose in the later subgame in comparison with an unchanged situation, two cases must be distinguished. If the later loss can be compensated in previous steps by a corresponding compensation payment, then an efficient solution will be realized. But, if the payoff space of the previous subgame is restricted and does not allow complete compensations[53], then in general suboptimal solutions result because the Pareto fontier of the total game cannot be reached[54].

Figure 7.1

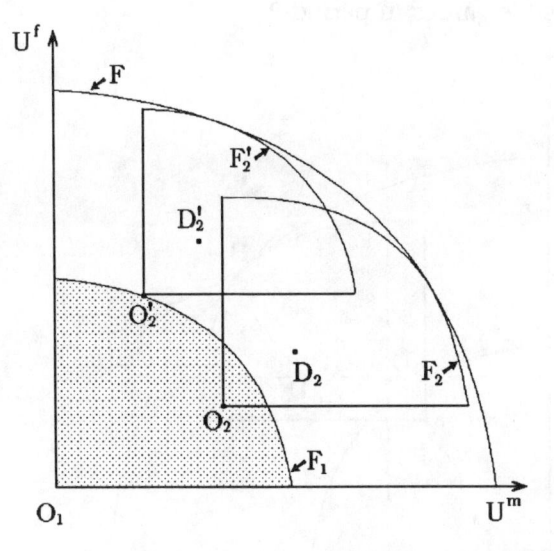

---

[53] Complete compensations may be impossible, if the feasible sets of the subgames differ greatly in their size. This is the case in the two period model of household decisions, because period one represents a relative short time period, while period two includes the remaining life cycle. Then the increases in productivity in period one do not turn out to be so large, that bigger losses in period two can be compensated in advance.

[54] The problem of ex-ante underinvestment in dynamic contracting with renegotiation is anlyzed by Rogerson (1984) or Hart/Moore (1988); see also Bolton (1990).

This is illustrated for the two-period model in figure 7.1. Because both the feasible set and the conflict point in period 2 are determined by the decision in period 1, this decision implies the selection of the game for period 2 from the set of different possible games. Each point in the payoff space of period 1 is linked with one of these possible games due to the specific time allocation. Different points can be linked with the same game for period 2, because the payoff in period 1 also depends on the distribution of consumption goods, which do not influence the later subgame. The feasible set of the total game then is determined by the payoff space of period 1 and the set of all corresponding games for period 2.

The shaded area in figure 7.1 represents the payoff space in period 1 with the utility possibility frontier F_1. Each point in this space (e.g. O_2 and O_2') is characterized by a specific allocation, which determines the payoff space (with respective UPF F_2 and F_2') as well as the conflict point (D_2 and D_2') of period 2. The utility possibility frontier F of the total game is defined by the envelope of all possible games in period 2.

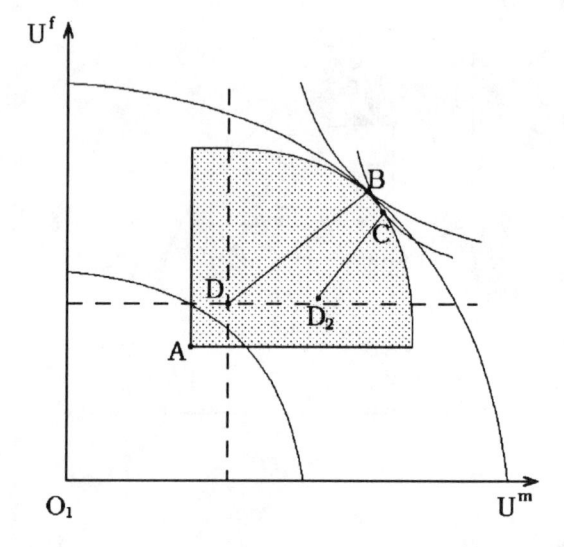

Figure 7.2

In the case of binding long-term contracts the game is played in one step, and the Nash solution (point B in figure 7.2) belonging to the conflict point at the beginning (point D) results. This means that an allocation for period 1 is chosen which implies that feasible set for period 2 which contributes the solution point B to the envelope F. In this case, in period 2 no new subgame is played, but the agreed solution B is realized independent of the actual conflict point D_2. If this allocation leads to a maximum production in both periods, then the origin of the second subgame lies on the Pareto frontier of period 1 F_1. However, this is not necessary for the optimal solution of the total game. The origin may be located inside the payoff space of period 1, when the chosen time allocation results in a different development of the productivities in the two periods. In this case, a different time allocation could increase the welfare production of the household in period 1, but would lead to a suboptimal solution in the long run. For example, an increase of welfare production may be possible in the short run by specialization in work at home. But, as discussed in chapter 5, the long-term losses of earning capacity might outweigh this gain, because total specialization in household work is an efficient production only for short periods in the life cycle. Then an allocation which realizes the maximum production in period 1 would imply the choice of a subgame for period 2 that does not allow an efficient solution. The origin of this subgame is located on the Pareto frontier of period 1, but the payoff space lies completely inside the feasible set of the total game.

If long-term contracts are not enforceable, both players know that in period 2 a new subgame will start, from which the Nash solution corresponding to the actual conflict point will result. In this case, the same allocation (A) as in the game with binding long-term contracts is chosen only if the corresponding subgame in period 2 has the solution B. This can occur only if the relative bargaining power of the players remains unchanged, i.e. D_2 is located on line DB. But, as discussed above, this situation is very unlikely. In general, a solution results from this allocation (A) which lies inside the Pareto frontier (e.g. Point C).

Because each possible subgame in period 2 has a unique solution, which does not lie, in general, on the envelope, not all points of the feasible set can be reached by rational players. Some points are available only through a long-term contract between the players. If such contracts are not enforceable, one player has the opportunity to win in period 2 by renegotiation, and a rational player will do so. Anticipating this, no such contract will be made by rational players. Therefore, all points which can be reached only through long-term contracts are irrelevant for the bargaining process of rational players. Thus, for the decision in period 1 not the whole feasible set of all possible subgames for period 2 is considered, but only their Nash solutions. Then the *rational feasible set* of the total game is the locus of all Nash solutions of possible subgames in period 2 with the frontier F' in figure 7.3.

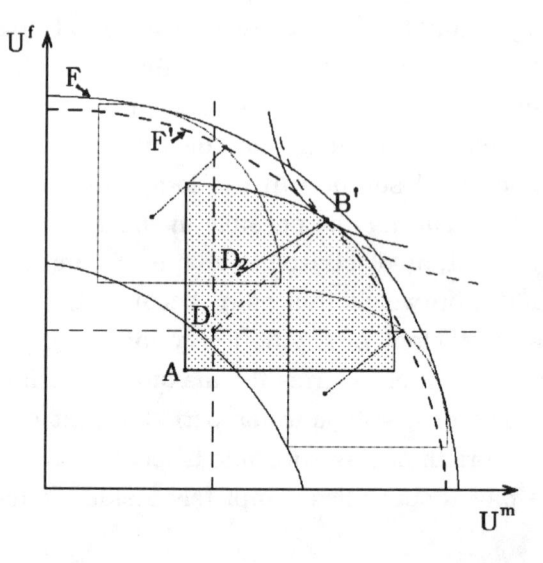

Figure 7.3

In this case, the Nash solution for this rational feasible set is the solution of the total game (point B'). This implies the choice of an allocation in period 1 linked to that subgame in period 2, that has a Nash solution identical with the Nash solution B' of the total game. If the bargaining power of the players change over time, this allocation is not the same as in the game with binding long-term contracts and generally does not maximize the welfare production which could be obtained given the household resources.

The lack of long-term contracts leads to an allocation which does not utilize the available resources efficiently. There are some allocations that in principle are feasible given the resources of the household, but cannot be reached by rational players. Without binding long-term contracts the *rational feasible set* lies completely inside the *technical feasible set*, because there are fewer points on which the partners can agree. The solution of the game always lie on the frontier of the rational feasible set. Nevertheless, given a world in which intrafamily long-term contracts are not enforceable, this solution satisfies the Pareto criterion, because there is no allocation which is preferred by both partners. Any other allocation that would increase the total output results in a distribution in later subgames that leaves one partner worse off.

However, this solution of the game without binding long-term contracts does not exhaust all production possibilities. To increase the welfare production within the household, long-term contracts must be enforceable.

7.2 Discrete choices

The problem of lacking enforceability of long-term contracts becomes more illustrative in discrete choices, for instance on a restricted labor market. In most cases an employed person cannot vary the hours of work continuously but has to choose between jobs with different working hours which are offered on the labor market. In this case, there is no continuum of different games. In period 1 the partners have to choose between some discrete situations with different subgames for period 2. The negotiation set has some gaps or it consists of singular points. A jump discontinuity also results if a marginal change in time allocation is linked with a change between very distinct subgames in period 2, which is likely for corner solutions.

Especially for irreversible decisions with long-term effects on the conflict outcomes like a disruption of working life imply a discrete choice. The losses in earning capacity due to foregone accumulation of market skills are *sunk costs* in the production of household skills, which have a low value in the case of conflict[55]. Therefore, each reduction in working time implies that the relative bargaining position is worsened (see the discussion in chapter 6). In general, a continuous variation in working time results in a continuous change in the earning capacity. However, a different situation results in the case when one partner leaves the workforce. Large reductions in the earning capacity may result even from short interruptions in working life due to the loss of firm specific human capital[56]. As a consequence, the conflict point as well as the possibilities of welfare production in the household will change substantially. In this case the household has to choose between two rather different situations as illustrated in figure 7.4.

---

[55] *Sunk costs* are expenditures in prior periods, which have no value in the actual situation. Already Becker (1962, p. 22) describes investments in human capital as sunk costs.

[56] See for losses in income following work disruptions Mincer/Polachek (1974), Corcoran/Duncan (1979), Mincer/Ofek (1982), Corcoran et al. (1983) and Galler (1988 and 1991).

Figure 7.4

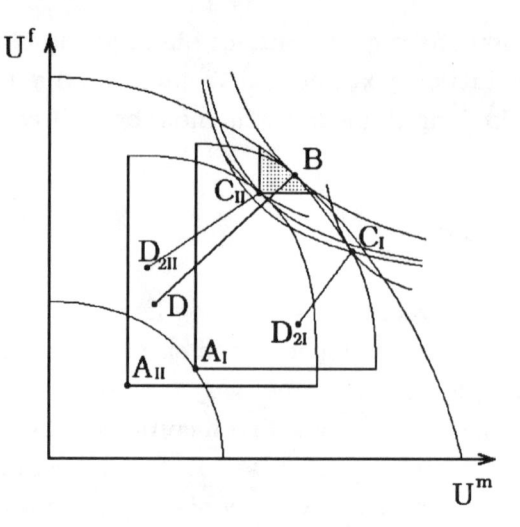

In period 1 the household can choose between allocation A_I and A_{II} with the respective solution points C_I and C_{II}. In this situation person f prefers solution C_{II}, which implies allocation A_{II}, and person m prefers solution C_I. Because in the total game the Nash solution is realized, that point with the larger Nash gain is chosen, which lies on the more outward 'household indifference curve' (hyperbola respective to the conflict point D of the total game). In the example of figure 7.4 the allocation A_{II} with solution point C_{II} results, because the following inequality holds:

$$(U_{II}^m - D^m) * (U_{II}^f - D^f) > (U_I^m - D^m) * (U_I^f - D^f) \tag{7.1}$$

But there are solutions in which both partners would be better off (the shaded area). A long-term contract in period 1 would allow to reach point B. Therefore, both partners are interested *ex ante* in such an agreement. However, person m can gain additional benefits, if he later breaks the contract and asks for renegotiation. If the contract is not binding there is a large incentive to break it, and *ex post* the solution C_{II} would result.

This situation is very similar to the well-known prisoner's dilemma. The cooperative solution is allocation A_I in period 1 and a fixed distribution in period 2 (point B) independent of the actual conflict point in period 2. If both partners choose the non-cooperative strategy, i.e. they do not agree to the contract, allocation A_{II} results. But, if person f behaves cooperatively and agrees to the contract, whereas person m plays in a non-cooperative manner demanding renegotiation, person m gets a higher payoff than he would by being cooperative. Person f, on the other hand, is worse off even in comparison to the non-cooperative solution.

Thus, if one spouse trusts in the realization of the agreed distribution and interrupts his or her working life, a great incentive exists for the other spouse to break the contract. In contrast to the classical prisoner's dilemma, only one partner can improve his payoff by breaking the contract later on. Thus, the non-cooperative strategy for the other spouse is to object to the contract and to remain in market work. Otherwise, he or she makes his or her contribution immediately, i.e. in period 1, and the loss in earning capacity is irreversible. Once this spouse has opted for a cooperative behavior, he or she cannot gain by a change toward non-cooperation[57]. Thus, if the contract is not enforceable and the risk of a break up is relatively large, the optimal strategy for f is not to agree to such a contract. As is well-known from the analysis of the prisoner's dilemma, the only equilibrium in such a situation is non-cooperative behavior on the part of both players. But then possible welfare gains will not be realized.

7.3   Fertility as a prisoner's dilemma

In particular, the decision on fertility may be such a situation. We will assume that a child would increase the utility of both spouses. We will also assume that the decision for a child results in a net welfare gain for the family, i.e. that the gains in the total welfare of the family are larger than all the costs (the direct expenditures for the child and the opportunity costs of child caring due to foregone income). Then, the traditional model would predict a positive decision for a child, since changes in conflict outcomes resulting from a birth are neglected.

---

[57] For this reason often a marriage stabilizing effect is expected from intrafamily specialization (see e.g. Pollak 1985, p. 601), because the losses in the case of conflict increase the interest in the joint household. That this is true only for the spouse specialized in household activities, is in general neglected. For the other spouse incentives exist for non-cooperative behavior resulting in a breach of the contract, which might increase the probability for a divorce due to the breach of trust.

Let us consider a situation where the wish for a child can be realized only by an interruption in the working life of one spouse, which is in most cases the wife. This is a typical situation in Germany and in many other countries because of a lack of institutions for child care. Then, the welfare gain of the household is combined with a large decrease in the bargaining position of the wife, and a situation comparable to the prisoner's dilemma may result.

Figure 7.5

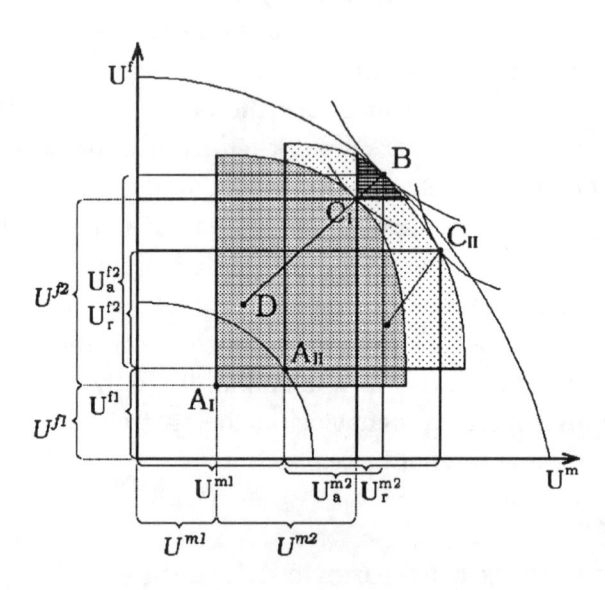

In figure 7.5 the point A_I represents the unchanged time allocation which can be maintained only without a child. From this allocation the solution C_I results. The decision for a child is linked with the allocation A_{II} in period 1. If long-term contracts are binding, the solution B could be realized. Otherwise the solution C_{II} results in period 2 due to the changed conflict point.

The prisoner's dilemma can be described as follows. Cooperative behavior implies that the couple makes a long-term contract and both spouses will carry it out. The contract requires the following contributions: the couple adjusts the distribution of the household production for the entire future; one spouse, denoted by f, interrupts her working life and specializes in child-caring and housework, which also means that she accepts a decrease in her earning capacity; the other spouse, denoted by m, specializes in market work and promises not to ask for renegotiation. Because the person who drops out of the market makes her contribution immediately, non-cooperative behavior of this person would imply not agreeing to the contract and continuing market work. The other spouse has to contribute later and can break the contract afterwards, when the additional welfare benefits have already been obtained and the conflict point has changed. Therefore, for this person non-cooperative behavior consists in the breach of the contract at any later point in time. Then the payoff matrix is as follows:

m \ f	cooperative	non-cooperative
cooperative	$U^{f1} + U_a^{f2}$ $U^{m1} + U_a^{m2}$	$U^{f1} + U^{f2}$ $U^{m1} + U^{m2}$
non-cooperative	$U^{f1} + U_r^{f2}$ $U^{m1} + U_r^{m2}$	$U^{f1} + U^{f2}$ $U^{m1} + U^{m2}$

(7.2)

where[58]

U^{i1} payoff in period 1, if decided for a child
U_a^{i2} payoff in period 2 as agreed
U_r^{i2} payoff in period 2 after renegotiation
U^{it} payoff in period t, if decided against a child

and

$$U^{m1} + U_r^{m2} > U^{m1} + U_a^{m2} > U^{m1} + U^{m2}$$
$$U^{f1} + U_a^{f2} > U^{f1} + U^{f2} > U^{f1} + U_r^{f2}$$

If the unchanged allocation (A_I in figure 7.5) represents the status quo, which the couple realize when deciding against a child, the payoff matrix describes the game completely and the status quo point is the only equilibrium. A decision against a child will always result whenever the outcome in the case of a renegotiation for one spouse would decrease below the status

---

[58] This correspond to the points B, C_I and C_{II} in figure 7.5:

$$B = (U^{m1} + U_a^{m2}, U^{f1} + U_a^{f2})$$
$$C_I = (U^{m1} + U^{m2}, U^{f1} + U^{f2})$$
$$C_{II} = (U^{m1} + U_r^{m2}, U^{f1} + U_r^{f2})$$

quo level. Now, it is not obvious that in the case of a decision against a child the hitherto allocation remains. But, as long as this decision is not irreversible and can be changed later, it is likely that the couple will agree to maintaining the status quo and to delaying the final decision.

Nevertheless, such a situation cannot be considered in the context of the two-period bargaining model. Here it is assumed that the allocation in period 1 determines exactly the outcome in period 2. With complete information, as assumed, no delay of the decision can result, because both spouses know the final decision from the beginning. Therefore, in the context of the model, time allocation in period 1 is always bargained with respect to the conflict point of the total game, and the couple will realize the allocation with the larger Nash gain, which may also be solution C_{II}. The prisoner's dilemma situation results only if

$$(U^{m1} + U^{m2} - D^m) * (U^{f1} + U^{f2} - D^f) > (U^{m1} + U^{m2}_r - D^m) * (U^{f1} + U^{f2}_r - D^f) \quad (7.3)$$

The addition of this constraint (7.3) to the system (7.2) completes the description of game. In this case the decision for a child will always be made when (7.3) does not hold, independent of whether the contract is enforceable or not. Therefore, in a discrete choice situation an efficient solution can be reached, even if one spouse does not gain. But, this can only occur, if the loss is small enough.

But, it is obvious that during the bargaining process the spouses do not threaten permanently with the conflict. In reality often a delay of decisions is observed, because the couples do not have complete information about the future. Here lie the limits of the chosen approach. In order to model such a behavior, an extension towards a multi-period model with incomplete information would be required. Nevertheless, the two-period model still may be an appropriate basis for empirical analyses. As we have seen, a delay results if in the actual period at least one partner would gain from a positive decision, and future situations are not completely known. But, for the actual period a prisoner's dilemma results, and we observe a decision against a child. The same will be observed, if a final decision against a child is made. In addition, it depends on the unobserveable utility functions of the spouses whether the solution point C_{II} lies on the inner or outer indifference curve. Because this point will never be realized in either game, it is not possible to distinguish what kind of prisoner's dilemma arises: one with or without complete information. In fact, it cannot be observed whether a prisoner's dilemma situation arises at all. However, with suitable variables the probability of a prisoner's dilemma can be modelled. But, it is not possible to distinguish empirically between a delayed and a final decision against a child. Therefore it is not problematical to use a more simple approach in the empirical analysis. The substantial argument, that situations like a prisoner's dilemma may influence fertility and lead to suboptimal solutions, can be modelled adequately by the two-period approach.

8 The binding force of intrafamily contracts

As we have seen in the previous chapter, the lack of enforceability of intrafamily long-term contracts may lead to solutions which do not allocate all resources efficiently. In particular, this may occur in the case of intrafamily specialization, because the contract is asymmetrical. It was argued, that only one spouse can gain by breaking the contract later on. The same is also true for many other intrafamily contracts, for example for some insurance contracts. Even contracts for joint consumption may be asymmetrical, if for instance one partner is the owner of a good, like a house. In all these cases there is an incentive for one partner to breach the contract when the other has made his contribution. Without sufficient possibilities to enforce those contracts, no such long-term agreements would be made by rational players. Therefore, we will investigate the binding force of intrafamily contracts.

Contracts can be made either explicitly or implicitly. Usually the two types are distinguished by the enforcement mechanism (see e.g. Parsons 1986, Klein 1985 or Carmichael 1989). A contract, which is enforceable by law, is called an *explicit* one. Such a contract must be complete, i.e. it must define an outcome for all possible states of the world, and it must be limited to observable outcomes in order to be enforceable by a third party. Contracts which do not fulfill these requirements are called *implicit*: not all terms are specified in detail, and often they are made tacidly. An implicit contract can be "interpreted in the 'as if' sense of an explicit one, as a mutual understanding ... that the invisible handshake implies" (Rosen 1985, p. 1149). In the literature endogenous enforcement mechanisms are assumed for implicit contracts[59]: either by the threat of termination of the transactional relationship or by reputational effects (see e.g. Bull 1987). If because of these or some other reasons both parties are interested in keeping their promises, the contract is called self-enforcing. Besides these self-enforcing implicit

---

[59] See e.g. Telser (1980). Surveys of implicit contract literature are given by Azariadis (1981) and Rosen (1985).

contracts, there is a second kind of contract which is not an explicit one. Implicit contracts may also be based on social norms, because the commonly agreed regularities imply a mutual understanding. However, these contracts based on social norms are not self-enforcing as defined above, but are enforced by sanctions of a third party, the public. Therefore, as far as the enforcement mechanism is concerned this kind of contract is more similar to contracts enforced by law.

Hence, the binding force of a contract depends either on endogenous enforcement mechanisms or on sanctions for the breach of the contract imposed by a third party. To what extent such enforcement mechanisms exist for intrafamily long-term contracts will be discussed in the next sections.

8.1 Self-enforcing contracts

A contract is called *self-enforcing* if none of the partners has an incentive to deviate from the contract at any time. This means that the mutual promises form a subgame perfect equilibrium (see Aumann 1974). As we have seen in chapter 6.2, the solution of the game without binding contracts for period 2 is a subgame perfect equilibrium, because the only promise for period 2 is to bargain with each other, from which both partners can gain[60]. But, the question arises: is that equilibrium unique or are there other subgame perfect equilibria? Are there incentives in the partnership itself to fulfill the contract in any case, even if the contract is asymmetrical and is not enforceable through a third party?

As we have seen, intrafamily contracts are often asymmetrical due to changes in the bargaining power resulting from actions agreed in the contract, and one spouse can gain from renegotiation about a new distribution. If the breach of the contract, i.e. renegotiation, is without costs there is an incentive for that partner to deviate, and a rational player would always do

---

[60] This is true, at least in the case of full information. In the case of uncertainty about the future, the game with the same partner will be gainfully compared with all known alternatives only with a certain probability, which will influence the subgame perfect equilibrium (see chapter 9).

so. Otherwise, the contract will be broken only if the gains exceed the cost of the breach.

Because the gains of a breach result from an intrafamily redistribution they depend on the change in the bargaining power. If this change is small, also the possible gains are small. On the other hand, some costs arise already through the renegotiation process itself: e.g. the time required for negotiation. Therefore, if the change in the bargaining power is small, in many cases there is no incentive to ask for renegotiation. But, if the change in the bargaining power is large as in the case of a disruption of the employment, the potential gains from renegotiation may be high[61]. Because a new distribution in favor of the spouse with the improved bargaining power will take place for the remaining time of the partnership, these gains may exceed the direct renegotiation costs[62]. Then, the contract will be fulfilled only if there are additional costs of the breach.

Such costs are not considered in the model described in chapter 6. In the context of the two-period model it cannot be done, because the contract can be gainfully deviated at the earlist in period 2 and costs arise in periods after the breach. In order to model the costs of a breach explicitly, at least a three-period model is required. But then, the difficulty arises that all possible contracts in the family must be modelled, because for different contracts different costs may arise. This cannot be done in a simple model, and it should be done only if there are sufficient indications, that such costs are relevant for the decisions analyzed in research. Therefore, we will discuss in the following whether and for which intrafamily long-term contracts costs arise out of a breach, which may be high enough to enforce the contract.

---

[61] How large these gains are, depends on the status quo: the amount of marriage gain and the marginal rate of substitution between the spouses. But, as argued in chapter 7, at least in about symmetrical status quo situations a large change of the conflict payoff results in a large redistribution after renegotiation.

[62] Since the direct renegotiation costs arise immediately, but most of the gain occur in the future, the gain-cost ratio depends on the remaining time and the rate of time preference. Usually the expected remaining time of the partnership after a birth and a simultaneous disruption of employment is relatively long, because those decisions are made by young couples. On the other hand, direct renegotiation costs are in general not very high. Therefore, in the case of the decision on fertility the potential gains may exceed these costs.

Usually, two kinds of costs of a breach are considered (e.g. Klein 1985, Bull 1987). Both result from lower gains in future negotiations as a consequence of the breach. On the one hand, possible gains from future cooperation with the same partner will be foregone, if the transactional relationship is terminated following the breach. On the other hand, the cooperative payoffs in future negotiations with the same or with other partners may be reduced due to reputational losses.

8.1.1 Threat by future non-cooperative behavior

If both partners have an interest in continuing the cooperative relationship in order to realize further gains, the breach of a contract can be punished with non-cooperative behavior in later periods. In this case, after a deviation from the agreements by one partner the possible gains from cooperation in future periods are foregone by both partners, at least for that time interval where the non-cooperative strategy is played. The threat of such a strategy will restrain a rational player to deviate from cooperative agreements if the losses in later periods are high enough. But, as the analysis of repeated games shows, cooperation gains from such strategies will be obtained in general[63] only if the game is repeated sufficiently often (see. e.g. Van Damme 1987, chap. 8). Especially if the players can communicate at any point in time, only such strategies which build a renegotiation-proof equilibrium force the players to cooperate (ibid., p. 203ff.). This means, that threats that hurt the threatener himself are not credible, because after a deviation there is no incentive to execute the punishment, but it would be profitable for both players to start a new cooperation.

In the family there are many situations in which these conditions are fulfilled: for example, the day to day allocation of income or the use of joint, but not really public goods (like a car) are games which are repeated nearly uncountably often. For these situations we can assume a sufficient incentive for cooperation, and we should expect a self-enforcement of these contracts. But, decisions which imply a large asymmetrical change in the bargaining power like the disruption of employment, are mostly singular in the family

---

[63] With the assumptions of fully rational players and complete information, only games with more than one equilibrium point may preserve cooperation if it is only finitely repeated.

and are seldom repeated[64]. Then a threat to behave non-cooperatively at the next decision of this type is either not relevant or forces cooperation only till the last decision of this type is made[65].

However, one could argue that the whole partnership with all negotiations can be interpreted as a permanent repetition of more or less similar games[66]. Therefore, the cheated spouse can punish with non-cooperative behavior in other areas within the scope of the relationship[67]. But, in asymmetrical situations with a decreasing conflict payoff for at least one partner, threatening with termination by this person is not credible, because it is not a renegotiation-proof equilibrium. In such a situation the breach of the contract is gainfully for the other spouse only after the changes in the bargaining power. But then, after the breach, the conflict payoff of the cheated spouse is worse than before the contract is made, and the execution of the punishment will hurt him- or herself possibly more than the partner. The cooperative outcome after renegotiation in period 2 is always better for the cheated spouse, and to cooperate further will be the only subgame perfect equilibrium after the breach.

On the other hand, the cheated spouse could punish a breach with partial non-cooperative behavior. This means, a non-cooperative equilibrium point within the actual feasible set with a better payoff for both spouses than their conflict payoff is chosen as threat point. But, as we have argued in chapter 3.3, equilibrium points will be formed only by those pairs of non-cooperative strategies which yield the same cooperative solution as the threat with

---

[64] Even, if the decision looks very similar like the decision for a further child which is linked with an additional work interruption, the situations may differ. Because the losses in earning capacity during the first interruption are nearly irreversible the additional change in the bargaining power will be much smaller.

[65] For example, if the spouse with the superior bargaining position is interested in several children, he will not break the contract till the decision for the last child is made.

[66] Such complex situations are rarely investigated with formal models. While game theory predominantly focuses on repeated games, i.e. the repetition of identical subgames, contract theory deals with more comprehensive transactual relationships. Here, the enforcement of implicit contracts by fear of losses in future cooperation gains is mostly explained based on plausibility arguments and not on formal models. Nevertheless, this argumentation indicates that the results of the game theoretic analysis of repeated games are also plausible for a sequence of non-identical subgames.

[67] This can also be seen as losses in internal reputation. Here, there is no clear distinction made in the literature.

separation. All non-cooperative equilibrium points are determined by the actual payoffs in the case of dissolution, and therefore can enforce only a cooperative outcome related to this conflict point, but not the ex-ante bargained distribution.

Therefore, within the family there is no credible threat with future non-cooperation which can enforce a contract with large asymmetrical changes in bargaining power. This implies, that the distribution for period 2 which was agreed to ex ante in the contract will not be performed, and renegotiation will take place in period 2, if no other enforcement mechanism exists.

8.1.2 Reputation

The other endogenous enforcement mechanism for implicit contracts usually mentioned is the players' concern about their reputation[68]. Reputation is seen as "a characteristic or attribute ascribed to one person by another" which depends on the person's previous behavior and affects future opportunities (Wilson 1985, p. 27f.). In the case of incomplete information the players' behavior also depends on the beliefs they have about their partners. If agreements are not enforceable by a third party, the players will cooperate only if they believe in the honesty of the partner. Therefore, the reputation of being honest allows the realization of some cooperative gains which cannot be obtained otherwise.

Because reputation depends on the history of previous observed actions, the beliefs and as a consequence the later behavior of the partner can be affected by current actions. This is not only true in a continued partnership with the same partner, but also for all possible future partners. In particular, market reputation, i.e. reputation in the view of a third party which is not involved in the actual transaction, is the most mentioned in the literature.

Regarding transactions with the same partner in a long-term partnership, reputation means to prevent the threat of non-cooperative behavior. Therefore it is almost the same endogenous enforcement mechanism, and in particular, it leads to the same result, because only for credible threats there is an incentive to prevent them. As was argued in the previous section, there

---

[68] See e.g. Wilson (1985), Bull (1987), Klein/Leffler (1981).

are no credible threats with non-cooperative behavior in the family which could enforce contracts with large asymmetry. Thus, also no enforcement of such contracts is constituted by internal reputation.

Reputation in the market - also called brand name - can be seen as an appeal to the market to enforce implicit contracts (Bull 1983, p. 659). But, these reputational effects are "only as strong as the information flows that support them" (Bull 1987, p. 149). For reputational effects to be effective, the information about a breach must flow rapidly and must be accurate. Both requirements are often not fulfilled. Information in large markets will flow slowly, especially if the person is not very well-known. Then, there may be no actual interest in any information about this person and potential future partners may not learn about a breach. The other problem is the accuracy of the information. In order to protect their reputation, after a breach both parties have an incentive to claim that the other side is at fault. Then, the third party often cannot evaluate these claims because the breach itself is not observable (see Bull 1983, p. 662). Therefore, market reputational effects alone may not be strong enough to enforce implicit agreements. Hence, Bull (1987) emphasizes the intrafirm reputation as the more effective enforcement mechanism. If there are more members in the transactual organization than the partners actually involved, these members have a direct interest in obtaining quick and accurate information about the honesty of both current players.

Regarding intrafamily contracts, however, market reputational effects play a subordinate role. Usually there is no great interest in the honesty of the spouses in any marriage, because the probability is very small that one of them will become a partner in the future. Moreover, after the breach usually each of the spouses claims to be the cheated person, which will in general be believed by the new partner.

More important may be the reputation within the transactual organization. If the family has other members beside the couple like children, there is an interest for the spouses to care for their intrafamily reputation, and the other family members have an interest in monitoring the performance of the contract, because they will be the partner in one of the next cooperative subgames. Therefore, intrafamily reputation could be an effective mechanism because the loss of this kind of reputation after a breach generates costs by losses in future cooperative gains. However, since children depend on their parents in many ways, their possibilities to behave non-cooperatively are limited. Hence, the costs may be not high enough to enforce all intrafamily contracts between the spouses.

8.1.3 Loyalty

Loyalty is a third endogenous enforcement mechanism for implicit contracts which is not often mentioned in theoretical analysis, but - as experimental studies show[69] - plays a significant role in real bargaining situations. Loyalty here is understood as the willingness "to trade off the certainty of exit against the uncertainties of an improvement in the deteriorated product" (Hirschmann 1970, p. 77). This means, that in the case of incomplete information about the characteristics of the partner the breach of an implicit contract is not always punished directly with termination of further cooperation (in Hirschmann's terminology the *exit* option), but the cheated player may try to reestablish the former situation through protest (the *voice* option). If the player is convinced that 'voice' will be effective, 'exit' may be postponed, but will be carried out after 'voice' has failed (ibid., p. 37). Thus, 'voice' can be interpreted as a new negotiation process after a breach, which takes place and can be successful only if there is an interest in the relationship which was not considered when making the contract. Thus, loyalty can be seen as the willingness to bargain again in order to avoid the termination, because the relationship itself is profitable for the individual. Then, a loyal person will not directly choose the exit option after a breach, and will not risk the partner's exit through a break by him- or herself.

Usually a person preserves different loyalties to several partners or groups. These differences are usually not explained in the literature. Regarding the family, emotional attachments like 'love', 'affection' and 'caring' are mentioned as the basis of loyalty (Becker 1974, Pollak 1985, p. 586, Ben-Porath 1980, p. 4, Lommerud 1989, p. 118). These attachments are specific characteristics of the individual, and usually they are treated as stable elements, which are sufficient to enforce intrafamily contracts. For example, Pollak (1985, p. 586) remarks: "The affectional relationships, whatever their basis, may provide a relatively secure and stable foundation for a wide range of

---

[69] See e.g. Shogren (1989) or Güth/Ockenfels/Wendel (1991).

activities". But, if these attachments are not independent from the circumstances in the relationship, their effectiveness in enforcement may change with the bahavior of the family members[70].

Some elements of family loyalty, e.g. caring, may result from internalizing social norms, so that "fulfilling family obligations becomes a source of pleasure, pride and satisfaction" (Pollak 1985, p. 586). Regarding these kind of idiosyncratic attitudes, we can assume that they are independent from the actions of the partner and may enforce implicit contracts to some degree. But, because these individual characteristics cannot be observed, and in particular they can hardly be distinguished from obeying social norms because of fear of sanctions (see chapter 8.2.3), the importance of this enforcement mechanism cannot be evaluated in general. However, although this kind of loyalty may improve intrafamily trust in implicit contracts in some special cases, there are no indications that such behavior is common.

The most important incentive to fulfill intrafamily contracts may be the affectional relationship, because both partners are interested in the well-being of the spouse and will prevent any damage of this relationship. This will increase the propensity to fulfill intrafamily contracts, once established. But, there is also an incentive not to agree to a very asymmetrical contract. In general, the emotional relationship implies an affectional exchange[71], which should be distinguished from usual economic exchanges. Normally, the mutual exchange of emotional grants is expected and no compensation by other benefits is accepted: partners[72] want to exchange love with love and nothing else, and one-sided emotions are usually not maintained over long

---

[70] In principle, such emotional attachments can be introduced in the formal model as additional elements of the individual utility functions, which may be interdependent. If there is a positive attachment, then the negotiation space and therefore the marital gain would be larger. However, for deriving the enforcement strength of such elements a model with asymmetrical information is required as an adequate approach to the concept of loyalty. But, if it cannot be assumed that these emotional attachments are independent from the family members' actions, this connection also has to be modelled. Without such a model for the development and change of emotional attachments, the introduction of these elements into the utility function gives no additional information on the enforcement strength, because the assumed influence is just as arbitrary as an assumption on the enforcement strength itself.

[71] Exceptions are partnerships with an emotional or sexually obsequious partner. But, decisions in those partnerships cannot be described as a cooperative bargaining game in general. They are more similar to an ultimatum game.

[72] But the relationship between parents and children is similar.

periods of time[73]. As a consequence the effect on intrafamily contracting may even be reversed. Because any breach of a contract will be punished with non-cooperative behavior in other transactional relations, also the exchange of emotional grants may be involved, in particular if other threats are not credible (see chapter 8.1.1). But, if the affectional relationship is the only enforcement mechanism, it may be damaged due to a lacking balance in that special exchange. When the contract is fulfilled solely by emotional reasons, the omitted redistribution of non-affectional benefits are included in the emotional exchange. Both, to waive potential gains solely due to affectional attachments as well as to depend on the good conduct of the partner, may produce dissatisfaction due to the feeling of imbalance in the relationship[74]. On the other hand, if the contract is broken, the cheated person has to punish with non-cooperative behavior, i.e. with reduction in emotional grants, from which a damage of the partnership may result. Therefore, if there is no other enforcement mechanism for asymmetrical contracts and the incentives for a breach are high, then the risk for a damage to the affectional relationship is also high. When this affectional relationship is highly valued by both partners, such risky contracts will not be made[75]. Under those circumstances, the possible damage to the affectional relationship may not enforce, but prevent asymmetrical contracts. Therefore, the high value of the emotional relationship by itself - which is usually seen as a guarantee for an efficient division of work in the family - may prevent such agreements and may force bargaining solutions without long-term contracts.

Concluding, the incentives to fulfill intrafamily contracts appear somewhat contrary. There are strong incentives in the permanently day to day bargaining not to deviate from agreements because the short-term gains are much lower than the costs in the long run. These contracts will be self-enforcing. But, for some particular decisions with nearly irreversible, asymmetrical effects on the bargaining power of the spouses, the gains from breaking the contract may be high and neither the interest in further

---

[73] Nevertheless, the exchange must not be symmetrical.

[74] See for the results of several empirical studies on satisfaction and dissatisfaction with the marital decision making process Kirchler (1988), p. 286.

[75] Simm (1989) shows that children are often seen as concurrence to the partnership, because a damage of the well-balanced relationship is feared.

cooperation nor reputational effects provide a sufficient enforcement mechanism. The affectional relationship - usually seen as the strongest endogenous enforcement mechanism - may even provide incentives to omit such contracts, if they are not enforced also due to other reasons. Therefore, there are no sufficient endogenous enforcement mechanisms for such asymmetrical contracts in the family. But, then non-efficient solutions will be chosen - except when the contracts are enforced by exogenous factors.

8.2 Enforcement by institutions

The failure of private exchange in reaching efficient allocations due to externalities is usually the argument for political interventions. While the Pigouvian proposal is to correct the exchange prices by taxes and subsidies directly, the Coase theorem (see Coase 1960) points out, that efficient solutions can be achieved by private agreements if property rights are well-defined and private contracts are enforced by law. As was shown, inefficient allocations in the family result from lacking enforcement of intrafamily long-term contracts. Therefore, public interventions in family decisions may be limited to the performance of intrafamily contracts.

In industrialized countries the aim of interventions in family decisions is to establish regulations in the Coasean sense. We do not observe specific regulations for intrafamily behavior[76], but a public marital contract with some general principles is provided. An alternative option is to enter into justiciable private contracts. In the public contract all regulations are implemented by the government, while the terms of a private contract are fixed by the contractual partners, but performance is guaranteed by the court.

8.2.1 The formal marriage contract

Justiciable contracts must be complete and observable for a third party. Because the breach of an intrafamily contract will always result in renegotiations and a new distribution of welfare, the intrafamily distribution is an

---

[76] In Europe as well as in the United States the strict rules for the spouses' behavior in past marriage law systems were resigned in the last decades and replaced by more general principles (see e.g. Cheadle 1981 for the development in the United States).

essential element of all contracts in the family. Therefore, completeness of the contract requires a well-defined sharing-rule. But, some difficulties arise in establishing such a sharing-rule due to problems of observability and measurement of the welfare distribution.

Individual welfare is not observable. Because it depends on individual preferences, it is a very private information which cannot be inspected by other persons. Therefore, a common sharing-rule established by law cannot be an optimal one for all families[77]. Nevertheless, in bilateral bargaining the spouses introduce their preferences into the negotiation about the distribution of goods, which could then be explicitely fixed in the contract.

But, even the distribution of goods cannot be fully observed. On one hand, a permanent monitoring by a third party would be necessary, because most of the goods will be consumed directly. But, such a monitoring would be very expensive. On the other hand, especially the measurement of private immaterial goods raises some problems, because they are often produced jointly with other home-produced goods, and therefore not even the input factors may be appropriate indicators for their valuation.

Thus, it seems impossible to make a justiciable complete marriage contract due to lacking observability and measurement. The breach of the contract, i.e. a redistribution, cannot be observed and therefore cannot be sanctioned by the court. Then, this kind of contract is not suitable for supporting efficient solutions.

8.2.2 Divorce law

If it is not possible to enforce asymmetrical intrafamily contracts directly, the political system can try to change the payoffs in such a way, that the efficient allocation will be an equilibrium point. Because the large incentive for breaking the contract results from the redistribution after changes in the bargaining power, the breach could be prevented if no such asymmetrical effects would be linked with the efficient allocation.

---

[77] Typically, there is no sharing-rule defined in the public contract, but only the liability for both spouses to share 'fairly'.

Interventions in the conflict payoffs, which determine the intrafamily bargaining power, already exist in form of the divorce law. In this way the restrictions for the internal optimization problem can be influenced in order to make intrafamily contracts self-enforcing. In the case of intrafamily specialization, maintaining the ex-ante bargaining power requires the redistribution of all returns and losses of accumulated and foregone human capital which are accrued after the divorce.

From the Coasean point of view these regulations can be interpreted in the sense, that not only property rights on the produce of the household are defined (as in the marriage contract), but also joint property rights of both spouses are established on all human capital accumulated during the marriage. The exercize of these rights is not controlled by law as long as the marriage continues, because consent decisions resulting from intrafamily bargaining are assumed[78]. In the case of divorce the decisions are no longer made jointly, and only one partner has the possibility of utilizing human capital. But, because both spouses have invested in the human capital stock and have a right on the returns on their investments, a sharing-rule for the returns which are accrued after divorce must be defined. This is usually done with alimony regulations. But here, a referability problem arises: what share of after-marriage income can be regarded as a return on marital investments? Furthermore, there is a moral hazard problem in such a regulation. Because after divorce only one partner decides on the utilization of human capital, but both spouses participate on the returns, there is an incentive to conceal some returns and even to forego some possible returns.

Another possibility for redistributing after-marriage returns on marital investment in human capital is to convey the property rights to the partner with the increased human capital stock. This partner would then have to purchase this exclusive right from the other spouse. Such a compensation for the lost investments in the spouse's human capital by a singular lump-sum payment has increasingly replaced the alimony rules in industrialized countries[79], because it makes a clear cut and prevents moral hazard.

---

[78] Nevertheless, in this case moral hazard also is possible due to assymetrical information. For example, human capital may be used for a more pleasureful job, i.e. for the production of a non-transferable immaterial good, instead of for a better payed job from which the outcome can be transferred to other family members.

[79] See e.g. Henrich (1986).

Nevertheless, a valuation problem also arises, because all expected future returns have to be summed up for an appropriate lump-sum payment.

Certainly, such regulations in divorce law, either alimony or lump-sum payments, change the conflict payoff, and make the breach of intrafamily contracts more unlikely. But, due to the problems of referability and valuation of after-marriage returns on marital investment in human capital, in general no optimal marital investments in human capital can be induced by such interventions. As Borenstein/Courant (1989) show, the existing divorce laws are far from being optimal in this sense.

8.2.3 Social norms

Finally, social norms provide another enforcement mechanism for contracts, which is also constituted by a third party. Social norms are usually defined as "regularities in behavior which are agreed to by all members of a society and specify behavior in specific recurrent situations" (Schotter 1981, p. 9). This specific behavior is either self-policing or enforced by external authority (ibid., p.11, see also Axelrod 1986)[80]. Similar to laws, social norms are seen as mechanisms which will improve the efficiency of the economic or social system (e.g. Ullmann-Margalit 1977)[81]. Social norms result from a social learning process in recurrent situations (see Schotter 1981, p. 39 or Witt 1986). Recurrent coordination problems and recurrent prisoner's dilemma situations are mentioned as the most relevant situations from which social norms emerge (Ullmann-Margalit 1977, Schotter 1981).

Coordination problems arise in situations with multiple equilibrium points. In order to reach one of these equilibria, the actions of the players must be coordinated. Otherwise all players would lose. If communication is impossible or the communication costs are prohibitively high, social norms can

---

[80] Social norms differ from moral norms which can be regarded as internalized penalties for breaking agreements (Harsanyi 1979, p. 111). Moral norms may be constituted by social norms, if a break would be sanctioned by a third party and these sanctiones are internalized. But, if there are no third party sanctions, moral norms are very specific characteristics of the individual and cannot be assumed in general. Then, they must be treated as an individual element of the utility function and form the basis for loyalty (see chapter 8.1.3).

[81] Although most of social norms are 'socially useful' in the sense of Pareto-improvement, Elster (1989) shows some examples which are not.

generate convergent expectation. Such situations are mostly self-policing (Schotter 1981, p. 10). Because all players gain from reaching one of the equilibrium points, and an equilibrium will be reached when all players act according to the norm, none of the players has an incentive to deviate from the norm.

Social norms may also help to solve a recurrent prisoner's dilemma, which is repeated in the society, but not between the same partners. Unlike the usual repeated games in such a generalized prisoner's dilemma there are no incentives to cooperate due to the interest of further cooperative solution with the same partner, and therefore no endogenous enforcement mechanism will arise (Ullmann-Margalit 1977, chap. 1). For the same reason a social norm is not self-policing in this case, because the individual can gain from breaking the norm, if all others fulfill them. Therefore, a breach of the norm must be punished by sanctions from a third party. Because 'private' sanctions by some other society members will in general not be strong enough, an organized action (e.g. from a governmental instance) is required (Vanberg 1984, p. 141ff.). If the punishment is too small and therefore moral hazard is observed frequently, the trust in the behavior of other society members is destroyed, and social norms will disappear by a social learning process (Witt 1986).

In the family we can find both coordination problems as well as prisoner's dilemma situations. Because communication is possible in the family, coordination problems could be solved directly. But, social norms may reduce the costs of coordination. Some norm directed gender specific behavior may be explained for this reason.

Prisoner's dilemma situations surely arise in insurance contracts, for example in the case of needing care. For such situations we observe strong social norms. A breach of those social norms will be punished by the disapproval of other society members with blame as well as by sanctions through social institutions like the church and the government. The latter imposes the costs which arise for the society upon the family. But, with increasing costs for the family to fulfill social norms[82], such sanctions lose importance and social norms begin to vanish.

Regarding the fertility decision and intrafamily division of work there are also social norms, but they do not apply to the whole contract. There are norms on how long a child should be cared for only by the parents and which spouse should stay at home. But, the other part of the contract, the intrafamily distribution of welfare is not considered in the norm, and a breach of that promise is not sanctioned. Surely, the same problems of lacking observability as for enforcing a formal contract arise here, and therefore also social norms are not suitable for enforcing such asymmetrical contracts.

However, the existing social norms have probably not been a response to such recurrent prisoner's dilemmas but to recurring coordination problems. Since in the past full specialization in household production has been an efficient allocation, i.e. also in households without small children, marriage gains were large and the losses in bargaining power were relatively small. In such a situation no prisoner's dilemma occures, and the efficient allocation is chosen, because even after redistribution both spouses gain as compared to their status quo outcomes (see chapter 7). In such a situation social norms may be an instrument for coordination of investments in human capital, which partially take place before marriage. But, if the terms of the contracts change due to the decreasing efficiency of household production, and the situation turns out to be a prisoner's dilemma, the social norms are no longer efficient and will disappear. This might explain some of the recent changes in societal values. However, the contract which would be required nowadays does not gain in binding force by social norms.

8.3   Remarks on policy options

As we have seen, there are many intrafamily contracts which are self-enforcing or enforced by a third party. The related decisions should therefore yield

---

[82] In the case of needing care such costs arise e.g. from long distances between the residences of children and parents or from an interruption of employment in order to take over this tasks.

to efficient solutions. But, regarding intrafamily contracts with large asymmetrical effects on the bargaining power (like fertility linked with an interruption of employment), the enforcement mechanism appears insufficient for enforcing them. Therefore, we should expect a trend not to make such contracts and to choose non-efficient allocations in the family. Surely, politics could try to prevent such a development by improving the enforcement by law. But, it is doubtful whether this would lead to a Pareto-improvement in the society. A basic assumption in the Coase theorem is that transactions and sanctions are without costs for the society. If this is not true, the costs must be compared with the improvement in efficiency. As we have seen, for the enforcement of intrafamily contracts at least a highly expensive monitoring would be required, and the possible improvement in efficiency may be not great enough. Then, it may be more efficient for society to transfer welfare production further from the family to other institutions, especially if it results in large asymmetrical changes in the intrafamily bargaining power. Such a solution requires substitutes - either provided by the market or the state - for household production in such a way that periods of full specialization in household production by one of the spouses can be avoided or shortened to a harmless extent. An example are child-care services that allow women to combine raising a family with a professional career.

9 Introducing uncertainty: the possibility of conflict

In chapter 6 a deterministic two-period model was developed for analyzing time allocation and intrafamily division of work in an existing household. For that purpose, a cooperative solution was assumed for period two as a subgame perfect equilibrium, because at any time the partners gain in the joint household compared with two single-person households. In such a model the conflict point has been important only for the internal distribution. The conflict payoffs themselves are never realized. In view of the observed growth of the number of divorces and separations this is a rather unrealistic assumption. In general, these dissolutions are not planned from the beginning of the partnership, but result from new knowledge about the characteristics of the partner or about external alternatives. As discussed in chapter 2, in view of an economic model a divorce can be seen as the revision of a miscalculation, which may occur if the individuals have no complete information.

Besides this, a theoretical problem also exists with axiomatic cooperative solutions. If the partners have complete information from the beginning and a cooperative solution is reached with certainty, the conflict point is irrelevant, because the threats are not credible, as Pen (1952, p. 38) already noted: "A subject that possesses full insight into his adversary's position cannot effectively be threatened within the contract zone. If we suppose perfect insight at both sides of the bargaining table, all threatening must necessarily be in vain, the execution of economic power is impossible, and the outcome is indeterminate." That the solution depends on the conflict point, is a reasonable assumption only when in the process of negotiation the possibility exists that each of the partners plays his non-cooperative strategy. Assuming rational players, this can occur only if the players act under uncertainty (see Harsanyi 1977, p. 143). In principle, a model of the bargaining process formulated as a sequence of proposals like in the Zeuthen game (see Zeuthen 1930, chap. 4 or Harsanyi 1977, p. 149ff.)

implies uncertainty, because the rule for making concessions depends on the individual risk, which can be interpreted as the subjective probability of a conflict (Harsanyi 1977, p. 151). A modification of this model with an explicit consideration of uncertainty was given by Harsanyi (1956). Another probabilistic model of a bargaining process based on the theory of 'convergent expectation'[83] is proposed by Anbar and Kalai (1978). In these models the Nash solution results, whenever the players find a cooperative solution. But, since in cooperative bargaining models only such cases are considered where no conflict occurs, the solution can be described adequately with an axiomatic approach.

Therefore, no problems arise for the static model, because the process of negotiation itself is not modelled and only partnerships are considered, for which a cooperative solution results. But, in the two-period model the assumption of a certain cooperative solution for period 2 poses problems. If the partners do not possess complete information in the beginning of a negotiation process, they can expect a cooperative outcome for period 2 only with a given probability. Then the question arises, whether the results about labor supply and intrafamily division of work derived from the deterministic model maintain, or whether the consideration of uncertainty will change the conclusions.

9.1 Exogenous probability of conflict

In a first step we will assume an exogenous probability of a conflict in period 2, which may arise from changes in the production technology or changes in the outside options. Because changes such as the possibility of an engagement in another partnership are not modelled explicitly, a resulting conflict must be treated as exogenous. In this case, the outcome for period 2 is given by the expected value of the cooperative and the conflict payoff.

---

[83] See for the probabilistic models of bargaining Roth (1979).

Then the expected outcome for player i in period 2 is given by

$$V^{i2} = qD^{i2} + (1-q)U^{i2} \tag{9.1}$$

where q   is the probability of conflict in period 2
U^{i2} is the cooperative outcome for period 2, and
D^{i2} is the conflict outcome for period 2,

and the game can be written as follows:

$$\max \quad N = (U^{m1} + V^{m2} - D^m) * (U^{f1} + V^{f2} - D^f) \tag{9.2}$$

subject to (6.7) - (6.14).

To analyze whether the results of the deterministic model referred to are maintained, we have to examine how the decisions in period 1 affect the expected payoff of the period 2, i.e. we have to derive

$$\frac{dV^{i2}}{dM^{i1}}, \frac{dV^{j2}}{dM^{i1}}, \frac{dV^{i2}}{dH^{i1}} \text{ and } \frac{dV^{j2}}{dH^{i1}}.$$

The changes of the individual cooperative outcomes in period 2 due to the changes of the conflict payoffs were essential for the results of the model without long-term binding contracts. These results were determined by the asymmetrical development of the human capital stocks of the spouses and their effects on the household production and the conflict payoffs. Assuming that productivity depends on human capital only in a 'technological' way, then the changes in productivity due to investments in human capital $\frac{dw^{i2}}{dM^{i1}}$ and $\frac{da^{i2}}{dH^{i1}}$ remain unaffected by the possibility of conflict. Therefore, we only have to see whether changes in wage rates or in the household productivity yield other effects in the model with uncertainty than in the deterministic model[84]. These are derived now as (the reactions on changes in household productivities result analogously):

---

[84] This results from
$\frac{dV^{i2}}{dM^{i1}} = \frac{dV^{i2}}{dw^{i2}} * \frac{dw^{i2}}{dM^{i1}}$ and $\frac{dV^{i2}}{dH^{i1}} = \frac{dV^{i2}}{da^{i2}} * \frac{da^{i2}}{dH^{i1}}$,
if $\frac{dw^{i2}}{dM^{i1}}$ and $\frac{da^{i2}}{dH^{i1}}$ are independent from the conflict outcome.

$$\frac{dV^{i2}}{dw^{i2}} = q\frac{dD^{i2}}{dw^{i2}} + (1-q)\frac{dU^{i2}}{dw^{i2}} \qquad (9.3)$$

$$= q\left[\frac{dD^{i2}}{dw^{i2}} - \frac{dU^{i2}}{dw^{i2}}\right] + \frac{dU^{i2}}{dw^{i2}}$$
$$> 0$$

and

$$\frac{dV^{j2}}{dw^{i2}} = q\frac{dD^{j2}}{dw^{i2}} + (1-q)\frac{dU^{j2}}{dw^{i2}} = (1-q)\frac{dU^{j2}}{dw^{i2}} \qquad (9.4)$$

In equation (9.3) which describes the reaction of the individual's own payoff, an additional positive term results, that works in the same direction as the bargaining effect (see chapter 5.2). On the other hand, the effect on the partner's payoff in equation (9.4) is less than in the deterministic model, because this is only affected via the household context. From (9.3) and (9.4) we can see that in comparison with the deterministic model the individual effects are weighted in a different way. But the principle results concerning the labor force participation and the intrafamily division of work in principle remain unchanged. However, the effects of a change in the conflict payoff gain more importance as compared to the effects on the household level.

In the model with binding long-term contracts, on the other hand, a changing outside option in period 2 has no effect on the intrafamily distribution of welfare and therefore is neglected in the deterministic model (see chapter 6). But, if there is a possibility of a conflict in period 2, then the actual conflict payoffs would be realized in the case of conflict. As a consequence, the future conflict point will be relevant for decision making also in the model with binding long-term contracts. In principle, such a model corresponds to that of Lommerud (1989), who analyzes the effects of the divorce probability on intrafamily time allocation in a model with a joint household welfare function which is formed by the sum of the individual utilities. With his model, where the distribution between the spouses does not depend on the conflict point, he comes to the conclusion that the probability of divorce influences the time allocation within the marriage. However, if conflicts cannot be ruled out with certainty, then the changes in the conflict payoffs will be considered in the decision on time allocation in period 1[85]. Then, also in the model with binding long-term contracts changing outside options have an effect similar to the bargaining effect.

But here it must be noted that the possibility of a conflict in a model with binding long-term agreements is logically inconsistent. Introducing a positive probability of conflict in such a model implies, that all contracts made in period 1 are binding with one exception: the agreement about the continuation of the partnership. If there are mechanisms to enforce all intrafamily contracts, then the case of conflict can also be ruled out with certainty. This shows the consistency problem of traditional approaches, that assume for an existing family a fixed internal distribution requiring binding agreements. But then, it is not clear why conflicts arise at all. In the end, it must be substantiated by incomplete information about the characteristics of the partner and the future states of the world. But then, it ought to be possible to model the conflict endogenously.

9.2 Causes of conflict and negotiation strategies

If one investigates the possible causes of conflicts one should consider incomplete information about the partners and about future environmental conditions as well as the external options with respect to other partnerships.

External options lead to a conflict, when the utility obtained from a new partnership is valued more highly than that of the present one. But, because all of the other options are not known at all times, the probability of finding a preferable relationship depends on the distribution of possible partners as well as on search behavior. Because other partners are not available at any given time, this probability is not fixed and the opportunity for other partnerships can be interpreted as a random deviation from the certain outcome when living alone.

Incomplete information about the characteristics of the partner results in an uncertain negotiation set. If the utility function of the partner is not known

---

[85] Also Marrewijk/Bergeijk (1990) show a less specialization in trades with an exogenous probability of trade disruption than in trades under certainty.

completely, or if based on erroneous assumptions about the characteristics of the partner the utility is wrongly evaluated, the utility possibility frontier cannot be exactly determined, and the cooperative outcomes are also uncertain. Therefore, it is possible that a situation occurs in which the condition for a cooperative solution - the existence of a marriage gain - no longer holds, and both partners would be better off with their conflict payoffs.

Indeed, even in the case of existing marriage gains a conflict can result directly out of the bargaining process due to incomplete information. Wrong estimates of the possible negotiation space, which can result through wrong estimates of the partner's conflict payoff, may possibly lead to incompatible demands of the partners. As a consequence, a cooperative agreement may be prevented even if a Pareto improvement is possible. Such an escalation of the threats up to the conflict point (see Schelling 1960, chapter 3) has been modelled formally by Chatterjee and Samuelson (1983) and by Crawford (1987). Chatterjee and Samuelson assume the conflict as soon as incompatible demands are put forward in the negotiation. Costs of backing down in incompatible demands are considered in the model of Crawford, from which the limits can be derived when no cooperative solutions are realized, even if they exist. In particular, the model of Crawford could provide a suitable approach for analyzing conflicts in the family that result out of the negotiation process itself. But, this shall be left to future research. In the following, only those conflicts are considered which result from the lack of cooperation gains in the joint household.

Uncertainties about the future exogenous factors can also be the cause of conflicts. Random variations in variables relevant for decision making, such as wages, alter the negotiation set as well as the conflict point. This can give rise to constellations in which the condition for a cooperative solution no longer holds.

If future states concerning the negotiation set or the conflict point are uncertain, two extreme negotiation strategies which define the range of possible behavior are available. Either the partners will wait until the uncertainties are resolved and will only negotiate the actual distribution, or they will agree on a distribution for the next period before the actual realization of the negotiation set and of the conflict point becomes known. In this case, the basis for the negotiation is the expected value of the conflict point of the next period, i.e. foreseeable systematic changes are anticipated and are taken into consideration. But, if the expected states are not realized later, one partner will be able to improve his situation by renegotiation. Therefore, renegotiations may be ruled out as one agreement in this ex ante negotiation.

For further analysis, it is assumed that there is only uncertainty about the conflict outcomes. One of the properties of cooperative bargaining games is the independence of equivalent utility representations (see Roth 1979, p. 6), i.e. the Nash solution is independent from monotonic affine transformations of the utility function. Based on this invariance, random deviations in the negotiation set can be represented as deviations in the conflict point and vice versa. This means, that uncertainties concerning the negotiation set may be modeled as uncertainties with regard to the conflict outcomes[86]. Then, the conflict payoffs can be modelled as random variables in a game with a certain negotiation set. With these assumptions the probability of conflict can be derived given different negotiation strategies.

Ex-ante negotiation

One of the possible negotiation strategies of the partners is to bargain in period 1 about the distribution in period 2. The aim is not to reach a distribution like in the game with binding contracts, but to reduce the negotiation costs. This means, that the partners agree on a distribution for period 2, in which systematic changes in the bargaining power are anticipated. Hence, in period 1, the cooperative solution for period 2 (U_a^{m2}, U_a^{f2}) is negotiated with regard to the expected conflict point ($E(D^{m2})$, $E(D^{f2})$). Given this, a breach of contract will be avoided. On the one hand, the spouses anticipate systematic changes in the conflict point and will make their decisions in period 1 in such a way, that no big incentives for renegotiations in period 2 result. On the other hand, negotiation costs can be reduced by such an ex-ante agreement, because no permanent negotiation is required when new information

---

[86] If uncertainty prevails on both the conflict point and the negotiation set, then in this interpretation no simple assumption about the distribution of the random deviations can be made in general. However, the problem is reduced when the uncertainty depends on factors that determine both the conflict point and the negotiation set, like wage rates or prices. In this case, the conflict point and the negotiation set are affected by random events in a similar way: a random increase of the wage rate increases both the conflict payoff and the household utility. Thus, only an assumption about the distribution of the balance is necessary.

becomes available. Renegotiations are ruled out, and it is presumed that a violation of this agreement immediately leads to conflict.

Figure 9.1

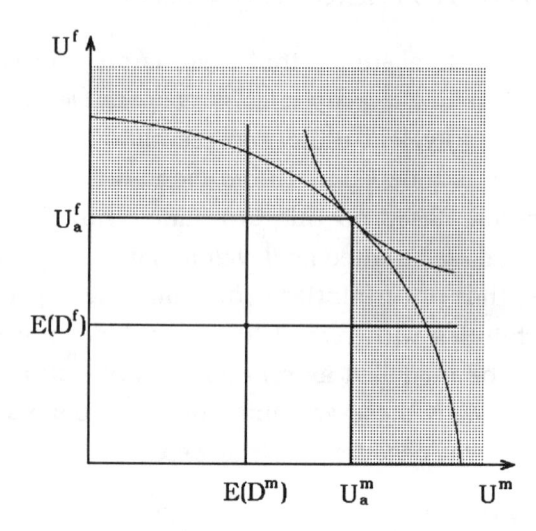

These rules lead to a realization of the ex ante negotiated distribution, if the actual conflict point in period 2 lies inside the Pareto frontier. But, if the random effect results in an actual conflict payoff for one partner which is better than his cooperative outcome, no renegotiation will take place, a conflict will arise. Consequently, the conflict probability is equal to the probability that the actual conflict payoff for at least one player exeeds his cooperative outcome (i.e. the actual conflict point falls in the shaded area in figure 9.1):

$$q = \text{prob}\{U_a^{m2} - D^{m2} < 0\} + \text{prob}\{U_a^{f2} - D^{f2} < 0\} \qquad (9.5)$$
$$- \text{prob}\{U_a^{m2} - D^{m2} < 0 \wedge U_a^{f2} - D^{f2} < 0\}$$

$$= 1 - \text{prob}\{U_a^{m2} - D^{m2} > 0 \wedge U_a^{f2} - D^{f2} > 0\}$$

Ex post-negotiation

Another negotiation strategy is to bargain at any point in time only about the actual distribution. This means that in period 1, as in the deterministic model without binding agreements, the future distribution is not yet decided on. But, the partners do take into account, that a new negotiation will take place in period 2, when the actual conflict point in period 2 is within the negotiation set. Then in period 2, the cooperative Nash solution (U^{m2}, U^{f2}) is realized relative to the actual conflict point (D^{m2}, D^{f2}).

Figure 9.2

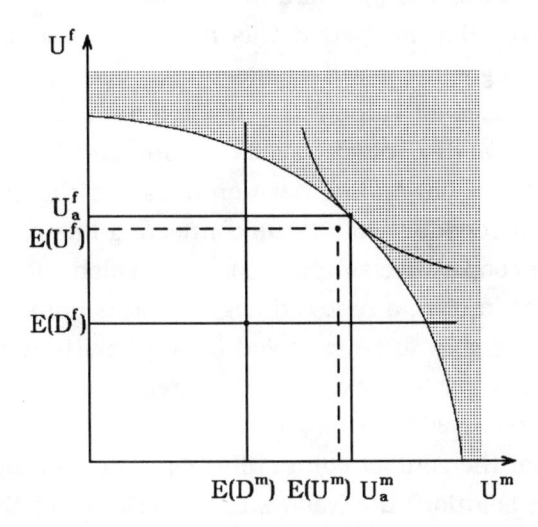

In this case, the probability of a conflict equals the probability that the actual conflict point lies outside of the negotiation set (in the shaded area in figure 9.2):

$$q = 1 - \text{prob}\{U^{m2} - D^{m2} > 0 \wedge U^{f2} - D^{f2} > 0\}$$

The expected value of the cooperative solution is the expected value of all possible cooperative outcomes $E(U^{12})$. But given a convex utility possibility frontier, this expected value is smaller than the outcome of the Nash solution relating to the expected value of the conflict point (see Chun/Tomson 1987 and Perles/Maschler 1981).

Mixed strategy

The two strategies mentioned are two extreme cases, which are not likely to be practiced in a pure form. On the contrary, we can expect that negotiations represent a mixed form of the two strategies. The ex-ante solution has advantages for both partners, because the expected outcome is larger than in the ex-post case. Furthermore, negotiation costs can be reduced, which increase the gain of both partners further. On the other hand, there are incentives for a partner to break the agreement ex post, because he can improve his position by renegotiations regarding the actual conflict point. However, this partner will only insist on a new negotiation, when his gains are sufficiently large. Therefore, the partners may proceed in the following way. In period 1, the distribution for period 2 is negotiated based on the expected conflict point. This agreement will be executed if both actual conflict payoffs are less than the expected value (area denoted with A in figure 9.3). It will also be executed, if both conflict payoffs do not exeed the cooperative outcomes and the relative bargaining position does not change too much (area B). Then, there is a corridor around the connecting line of the expected conflict point and the cooperative solution point, in which, when the actual conflict payoffs become known, a renewed negotiation is not rewarding for either partner, because the gain to be expected is only relatively small. But, if the conflict payoff of one partner exceeds his agreed cooperative outcome or if the change in the relative bargaining position is large, renegotiation will take place. Provided that the conflict point still is contained in the negotiation set, a new cooperative solution, the Nash solution relative to the actual conflict point, is realized. A conflict will only occur, if the conflict point lies outside of the negotiation set.

Figure 9.3

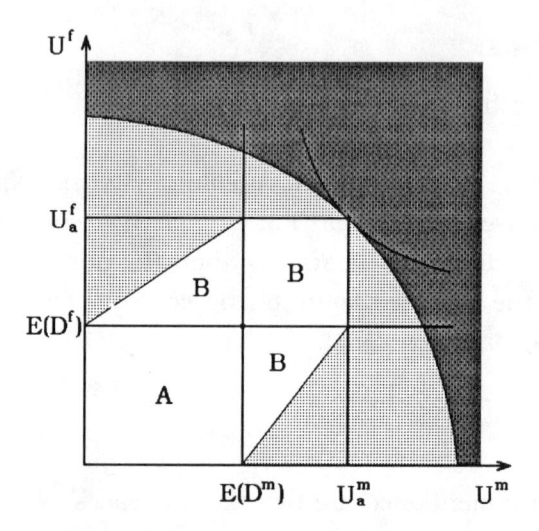

This mixed strategy results in larger outcomes than the pure strategies, because in many cases the ex-ante solution will be realized with higher expected outcomes for both partners than the pure ex-post strategy. On the other hand, the conflict probability is lower in comparison to that of the ex-ante game due to the possibility of renegotiation. Like in the pure ex-post game, the conflict occurs only when the conflict point lies outside of the negotiation set. From this it is intuitively plausible that the probability of a conflict increases, the smaller the difference between the cooperative ex-ante solution and the expected conflict point. This is the case, if the expected gains of cooperation are small. But, because these gains are determined by previous decisions, these decisions also influence the probability of conflict. Therefore, the probability of a conflict depends not only on exogenous factors which are not considered in the model, but also on the negotiation process itself and should be modelled endogenously.

9.3 Endogenous probability of conflict

Let the conflict payoff be defined as a random variable in the following form:

$$D^i = D_0^i + \varepsilon^i \qquad (9.7)$$

where D_0^i is the deterministic part of the conflict payoff for person i and

ε^i is a random variable with the expected value 0, density function f and distribution function F.

If we assume the described mixed or ex-post negotiation strategy for both partners the conflict will occur only when no gain can be realized from cooperation, i.e. that the conflict point lies outside the negotiation set. A sufficient condition for this is that the actual conflict payment D^i of at least one partner is larger than his maximum cooperative outcome $\bar{D}^i$. This maximum cooperative outcome $\bar{D}^i$ is defined by an intrafamily distribution where person i gets the total gain from cooperation, i.e. when person j receives not more than the conflict payment D^j (see figure 9.4). Hence, the maximum outcome $\bar{D}^i$ depends on the conflict payoff D^j of the partner. The actual conflict payment D^i can exceed the maximum payment $\bar{D}^i$ only if the conflict point D lies outside of the negotiation set. But then also $D^j > \bar{D}^j$ results (see figure 9.5).

Figure 9.4

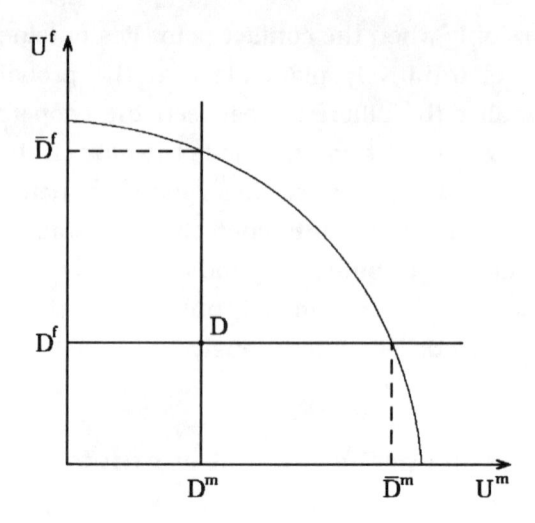

Figure 9.5

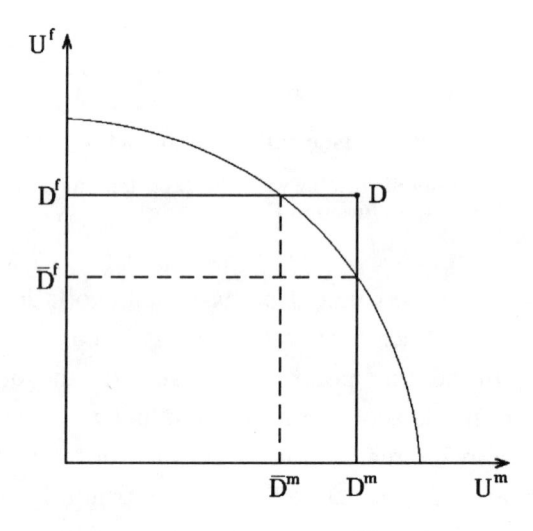

9.3.1 Conflict probability and wage changes

At this point, the conflict probability can be defined as the probability that the condition $D^i > \bar{D}^i$ holds for at least one partner. Because the maximum cooperative outcome depends on the actual realization of the partner's conflict payoff, it depends on the random term ε^j affecting ($\bar{D}^i = \bar{D}^i(\varepsilon^j)$). Assuming independency of the random terms in the conflict payoffs of both partners, then the conflict probability results in

$$q = \text{prob}\{D^i > \bar{D}^i\} \tag{9.8}$$
$$= \text{prob}\{D_0^i + \varepsilon^i > \bar{D}^i(\varepsilon^j)\}$$
$$= \text{prob}\{\varepsilon^i > \bar{D}^i(\varepsilon^j) - D_0^i\}$$
$$= \int_{-\infty}^{+\infty} \int_{\bar{D}^i(\varepsilon^j) - D_0^i}^{+\infty} dF(\varepsilon^i)\, dF^j(\varepsilon^j)$$

The conflict probability increases the smaller the difference $\bar{D}^i(\varepsilon^j) - D_0^i$ is. Because, this expression is identical to the total possible gain from the joint household the conflict probability rises the smaller the cooperation gain turns out to be. Then, the reaction of the conflict probability on wage changes is given by:

(9.9)

$$\frac{dq}{dw^{i2}} = \int_{-\infty}^{+\infty} \left[\int_{\bar{D}^i(\varepsilon^j) - D_0^i}^{+\infty} \frac{df(\varepsilon^i)}{dw^{i2}} dF(\varepsilon^i) - f(\bar{D}^i(\varepsilon^j) - D_0^i) \left[\frac{d\bar{D}^i(\varepsilon^j)}{dw^{i2}} - \frac{dD_0^i}{dw^{i2}} \right] \right] dF^j(\varepsilon^j)$$

Assuming that the random terms do not depend on human capital, the first term drops out and the reaction of the conflict probability on a wage change is

$$\frac{dq}{dw^{i2}} = - \int_{-\infty}^{+\infty} f(\bar{D}^i(\varepsilon^j) - D_0^i) \left[\frac{d\bar{D}^i(\varepsilon^j)}{dw^{i2}} - \frac{dD_0^i}{dw^{i2}} \right] dF^j(\varepsilon^j) \tag{9.10}$$

$$> 0 \qquad\qquad ?$$

In this equation the sign of the term in parenthesis is still unknown. In order to derive it, we will consider the maximum payoff $\bar{D}^j$ as the limit of the solution of an asymmetrical generalized bargaining game (see i.e. Roth 1979,

p. 18), in which the weight for person i approaches 1, i.e. in which a partner can fully realize his interests. In the game

$$\max \ (U^i - D^i)^\alpha (U^j - D^j)^{1-\alpha} \qquad (9.11)$$

subject to (5.4) to (5.7)

the maximum cooperative outcome is given by

$$\bar{D}^i = \lim_{\alpha \to 1} U^i(\alpha, D^i, D^j). \qquad (9.12)$$

This implies that $\bar{D}^i - D^i = N$ (see appendix 8) and

$$\bar{D}^i(e^j) - D^i_0 = E(N|e^j). \qquad (9.13)$$

From this follows that

$$\frac{d\bar{D}^i(e^j)}{dw^{j2}} - \frac{dD^i_0}{dw^{j2}} \qquad (9.14)$$

will be negative, if a wage change has a stronger effect on the conflict payoff than on the welfare production of the joint household and the gain from a joint household is sufficiently large for the partner j (see appendix 8). As discussed in chapter 6 this will be the case in general. Hence, from this it can be concluded that an increase of the human capital stock by employment in period 1 will lead in general to an increase of the conflict probability.

A change in the productivity for household production will have a reverse effect on the conflict probability. Because the conflict payoffs can hardly be increased by work at home, the effect on the household level will be in general larger than the effect on the conflict payoff. Then, the counterpart to (9.14) will be positive. Therefore, an increased participation in housework can promote the lowering of the conflict probability.

9.3.2 Time allocation and conflict probability

In studying the effect of a specific time allocation on the conflict probability both effects must be considered jointly. In the case that on the household level a specialization of one person in housework is efficient in the long run, the long-term Nash gain is large. Then, an extension of market work by the individual decreases the Nash gain and as a consequence will increase the conflict probability.

But, if the gains from specialization in housework result for the most part in the short term, and if market work is the more efficient use of time in the long run even on the household level (= positive welfare effect of market work), then, with a specialization on housework, the Nash gain in period 2 is comparatively small. Then, expression (9.14) may be positive, and an increase of market work may reduce the conflict probability more than specialization in housework. Therefore, a time allocation in period 1, which results in a game for period 2 with a relatively small negotiation set, is connected with a relatively large conflict probability. However, the conflict probability can be reduced by a time allocation, which maintains or increases the earning capacity of both partners. Hence, if specialization on housework is not efficient in the long run even in the joint household, a traditional division of work in the family may result in a higher conflict probability than a time allocation, that maintains the earning capacity of both partners.

In order to analyze the effect of the conflict probability on the decision in period 1, the expected outcomes in period 2 (V^{i2}) have to be considered. Assuming ex-post negotiation (i.e. when the actual conflict point is known) the expected individual cooperative payoff in period 2 can be represented as a function of the random variables ε^i and ε^j:

$$V^i(\varepsilon^i, \varepsilon^j) = \delta D^i(\varepsilon^i) + (1-\delta) U^i(D_0^i + \varepsilon^i, D_0^j + \varepsilon^j) \qquad (9.15)$$

where

$$\delta = \begin{cases} 1 & \text{in the case } D^i > \bar{D}^i \\ 0 & \text{otherwise} \end{cases}$$

Hence, the expected value of this outcome can be derived:

(9.16)

$$V_E^i = E(V^i) = \int_{-\infty}^{+\infty} \left[\int_{\bar{D}^i(\varepsilon^j) - D_0^i}^{+\infty} (D_0^i + \varepsilon^i) \, dF(\varepsilon^i) + \int_{-\infty}^{\bar{D}^i(\varepsilon^j) - D_0^i} U^i(D_0^i + \varepsilon^i, D_0^j + \varepsilon^j) \, dF(\varepsilon^i) \right] dF^j(\varepsilon^j)$$

and the derivative of this expected value with respect to a wage change gives the following expression (see appendix 9):

$$\frac{dV_E^i}{dw^{i2}} = \int_{-\infty}^{+\infty} \left[\int_{\bar{D}^i(\varepsilon^j) - D_0^i}^{+\infty} \frac{dD_0^i}{dw^{i2}} \, dF(\varepsilon^i) + \int_{-\infty}^{\bar{D}^i(\varepsilon^j) - D_0^i} \frac{dU^i(\varepsilon^i, \varepsilon^j)}{dw^{i2}} \, dF(\varepsilon^i) \right] dF^j(\varepsilon^j) \quad (9.17)$$

$$= q * \frac{dD_0^i}{dw^{i2}} + (1 - q) * E\left(\frac{dU^{i2}}{dw^{i2}}\bigg|_{D^i < \bar{D}^i}\right).$$

The effect of a wage change in period 2 on the expected outcome depends on the change of the expected conflict payoff (D_0^i) and on the expected change of the cooperative outcome $E(U^{i2})$. Because the random deviations affect the cooperative outcome only by changing the weights of the singular effects (see equation (5.25)), in principle the results of the deterministic model carry over to the stochastic approach. However, due to the first summand in (9.17) the change of the conflict payoff becomes more important the larger the conflict probability is. From this, an effect on time allocation in period 1 results which strengthens the bargaining effect.

But, a principle problem arises in such model. The marginal change of the conflict probability $\frac{dq}{dw^{i2}}$ has no effect on the change of the expected outcome, because on the threshold to conflict the cooperative and the conflict outcome are identical ($\bar{D}^i = D^i$). In this case, the marginal loss and the marginal gain counterbalance each other[87]. Calling to mind the discussion in the previous section, it is surpring that the marginal change of the conflict probability in equation (9.15) vanishes. The reaction of the expected outcome in period 2 depends on the absolute size of the conflict probability, which again also depends on earlier human capital accumulation. Consequently, a change of the conflict probability in a dynamic approach should show an effect on the future outcome. However, here the two-period approach clearly reaches its limits. For analyzing such feedback effect at least three periods have to been considered.

---

[87] However, this is only true if the utility functions are complete and include all utility bearing arguments, i.e. the affective components, too. In the model described in chapter 5 and 6 only the material situation is considered ($U^i U^i(L^i, C^i)$), i.e. that this aspect is missing and $U^i(\bar{D}^i) = \bar{D}^i$ does no longer hold. The terms, which influence the conflict probability, do not compensate each other. Then, the conflict probabilities based on such utility functions are not identical with divorce probabilities but they are at least correlated with them.

10 Empirical tests of the bargaining approach

In the previous chapters a theoretical bargaining model for family decisions was developed, which was applied to questions on labor supply and intra-family division of work. Also some hypotheses regarding fertility and divorce behavior were derived. For all these questions the model provides a consistent analytical framework. As was shown, the results differ from those of traditional models with a joint household utility function. Nevertheless, the empirical relevance of the bargaining approach has yet to be shown. Differences to the traditional approaches as seen in the theoretical derivation should also become apparent in the empirical analysis. In particular, based on the different results, it should be possible to test which approach is able to provide a better explanation model for observed behavior.

10.1 Tests based on the Slutsky restrictions

A formalization of household decisions as a bargaining model was first attempted by Manser/Brown (1979) and McElroy/Horney (1981). They analyzed labor supply with a static Nash model very similar to that described in chapter 5, but without household production. From this model they derived restrictions in order to test the bargaining approach against the traditional model with a household utility function. Due to the threat point the explanatory variables have additional influences in the demand functions derived from a bargaining model. Then, the estimated parameters for variables which affect the common household production as well as the conflict point, must be interpreted as compound parameters. Because the effect resulting from changes in the conflict point is neglected in the traditional model, this can be used as basis for generating testable hypotheses.

10.1.1 Derivation of testable hypotheses

Manser/Brown (1979) and McElroy/Horney (1981 and 1988) suggest three tests based on the Slutsky decomposition: a test on equal individual non-wage income effects and two tests on the symmetry and the semidefiniteness of the substitution matrix respectively. In comparison to equation (4.15) derived in chapter 4 they decompose also the bargaining effect into an income and a substitution effect. This means, that the effects of the conflict point are not estimated directly, but rather by a deviation from the properties of the traditional model. McElroy and Horney (1981, p. 341) use a model without household production based on a five good economy: one household public good, private market goods and leisure for both spouses. From this, they derive the following Nash generalization of the Slutsky equation:

$$\begin{bmatrix} X_p \\ -\lambda'_p \end{bmatrix} = \begin{bmatrix} (\tilde{X}_p - \lambda^{-1} b g' D_p) - \frac{1}{2}(X_I - BUD_I) eq' \\ (\lambda_p^{-1} - (c\lambda)^{-1} g' D_p) + \frac{1}{2}(\lambda_I - bUD_I) eq' \end{bmatrix} \quad (10.11)$$

where $X_p = \begin{bmatrix} \dfrac{\partial x_k}{\partial p_l} \end{bmatrix}$ $k, l = 1,...,5,$ $\quad \lambda_p = \begin{bmatrix} \dfrac{\partial \lambda}{\partial p_l} \end{bmatrix}$ $l = 1,...,5$

$\tilde{X}_p = \begin{bmatrix} \dfrac{\partial x_k}{\partial p_l} \end{bmatrix}$ with N = const., $\quad \tilde{\lambda}_p = \begin{bmatrix} \dfrac{\partial \lambda}{\partial p_l} \end{bmatrix}$ with N = const.

$D_p = \begin{bmatrix} \dfrac{\partial D^i}{\partial p_l} \end{bmatrix}$ i = m, f, $\quad D_I = \begin{bmatrix} \dfrac{\partial D^i}{\partial I^j} \end{bmatrix}$ i, j = m, f

$X_I = \begin{bmatrix} \dfrac{\partial x_k}{\partial I^j} \end{bmatrix} = BUD_I + be',$ $\quad \lambda_I = \begin{bmatrix} \dfrac{\partial \lambda}{\partial I^j} \end{bmatrix}$

$q' = X' - [0,0,0,T,T]$

with x_1: household public good
x_2, x_3: private goods of m and f
x_4, x_5: leisure of m and f

I^i the non-wage income of person i

e the unit vector.

(regarding additional notation see chapter 4).

The Slutsky decomposition of the traditional model results from (10.1) for

$$D_p = 0, \quad D_I = 0 \quad \text{and} \quad \frac{\partial x_k}{\partial I^i} = \frac{\partial x_k}{\partial I^j}.$$

Thus, the traditional model is nested in the bargaining model. Using this result, McElroy and Horney (1981, p. 343) suggest to test the following hypotheses:

1) Equal effects of the individual non-wage income:

H_0: $\quad X_I^m = X_I^f = x_I$ \hfill (10.2)

versus

H_1: $\quad X_I^m \neq X_I^f$ \hfill (10.3)

where $\quad X_I = [X_I^m, X_I^f] = BUD_I + be'$ \hfill (10.4)

2) Symmetry of the substitution matrix ($B = B'$):

H_0: $\quad (X_p + x_I q') = (X_p + x_I q')'$ \hfill (10.5)

versus

H_1: $\quad (X_p + \frac{1}{2} X_I eq') G^{-1} = G^{-1} (X_p + \frac{1}{2} X_I eq')'$ \hfill (10.6)

where $\quad G = \lambda I + UD_p + \frac{1}{2} UD_I eq'$ \hfill (10.7)

Equation (10.5) satisfies the substitution symmetry in the traditional model, and results from (10.6) for equal income effects and no influence of the threat point.

3) Negative semidefiniteness of the substitution matrix:

H_0: $\quad (X_p + x_I q')_{ii} < 0$ \hfill (10.8)

versus

H_1: $\quad (X_p + x_I q')_{ii} > 0$ \hfill (10.9)

(10.8) is a necessary condition for negative semidefiniteness of the substitution matrix in the traditional model.

A rejection of any of these hypotheses implies a rejection of the traditional approach, and is interpreted by McElroy and Horney (1981, p. 343) as contradicting "that the Nash demand model collapses to the neoclassical one".

10.1.2 Empirical results of Manser/Brown and Horney/McElroy

Both Manser/Brown (1979) and Horney/McElroy (1988) test these hypotheses in their empirical studies[88]. For this purpose, Horney and McElroy use a

Table 10.1 Estimation results of Horney und McElroy		
Equality of the income effects	Men	Women
$\dfrac{dL^i}{dI^i}$	-0.97	-0.15
$\dfrac{dL^i}{dI^j}$	-0.20	-0.05
$\dfrac{dL^i}{dI^i} \neq \dfrac{dL^i}{dI^j}$ (F-stat.)	2.12	0.02
Substitution matrix	w^m	w^f
	(t-value)	
L^m	-366.94	-311.11
	(2.39)	*(2.67)*
L^f	-42.64	-127.83
	(0.15)	*(0.62)*
$S^{ij} = S^{ji}$ (t-stat.)	0.89	
$\|S\|$	80546	
	=>[S^{ij}] is negative definite	
Source: Horney/McElroy (1988, p. 23 and 25)		

---

[88] Both studies use the data of the US National Longitudinal Survey, from which only married women were selected, who were between 30 and 44 years old, were working and had a working husband.

linear expenditure system[89], while Manser and Brown employ demand functions based on the Rotterdam approach (cf. e.g. Barten 1967).

Horney and McElroy carry out all three tests and obtain significant differences in the individual non-wage income effects only in the husband's labor supply equation (Table 10.1). The results of the other tests are not significant. Thus, the traditional model is not to be rejected.

Manser and Brown only test the equality of the non-wage income effects and the symmetry of the substitution matrix. The symmetry property is tested based on the bargaining model as well as based on the traditional model. For the latter a restricted model with equal income effects was estimated.

Table 10.2   Estimation results of Manser and Brown
Likelihood ratio test statistics

	Number of restrictions	$-2\log\mu$	$\chi^2(.01)$
Equal non-wage income effects	2	25.22	9.210
Symmetry conditional on the unrestricted model	3	25.29	11.341
Symmetry conditional on equal income effects	1	0.07	6.635

Source: Manser/Brown (1979, S. 22)

---

[89] McElroy and Horney do not derive the demand system from an explicit utility function, but they use a linear approximation. Although this is a common procedure, it is problematical in using the parameters in tests based on elasticities. If the basic relation is non-linear, the parameter estimates may strongly deviate from the true elasticities (e.g. White 1980). While even in a simple demand model with linear budget restrictions, a linear expenditure system can only be derived with rather specific assumptions (see Phlips 1974, chap. 4), the restrictions in the Nash bargaining model are high non-linear. Thus, the analytical derivation of an expenditure system is not simple, and it is not possible to specify conditions for linear demand functions in general (see for the general problem in the case of non-linear restriction Edlefsen 1981). Then, if the theoretical demand function is approximated by an arbitrary functional form - e.g. as linear demand function -, the relations found in the marginal analysis may be not correctly represented in this special functional form.

In the unrestricted model, both the hypothesis of equal non-wage income effects and that of the symmetry of the neoclassical substitution matrix are rejected. However, this does not result from the test based on the traditional approach. Hence, Manser and Brown (p. 19) get the surprising finding, that "the neoclassical model can be rejected on the basis of our bargaining model but not on the bases of the usual approach". This result also coincides with other empirical studies regarding cross substitution effects in family labor supply. Ashenfelter and Heckman (1974) test the symmetry conditions with a traditional approach and find no rejection of the model. Ashworth and Ulph (1981) estimate both a traditional and the Leuthold model (Leuthold, 1968), which describes a non-cooperative game. They obtain very small differences[90] between the compensated cross substitution effects in the traditional approach, but very large deviations in the model with two separate utility functions.

10.1.3 Some critical remarks

This result, that symmetry of the substitution matrix holds in a traditional model, but not for the counterpart nested in the bargaining model, points to some basic problems of the tests suggested by Manser/Brown and Horney/McElroy. It is in question whether these tests are well suited to test the bargaining model against the traditional one, and which the appropriate hypotheses are. In addition, there are some practical problems.

Relevance of the symmetry condition

First, the apparently inconsistent results regarding the symmetry of the substitution matrix brings up the question what we can actually conclude from the results of the symmetry test. What can be gathered from symmetry found in the restricted model (equation (10.5)) or in the unrestricted model (test on equality of the terms in parantheses of equation (10.6)), and what is the connection to the test on equality of income effects?

---

[90] Unfortunately the test statistic is not given.

Let us start with a traditional demand system in the following form which is often used in estimation:

$$X^m = a_1 w^m + a_2 w^f + a_3 I + \ldots \qquad (10.10)$$

$$X^f = b_1 w^f + b_2 w^m + b_3 I + \ldots$$

$$X^i = \ldots$$

Usually the estimated parameters of the system are interpreted as the marginal changes in demand, which should have the properties derived in the theoretical model:

$$a_2 = \frac{dX^m}{dw^f}, \quad b_2 = \frac{dX^f}{dw^m}, \quad a_3 = \frac{dX^m}{dI}, \quad b_3 = \frac{dX^f}{dI}$$

Let us assume that for a given data base the following relationship holds, which means that symmetry of the substitution matrix is found in the restricted model:

$$a_2 + a_3 X^m = b_2 + b_3 X^f. \qquad (10.11)$$

Usually, this is viewed to support the traditional model, since the symmetry of the substitution matrix appears to be given. But, because only the joint non-wage income $I = I^m + I^f$ is a regressor in the model the equality of the income effects

$$\frac{dX^i}{dI} = \frac{dX^i}{dI^m} = \frac{dX^i}{dI^f} \qquad i = m, f \qquad (10.12)$$

is introduced by definition without testing its validity.

Let us assume further, that the true model is described by the following functions:

$$X^m = \tilde{a}_1 w^m + \tilde{a}_2 w^f + \tilde{a}_3 I^m + \tilde{a}_4 I^f + \ldots \qquad (10.13)$$

$$X^f = \tilde{b}_1 w^f + \tilde{b}_2 w^m + \tilde{b}_3 I^m + \tilde{b}_4 I^f + \ldots$$

$$X^i = \ldots$$

Given the usual assumption of independence between the explanatory variables[91] it is to be seen from the comparison of the two systems, that the estimated parameters a_3 and b_3 in the traditional model represent the weighted mean of the two individual effects:

$$a_3 = \frac{I^m}{I^m + I^f} \tilde{a}_3 + \frac{I^f}{I^m + I^f} \tilde{a}_4$$

$$b_3 = \frac{I^m}{I^m + I^f} \tilde{b}_3 + \frac{I^f}{I^m + I^f} \tilde{b}_4$$

Then in the case of different individual income effects in the true model, these parameters of the restricted model do not measure the income effect as is presumed in the traditional model, because a different estimated value results from different income shares of the household members. Therefore, the parameters represent not only the change in demand that results from an income change, but also the effect of a change in income shares. Thus, without a test of the equality of the income effects (10.12), the symmetry of the substitution matrix in a restricted model does not tell us much about the validity of the traditional approach.

As will be shown in the following, the individual income effects are essential in both the equality and the symmetry test in the unrestricted model, too. The equality of the income effects is sufficient to reject the bargaining model. If it does not hold, in general no symmetry is to be expected for the traditional substitution matrix nested in the bargaining model.

In order to investigate the symmetry of the traditional substitution matrix based on an unrestricted model the following relationship is tested (Horney/McElroy 1988, p. 26):

$$\tilde{a}_2 + \frac{1}{2} X^m (\tilde{a}_3 + \tilde{a}_4) = \tilde{b}_2 + \frac{1}{2} X^m (\tilde{b}_3 + \tilde{b}_4) \tag{10.16}$$

Comparing with the symmetry condition in the bargaining model (10.6) this implies a test on the symmetry of matrix G. This matrix (see equation (10.7)) is the sum of the diagonal matrix μI and two matrices UD_p and $\frac{1}{2} UD_I eq'$

---

[91] From this assumption follows: $a_1 = \tilde{a}_1$, $a_2 = \tilde{a}_2$, $b_1 = \tilde{b}_1$ and $b_2 = \tilde{b}_2$.

which represent the influence of the threat point and are not necessary symmetrical. Furthermore, they are directly connected to the income effect.

As we can see from equation (10.4), $D_I = 0$ is a sufficient condition for the equality of the income effects, and in general, i.e. in a non degenerated case, it is also necessary. This means, that the income effects are equal if (and in general only if) the individual non-wage income does not affect the threat point. If the threat point is modelled as the solution of the maximizing problem in the one-person household, as it is done by McElroy and Horney, then $D_I = 0$ implies in general $D_p = 0$. Because earned income and non-wage income are substitutes in buying consumption goods, either both earned income and non-wage income or none of them affects the threat point[92]. Then, equality of the non-wage income effects implies that either income, wages and prices have no effect on the threat point or the threat point has no influence on the cooperative outcome. But, both are essential assumptions in the bargaining model. Thus, finding an equality of income effects, the bargaining model must be rejected.

If this is not the case, the bargaining model predicts $D_I \neq 0$ and $D_p \neq 0$, and matrix G will not be symmetrical in general. Therefore, finding different income effects it cannot be expected with the assumptions of the bargaining model that the part of the substitution matrix corresponding with the traditional model is symmetrical[93]. Thus, from the view point of the bargaining model, the equality and symmetry test are not independent[94].

Nevertheless, lacking symmetry of the traditional part of the substitution matrix is sufficient to reject the traditional model. But, this says little about the empirical relevance of the bargaining model, because other models are

---

[92] With the usual assumption of nonsatiation, income will always have an influence on the utility level. Then $D_I = 0$ can hold, only if the non-wage income of the joint household is not available for the separated households or if there are compensations in the case of conflict for every change in non-wage income. In this case $D_p = 0$ is not a necessary consequence. But, both alternatives are very unlikely.

[93] Nevertheless, it is surprising that symmetry of the substitution matrix is not be rejected for the restricted estimation, but is rejected for the unrestricted model. It is not clear whether there is a systematic relation behind this finding or whether it results from statistical problems.

[94] However, equality of the income effects does not imply a symmetric traditional substitution matrix. Therefore, even in the case of equal income effects the symmetry condition does not necessarily hold.

also consistent with the results. Chiappori (1988a) argues that for all data sets a matrix G can be found that obeys condition (10.6). But, if the utility function or at least the indirect utility function for the threat point is not known, no testable restrictions for the matrix G can be derived from the bargaining model. Therefore, it cannot be decided whether the deviations from the traditional model result from a bargaining or some other model structure.

This can be easily seen by writing the bargaining model as a model with preference changes like in chapter 4. Using the condition derived from (4.15)

$$X_Y = b \tag{10.17}$$

in equation (4.16) and solving for B, the symmetry condition equivalent to (10.6) results:

$$B = (X_p + X_Y X' - X_Y X_p)(\lambda I + UD_p)^{-1} = \tag{10.18}$$

$$[(\lambda I + UD_p)^{-1}]'(X_p + X_Y X' - X_Y X_p)' = B'$$

The term UD_p that is additional as compared to the traditional approach, results in every model with an additional price dependent term D in the utility function, and it does not necessarily indicate bargaining. As Pollak (1977) already showed, in models with price dependent utility functions the traditional substitution matrix neither has to be symmetrical nor negative semidefinite.

Concluding we see that the equality of the income effects and the symmetry of the substitution matrix do not provide independent tests for the traditional model (see also Ashenfelter 1979). The equality of the income effects is a necessary condition for supporting the traditional approach and it is sufficient to reject the bargaining model, while the symmetry condition alone does not provide a conclusive test.

Practical problems

Since the equality of the income effects is very important, the quality of the tests depends on the quality of the estimated parameters of the non-wage income. But, precisely at this point there are problems in the estimates of

Manser/Brown and Horney/McElroy. Some sources of non-wage income in the data base used cannot be identified as individual income of the wife or the husband. Therefore, Manser and Brown use information on single persons in order to split up the non-wage income between the partners. Horney and McElroy dispense with such a division, but they complement the individual incomes with individual transfer claims, which are, in part, never taken up. Both constructions are problematical and can strongly bias the results.

In addition, there is a general problem in the application of the tests, which also appears with correctly measured non-wage income. Both the test of the equality of the income effects and the test of the symmetry of the substitution matrix can only be carried out when the non-wage income is observed. For households without non-wage income the model is not identified, because only the total effect of the earned income is observed. Without additional information it cannot be decomposed into the income- and the compensated substitution effect. The isolated income effect can be estimated on the basis of an observed non-wage income, and is determined by the data of the subgroup with non-wage income. Now, the share of households that receive non-wage income is relatively small[95]. Using data on both households with and without non-wage income implies supposing the same income elasticity for the two subgroups. This is based on the assumption that there are no uncontrolled, systematic preference differences between the subgroupes. However, if these assumptions are incorrect, then the sample consists of a mixture of the two groups, and the results are biased.

Considering the sources of non-wage income, there are some arguments to suspect unobserved heterogeneity between the groups. In most cases, non-wage income consists of property income or transfer payments from the social security system. Now, both groups of non-wage income recipients show, in general, a different employment structure than households which only receive earned income. This may result from a dependency of the non-wage income on the actual labor supply (see Killingsworth 1983, p. 92ff.). Some kinds of non-wage income - especially transfers from the social

---

[95] In a sample for Germany corresponding to the data record of Manser/Brown and Horney/McElroy, 53% of the households in which both partners are employed receive no non-wage income.

security system - depend on the employment status or on the amount of earned income, and therefore cannot be considered as exogenous. Also actual property income itself may be endogenous, because it is simultaneously determined with labor supply in the process of asset accumulation, and should be modelled in a dynamic setting. On the other hand, non-wage income may be measured incorrectly, if only monetary income is considered. Especially with durable goods (e.g. a home of one's own) often non-monetary benefits are accrued, which represent quasi non-wage income for the labor supply decision. For households, which invest their capital in such durable goods, the non-wage income is not observed.

If there are differences between several subgroups in the sample, then at least for the households without non-wage income the decomposed effects cannot be estimated, and the tests proposed are not practicable. Thus, neither the one nor the other model can be clearly rejected based on these tests. But despite of these problems, the results of Manser and Brown do not support the traditional model, while they at least do not contradict the bargaining approach.

Additional explanatory variables

The various income components are not the only factors that affect labor supply. It should be possible to prove the influence of the conflict point using other explanatory variables. Both Manser/Brown (1979) and Horney/ McElroy (1988) have included various additional explanatory variables in their models. But, in contrast to the effects of income, prices and wages, for which the deviations from the traditional model are described by the generalized Slutsky decomposition, no comparable theoretical concept for separating the bargaining effect has been developed for other explanatory variables (like education, age, number and age of children, etc.)[96]. Referring to these variables similar results to those in other labor supply studies were obtained

---

[96] An additional problem arises from this lack of a theoretical concept, because the additional variables are included rather arbitrarily by simply adding them into the demand functions. In addition to the possibly biased estimate of the corresponding parameters, this also implies the assumption that the wage- and income elasticities do not depend on the additional explanatory variables. As Pollak/Wales (1981) and Barnes/Gillingham (1984) show the estimated value of the elasticities may strongly be influenced by the method of including additional variables. Therefore, it seems necessary to choose a model derived from the theory.

by Manser/Brown and McElroy/Horney, and they can be explained with the traditional approach as well as with the bargaining approach. Children in the household reduce the labor supply of women, while that of men remains unaffected. The working time of the husband increases with his own education level as well as with that of his wife, while the working time of the wife decreases with higher education of the husband. Care for children increases the labor supply of the husband and reduces that of the wife. Women are gainfully employed to a greater extent with higher age and when a greater demand for female labor exists. For men, increasing age, health limitations, and a high regional unemployment rate leads to a smaller labor force participation rate. Specific effects of the conflict point cannot be seen in the results even though they also do not contradict the bargaining model. Considerable difficulties in the interpretation of the parameters result from the fact that the household production is not explicitly considered in the models. Reducing work hours, then, can signify an increase in leisure time as well as in household production and tells nothing about the internal distribution.

Variables that, in theory, only affect the conflict point are included by Manser and Brown. They use data on the regional demographic structure as an indicator for search costs on external alternatives. However, they find an effect of the variables only at a significance level of 10%. The labor force participation rate of men becomes smaller the larger the number of single women relative to men is. If one assumes that for men less hours of work imply more leisure, this would be a weak indication for the bargaining model[97]. Nevertheless, the only way for strong tests of the bargaining model may be to include such variables which influence only the threat point. In the case of such 'extrahousehold environmental' influences the matrix G (10.7), which is relevant for the symmetry test, is no longer fully indeterminated (McElroy/Horney 1990). Then, modified testable hypotheses can be derived as is done by McElroy (1990). Starting from a Nash generalization of a general consumer demand model (similar to the description as model with preference changes in chapter 4), some properties directly based on the effect of variables only affecting the threat point are derived which can be tested for example with the Barten (1969) approach. Nevertheless, tests of

---

[97] According to the bargaining model the partner with the better bargaining position - i.e. that with the better chances in the case of conflict - is favored in the internal distribution.

such hypotheses depend on the availability of variables which influence only the threat point.

10.2 Test of Pareto efficiency

Since the tests based on the Slutsky decomposition do not provide strong tests of the bargaining approach against the traditional model, an approach will be considered that solely focuses on Pareto efficiency, which is a trait of all cooperative solution concepts. Chiappori (1988a, p. 794) points out that if the conflict point cannot be observed, the only testable property of the Nash bargaining solution is Pareto efficiency. He asserts further that for questions of labor supply, Pareto efficiency is sufficient to test a collective decision against the traditional approach, so that the intra-household distribution of consumption is not required to be known. From the assumption of Pareto efficiency he derives falsifiable conditions for household labor supply within a parametric and non-parametric context (Chiappori 1988b).

10.2.1 The parametric approach

Starting with a two-person household in a three-good economy Chiappori (1988b) considers the collective decision of the members whose utility functions depend on consumption und leisure. He distinguishes two cases, 'egoistic agents' whose utilities only depend on their own goods $U^i(L^i,C^i)$, and 'altruistic agents' whose utility functions also contain the goods of the partner $U^i(L^i,C^i,L^j,C^j)$. Household production is not considered in the model. Then, the budget restriction of the household reads $C^f+C^m=w^f M^f+w^m M^m+y$. For the case of egoistic agents the conditions for Pareto efficiency, called collective conditions, can be derived from specific functional forms of the utility or demand functions. A comparison of these conditions with the traditional Slutsky relations makes it possible to construct tests of different models.

However, these parametric tests are based on very restrictive assumptions. Egoistic agents are supposed in a simple model without household production. An explicit model of household production would lead to non-linear restrictions, from which labor supply functions cannot be derived easily (see Edlefsen 1981). Chiappori (1988b, app. I) also assumes linearity in the derivation of his collective conditions, and it is unclear whether comparable, well-defined conditions can be derived also for a model with non-linear restrictions.

Table 10.3 Comparison between neoclassical and collective conditions

Functional form for labor supply or demand for leisure	Slutsky conditions of the traditional model	Conditions for Pareto efficiency (egoistic agents)
Log-linear $M^i = k_i w_m^{a_i} w_f^{b_i} y^{c_i}$	$c_m = c_f$ and {$a_m = b_f = 0$ or ($k_m a_m = k_f a_f$ and $1+a_f = a_m$ and $1+b_m = b_f$)} plus concavity	$a_m = 0$ or $b_f = 0$
Semi Log $M^i = a_i \log w_f + b_i \log w_m + c_i y$	$a_m = b_f = 0$, $a_f c_m = 0$, $b_m c_f = 0$ plus concavity	Special cases always satisfied
LES $w_i L^i = b_i(w_m + w_f)T - C_0 + y$	always satisfied	Special cases always satisfied
Rotterdam-model $\dfrac{w_i M^i}{y} = a_i y + b_i \log y + c_i^f \log w_f + c_i^m \log w_m$	$c_f^m a_m(a_f+b_f) = c_m^f a_f(a_m+b_m)$ $c_i^f(a_m+b_m) + a_f c_m^i =$ $\quad = c_i^m(a_f+b_f) + a_m c_f^i$ $b_m c_f^i + b_f c_f^j = b_f c_i^m + b_m c_m^j$	$c_f^m = c_m^f = 0$ or $c_f^m = c_m^f = c_f^f = c_m^m = b_f = b_m$
Linear in Log. $L^i = a_i y + b_i y \log y + c_i \log w_f + d_i \log w_m$	($a_f = a_m$, $b_f = b_m$, and $c_f = c_m = d_f = d_m = 0$) or $a_f = b_f = a_m = b_m = c_m = d_f = 0$ plus concavity	$a_f b_m - a_m b_f \geq 0$, $b_m \geq 0$, $c_f b_m - c_m b_f \leq 0$, $b_f \leq 0$, $d_f b_m - d_m b_f \geq 0$

Source: Chiappori (1988b, pp. 72-73)

But, if the household production is not explicitly modelled, it is contained implicitly in leisure time. But then the assumption that the utility functions depend only on one's own leisure cannot be maintained any more, because the household production of a family member also benefits the others. Thus, the assumption of 'egoistic' agents has to be abandoned. But, for the case of individual utility functions called 'altruistic'[98], Chiappori does not derive collective conditions in a parametric context. Therefore, it is not clear whether a parametric test can be derived based on a model which describes household decisions in an appropriate way.

10.2.2 The non-parametric approach

Chiappori also points out the collective conditions in a non-parametric context[99]. In analogy to the usual revealed preferences conditions, he defines *collective rationalization* (CR) for household behavior from a pair of utility functions whose optimal solutions could have generated the observed data. For this the following proposition results (p. 79):

There exist a pair of strongly concave, strictly monotonic, infinitely differentiable utility functions which provide a CR of the data $D = \{(C_i, L_i^m, L_i^f, w_i^m, w_i^f), j = 1,...,n\}$ if and only if there exist nonnegative numbers $(Z_i, \alpha_i^m, \alpha_i^f, \beta_i^m, \beta_i^f), j = 1,...,n$ with $Z_i \leq C_i$, $\alpha_i^m \leq w_i^m$, $\alpha_i^f \leq w_i^f$, $\beta_i^m \leq 1$, $\beta_i^f \leq 1$ such that one of the following equivalent conditions is fulfilled:

(a) The data $(Z_i, C_i - Z_i, L_i^m, L_i^f; \alpha_i^m, \alpha_i^f, \beta_i^m, \beta_i^f)$ on the one hand and $(Z_i, C_i - Z_i, L_i^m, L_i^f; w_i^m - \alpha_i^m, w_i^f - \alpha_i^f, 1 - \beta_i^m, 1 - \beta_i^f)$ on the other hand, both satisfy the Strong Axiom of Revealed Preferences (SARP)[100].

(b) There exist numbers U_i^m, U_i^f and $\lambda_i, \mu_i > 0$, such that for each i,j in $\{1,...,n\}$, $i \neq j$:

---

[98] Note, 'altruistic' utility functions have to be proposed already due to a lacking modelling of household production, because we must assume an interest of all family members in the 'leisure' of that person working at home. But, this interest is surely not altruistic in the usual sense.

[99] To the non-parametric approach in demand analysis cf. Varian (1982 and 1983).

[100] See for the definition e.g. Varian (1978), ch. 3.12.

$$U_i^m - U_j^m < \lambda_i \alpha_i^m (L_i^m - L_j^m) + \lambda_i \alpha_i^f (L_i^f - L_j^f) +$$
$$\lambda_i \beta_i^m (Z_i - Z_j) + \lambda_i \beta_i^f (C_i - Z_i - C_j + Z_j)$$

and

$$U_i^f - U_j^f < \mu_i (w_i^m - \alpha_i^m)(L_i^m - L_j^m) + \mu_i (w_i^f - \alpha_i^f)(L_i^f - L_j^f) +$$
$$\mu_i (1 - \beta_i^m)(Z_i - Z_j) + \mu_i (1 - \beta_i^f)(C_i - Z_i - C_j + Z_j).$$

These conditions can be tested against the traditional model with a joint household utility function. The traditional model implies SARP for the full data set D. This is a special case of the collective conditions, because CR collapses to the Afriat conditions[101] if

$$\alpha_i^m = \frac{w_i^m}{2}, \quad \alpha_i^f = \frac{w_i^f}{2} \quad \text{and} \quad \beta_i^m = \beta_i^f = \frac{1}{2}.$$

On the other hand, for

$$\alpha_i^m = w_i^m, \quad \alpha_i^f = 0, \quad \beta_i^m = 1 \quad \text{and} \quad \beta_i^f = 0$$

the case of egoistic agents results. In principle, this allows to construct a test for the different models[102].

Chiappori himself conducts no empirical research so that no results can be presented. However, he shows a way to test whether family decisions can be appropriately described by a traditional model with a joint household utility function, or whether a model based on individual utility functions should be used. Chiappori's approach is suitable for tests if observed household behavior satisfies Pareto efficiency. Hence, such tests can form the basis for judging whether the family behavior can be appropriately described by a cooperative equilibrium as is done in static bargaining models. If neither the traditional nor the collective conditions are fulfilled, at least the observable short-term outcome is not Pareto efficient. This may arise, if future aspects which are evaluated in the utility functions are essential for the behavior, but are not modelled in a static approach. Or the solution is not Pareto optimal at all, because it results from (partial) non-cooperative behavior. In any case a dynamic approach seems to be more appropriate for modelling household behavior.

---

[101] See e.g. Diewert (1973)

[102] A practical estimation procedure for such tests is described by Varian (1982 and 1983).

11 Survey of empirical bargaining models

This chapter includes a short survey of further empirical research that is based on the idea of intrafamily bargaining. These models do not provide a strong test of bargaining models against traditional approaches, but give at least some indirect evidence. They are based on individual utility functions and reject the hypothesis of a joint household utility function. Some approaches focus primarily on Pareto efficiency, but there are also empirical studies in which the threat point or the intrafamily bargaining power are modelled explicitly as functions of some exogenous variables[103].

11.1 Household labor supply: a model with fixed bargaining power

A household labor supply model for estimating the chosen Pareto optimal allocation has been developed by Kooreman and Kapteyn (1985). They presume that the actual allocation results from a bargaining process and present a model for estimating the individual utility functions and the bargaining power from data on actual and preferred working hours. The preferred hours of work are interpreted as individual preferences, while the actual hours are treated as the negotiation result. The allocation favored by each partner is described as the result from a dictatorial model:

$$\max_{L^m, L^f, y} U^i(L^m, L^f, y) \qquad i = m, f \qquad (11.1)$$

subject to

$$w^m L^m + w^f L^f + y = Y = w^m T + w^f T + I \qquad (11.2)$$

---

[103] Extensive empirical research based on the Nash bargaining model of Manser and Brown (1979 and 1980) was also made by Carlin (1985). But, because his assumptions are very problematical the results cannot be interpreted unambigously (see Ott 1989a). For this reason, his research is not discussed here.

Kooreman and Kapteyn consider only two possible uses of time, market work and leisure, and presume individual Stone-Geary utility functions which depend on the individual leisure and household income:

$$U^i = \alpha_i^i \log(L^i - \gamma_i^i) + \alpha_j^i \log(L^j - \gamma_j^i) + \alpha_y^i \log(y - \gamma_y^i) \quad i = m, f \qquad (11.3)$$

where γ_k^i subsistence quantity of good k for person i, (k = L^m, L^f, y)

α_k^i weighting factor for good k, with $\alpha_i^i + \alpha_j^i + \alpha_y^i = 1$.

From this the demand functions for leisure result:

$$w^i L_p^i = w_i \gamma_i^i + \alpha_i^i (Y - w^m \gamma_m^i - w^f \gamma_f^i - \gamma_y^i) + \varepsilon_p^i \quad i = m, f \qquad (11.4)$$

where ε_p^i is a random error.

On the other hand, the actual hours of work are treated as the result of a bargaining process. Given the relative bargaining power, denoted by a parameter δ with $0 \leq \delta \leq 1$, the cooperative solution lies on the contract curve between both dictatorial points and results from

$$\max_{L^m, L^f, y} (1 - \delta)U^m + \delta U^f \qquad (11.5)$$

subject to (11.2).

The relative bargaining power is treated as exogenously given and independent of the characteristics of the partners. With the assumption that the spouses agree to the higher subsistence quantity γ^i, the following demand functions result:

$$w^i L_r^i = w_i \gamma_i^i + [\alpha_i^i + \delta^i (\alpha_i^j - \alpha_i^i)](Y - w^m \gamma_m - w^f \gamma_f - \gamma_y) + \varepsilon_r^i \qquad (11.6)$$

where $\gamma_k = \max(\gamma_k^m, \gamma_k^f)$

$$\delta^i = \begin{cases} \delta & \text{for } i = m \\ 1 - \delta & \text{for } I = f. \end{cases}$$

With these four demand functions (11.4) and (11.6) for i=m,f and the additional restriction $\alpha_m^y = \alpha_f^y$, which is necessary for identification, the parameters α_k^i and μ_k^y of the individual utility functions as well as δ can be estimated from the data about actual and preferred hours of work.

The estimated parameters, based on a sample of 139 households in which both spouses are employed, fall into the expected ranges, but some, especially δ, the estimate for the bargaining power, are not statistically significant. Therefore, no interpretation of δ in terms of relative bargaining power is possible (p. 16). However, the test on equality of the individual utility functions indicates, that a traditional model with a joint household utility function does not represent household labor supply in an appropriate way.

Table 11.1 Estimation results of Kooreman and Kapteyn

	male		female	
	coeff.	std.dev.	coeff.	std.dev.
α_i^1	0.29	0.10	0.14	0.05
α_j^1	0.02	0.13	0.17	0.07
μ_m^1	119.2	8.1	123.4	3.3
μ_f^1	140.8	22.4	141.3	2.6
μ_y^1	348.1	249.7	644.6	91.9
δ	0.64	0.74		

Source: Kooreman/Kapteyn (1985, p. 16)

Nevertheless, there are some problems in interpreting these results, because Kooreman and Kapteyn use a very simple specification and some important influences are neglected. In particular, the composition of the household is not considered. On the other hand, the model regards only two types of using time - market work and leisure -, which means that time for household production is implicitly included in leisure time. But, because the extent of household production depends on the household size and the age of the children, we should expect that the preferences vary with household composition. Such dependencies could be introduced easily by modelling the subsistence quantities as functions of the household composition. Then, the model of Kooreman and Kapteyn seems to be an appropriate way for estimating individual utility functions and the cooperative solution.

But, by applying this approach in empirical research some practical problems arise. First, the estimated parameters for the non-wage income play an important rule in the model of Kooreman and Kapteyn, because they are needed to identify the weighting factors α_i^l for own leisure in the individual utility functions. As discussed in the previous chapter, the assumption of equal preferences of households with and without non-wage income is problematical, and unobserved heterogeneity may affect the results in an essential way.

But the most important problem is the question of whether the preferred and actual hours of work can be interpreted in the supposed way. Since the work time in many jobs is determined by institutional restrictions, the actual hours of work do not represent the optimal unrationed time allocation[104]. In that case, the estimation results would be biased, and a discrete choice model would be a more appropriate approach. But, also the preferred hours of work might not reflect the individual optimum in terms of a dictatorial point, because the individuals may anticipate labor market restrictions as well as reactions of other family members. For example, knowing that her husband cannot or does not want to reduce his work time, a woman may wish to diminish her own hours of market work in order to avoid a double burden for herself. This may, however, differ widely from her real preferences concerning the intrafamily division of work. Surely, the meaning of the 'preferred hours' depends on the detailed formulation of the questionnaire, and labor market restrictions are different in many countries. Therefore, the problems may not be important in each case, but they should be checked carefully. A replication of the estimates with German data[105] was not successful due to these problems.

Nevertheless, for problems with inner solutions the model of Kooreman and Kapteyn seems to be an appropriate instrument for estimating bargaining power and its influence on the allocation in the family. For example, given the hours of work, the conditional division of non-market time in work at home and leisure could be analyzed with this approach, if commensurate data about preferred hours are available.

---

[104] See for this problem e.g. Killingsworth (1983), p. 45-66, 97-100.

[105] Based on the data from the German Socio Economic Panel the same and an extended model, controlling also household composition, were estimated. But, for both models the estimation yields paradoxal parameters like negative subsistence quantities.

11.2 Household labor supply: a game theoretic model in a discrete choice setting

Besides the possibility to detect the realized Pareto efficient solution by estimating the relative power of the spouses, the rules of the game which determine the decision can also be modelled explicitly. Whereas with the former proceeding the bargaining power can be discovered only at the sample mean, a model of the rules allows different bargaining weights for the several households.

Such a model for estimating household labor supply was developed by Kooreman (1988), who considers a discrete choice problem. Each of the partners has two alternatives for working hours. The husband can choose between fulltime employment ($y^m=1$) and reduced hours of work ($y^m=0$), and the wife between any employment ($y^f=1$) and solely household work ($y^f=0$). With that, four different combinations of the individual actions result for the household. Furthermore, Kooreman assumes that each of the partners has a well-defined preference order concerning these four alternatives. Since 4! different orders are possible for each partner, there are $(4!)^2=576$ possible combinations for the household. Any combination of two individual preference orders represent a bargaining game, for which a unique solution has to be selected. For this, Kooreman assumes cooperative behavior and supposes Pareto efficient solutions. Therefore, a Nash equilibrium of the strategic game is chosen only if it is not dominated by a Pareto-optimal allocation.

In the following the utility of person i of the combination (y^m,y^f) is denoted by $U(y^m,y^f)$. In the example

$$U^m(0,0) < U^m(1,0) < U^m(1,1) < U^m(0,1)$$
$$U^f(0,0) < U^f(0,1) < U^f(1,0) < U^f(1,1)$$
(11.7)

allocation (0,1) is an equilibrium point of the strategic game, because there is no incentive for any person to deviate by choosing the other alternative. This allocation is also Pareto optimal, because there is no other allocation which would be better for both partners. On the other hand, if all equilibrium points are not Pareto optimal, then Kooreman assumes that the partners agree on a Pareto optimal allocation. In the case of four alternatives this is a unique solution. The example

$$U^m(1,0) < U^m(0,0) < U^m(1,1) < U^m(0,1) \quad (11.8)$$
$$U^f(0,1) < U^f(0,0) < U^f(1,1) < U^f(1,0)$$

has an equilibrium point in (0,0), but (1,1) is the Pareto optimal solution. If there are multiple equilibrium points which are all Pareto optimal, then one of these is selected with equal probability. Also in the case of a non-existing equilibrium point the solution is selected from the Pareto-optimal allocations with equal probability. With this procedure a unique solution can be found for each combination of individual preference orders.

The utility which the individual can derive from the different allocations is described as a function of several observed variables and a random term (ibid., p. 8):

$$U^i(k,l) = x'\beta^i_{kl} + \varepsilon^i_{kl}. \quad (11.9)$$

Given the distribution of the ε's the probability of a certain preference order can be derived[106]. With this, the probability for any combination of the spouses' preference orders - i.e. the probability that a certain number of the 576 games will be played - can be calculated. Then, the probability of observing a certain allocation (y^m, y^f) for a given combination of exogenous variables can be derived. Because each of the games has a unique solution, the probability results from the sum of the probabilities of all games with outcome (y^m, y^f).

In order to compare his approach with usual estimation models of simultaneous family member's labor supply, Kooreman interprets Heckman's (1976) *simultaneous model for dummy endogenous variables* in the context of his game theoretic model (see Kooreman 1988, p. 9ff.). It is described as follows:

$$\tilde{y}^m = x'\beta^m + \delta^m y^m + \varepsilon^m \quad (11.10)$$
$$\tilde{y}^f = x'\beta^f + \delta^f y^f + \varepsilon^f$$

with $\quad y^i = 1$, if $\tilde{y}^i > 0 \qquad\qquad$ i=m,f,
$\qquad\quad y^i = 1$, if $\tilde{y}^i \leq 0$
$\qquad\quad \delta^m \delta^f = 0.$ [107]

---

[106] Kooreman assumes that the ε's are independently Extreme Value distributed.

[107] The restriction $\delta^m \delta^f = 0$ is necessary for logical consistency, but cannot be motivated from economic theory (Kooreman 1988, p. 10).

The $\tilde{y}^i$ can be interpreted as the difference between the utilities of the two working alternatives, given the decision of the partner

$$\tilde{y}^m = U^m(1,y^f) - U^m(0,y^f) \tag{11.11}$$
$$\tilde{y}^f = U^f(y^m,1) - U^f(y^m,0).$$

From (11.11) and (11.9) a comparable system of functions for the differences in utility can be derived also for the game theoretic model. The restriction

$$x'(\beta_{11}^i - \beta_{01}^i) = x'(\beta_{10}^i - \beta_{00}^i) + \delta^i \qquad i=m,f \tag{11.12}$$

by which both systems become equivalent, can be used for empirical testing of the traditional approach.

Table 11.2   Estimation results of Kooreman

	male (i=m) β_{10}^m	β_{01}^m	female (i=f) β_{10}^f	β_{01}^f
		(t-value)		
constant	-1.01	52.67	2.56	-12.12
	(-0.72)	(1.59)	(1.29)	(-2.25)
children younger than 6	0.33	-2.53	-4.14	-0.57
	(2.04)	(-1.58)	(-2.79)	(-3.32)
number of household members	-0.01	0.06	0.03	-0.78
	(-0.03)	(0.07)	(0.06)	(-4.56)
age of person i	0.02	-0.83	-0.07	-0.02
	(1.16)	(-1.65)	(-1.91)	(-1.54)
education index of person i	0.46	-1.42	-0.23	0.57
	(4.18)	(-1.31)	(-0.80)	(5.10)
non-wage income	-0.11	-0.64	0.44	0.01
	(-1.33)	(-1.19)	(1.30)	(0.08)
δ^i		-2.17		14.32
		(-6.77)		(2.67)

Source: Kooreman (1988, p. 13)

Table 11.2 contains the estimated parameters of Kooremans model. The δ^i describe the influence of one spouse's employment on the propensity for employment of the other. Both parameters are significantly different from zero, which means that the restriction $\delta^m\delta^f=0$ must be rejected. Therefore, the simultaneous model with structural shift may be an unsuitable appoach for estimating household labor supply.

The parameter δ^m is negativ. This indicates a lower propensity of the husband for full time work if the wife is employed than if she works at home. On the other hand, the positive parameter δ^f implies that full time work of the husband increases the propensity of the wife for market work in comparison to part time working men.

In interpreting the estimated parameters of the independent variables Kooreman focuses primarily on the utility difference $U^i(1,0)-U^i(0,1)$ which represents the preference for traditional gender rules (husband works full time, wife does not work in the market) against a more equal division of work (husband works part time, wife works in the market)[108]. If there are young children in the household, men have a stronger preference for traditional gender rules, while this preference for women decreases. The same result holds for the individual's own education level. Both effects are consistent with the results of the dynamic bargaining model derived in chapter 6, from which we should expect that women try to avoid losses in their earning capacity, whereas men would profit from high specialization.

However, the results derived from the theoretical model cannot be compared directly with the empirical results of Kooreman, because there are some problems with his estimation approach, in principle. Like all non-cooperative models of family decision (see chapter 3) he assumes the family as given, and neglects the possibility of a conflict. But, if the conflict is not excluded by exogenous factors, not all possible alternatives are regarded and the individual preference orders are not described completely. In this case, other equilibrium points may result from the different games. For instance, if the complete preference orders of example (11.7) are described as follows

---

[108] The influence of the independent variables is measured by the difference of the parameter $\beta^i_{10} - \beta^i_{01}$.

$$U^m(0,0) < U^m(1,0) < U^m(1,-) < U^m(1,1) < U^m(0,1) \tag{11.13}$$
$$U^f(0,0) < U^f(0,1) < U^f(-,1) < U^f(1,0) < U^f(1,1)$$

with $U^m(1,-)$ and $U^f(-,1)$ being the individual utility levels in the case of conflict,

then allocation (0,1) is not an equilibrium point, because individual f could improve her situation by leaving the family. In this case, dissolution is a credible threat and prevents the allocation (0,1). The Pareto-efficient solution is now allocation (1,1), which can only be reached by cooperation. But then, in order to realize allocation (0,1) individual m can offer an intrafamily compensation which will change the preference order of individual f.

This leads to the second conceptual problem. Kooreman does not discuss the variables, that determine the individual utility function (11.9). Assuming that the time allocation itself is not utility bearing, but rather the commodities which are produced with that allocation, then the individual preference order reflects the valuation of the individual payoffs linked with each allocation. In turn, these individual payoffs depend on the intrafamily distribution of the total production.

This can be interpreted as a two step bargaining process. First, the spouses will bargain about the time allocation. Then given any allocation, they will bargain about the distribution of the total output which can be produced with this allocation. Thus, each of the possible combinations of employment behavior is linked with a unique outcome which results from that particular distribution game. This final outcome will be taken into consideration by the spouses when deciding upon time allocation. The conflict payoffs play a role only in the distribution game, whereas in the allocation game only final outcomes are considered, which will exceed the conflict payoffs for both spouses.

With this interpretation, the game modelled by Kooreman represents the allocation game given the final outcome which is linked with each allocation. The distribution game is not considered, but its solution is represented by equation (11.9). Therefore, the results cannot be interpreted without hesitation in the sense of a dynamic bargaining model, because they might also be explained by other models of intrafamily distribution. Nevertheless, they are consistent with the dynamic bargaining approach and do not contradict this model.

Beyond that, Kooreman's results indicate that family labor supply should be analyzed on the basis of a model with individual utility functions. His approach appears as a fruitful way to estimate family labor supply as a bargaining game for discrete choices.

11.3 The distribution of welfare in the household: measuring the bargaining power

A model for measuring the welfare distribution within the household has been developed by Antonides and Hagenaars (1990). Starting with individual utility functions, specified in a rather general form, they derive different estimation models corresponding to different theoretic approaches, which can be compared directly.

The basic general individual utility function is modelled as a Cobb-Douglas function which depends on household public goods, the individual's own consumption and the consumption of the spouse:

$$U^i = [(1 - \Phi)\pi y]^{\beta_1^i} [(1 - \Phi)(1 - \pi)y]^{\beta_2^i} (\Phi y)^{\beta_3^i} \qquad (11.14)$$

where Φ is the proportion of total income spent on public goods
 π is the proportion of the expenditures for privat consumption, spent on husband's goods

From this basic utility function different models are derived with additional restrictions:

- a household utility function which depends on the distribution of income between household public goods and other expenditures:

$$U = \delta_0 [(1 - \Phi)y]^{\delta_1} (\Phi y)^{\delta_3} \qquad (11.15)$$

- a household utility function which depends on the distribution of income between public goods and the private consumption of husband and wife

$$U = [(1 - \Phi)\pi y]^{\beta_1} [(1 - \Phi)(1 - \pi)y]^{\beta_2} (\Phi y)^{\beta_3} \qquad (11.16)$$

- individual utility functions which depend on the distribution of income between public goods and other expenditures:

$$U^i = \delta_0[(1-\Phi)\pi y]^{\delta_1^i} (\Phi y)^{\delta_3^i} \tag{11.17}$$

Based on the 'Income Evaluation Question', a question for the subjective satisfaction with income, a welfare function of income is derived which is used as a measure of utility (U^i)[109]. The husband's share on private goods is modelled as a function of the spouse's characteristics which determine the intrafamily bargaining power ($\pi = f(\gamma'X)$). The proportion of income spent for public goods was estimated separately from budget data as a function of various household characteristics ($\Phi = g(\delta'Z)$), and was imputed into the data used for the regressions of the models (11.14) to (11.17).

The results of Antonides and Hagenaars are presented in table 11.3. Regarding the distribution between public and private goods there is no significant difference between the spouses. Nearly the same estimated parameters result from a model with household utility function (11.15) as from the model with individual utilities (11.17). But, with respect to the division of private goods (model (11.14) and (11.16)) significant differences are seen between the weights for the own and the spouse's consumption. The individual's own share of income has a positive effect on the utility level, while the other's share is not significant. This implies that "the households should be considered as individualistic" (ibid., p. 25).

From the viewpoint of the bargaining model the independent variables show the expected effects on the distribution of income. The husband's share decreases with higher education, more working hours and higher personal income of the wife. Thus, the results of Antonides and Hagenaars show the dependence of the intrafamily distribution on the individual resources.

---

[109] Assuming that the subjective evaluations u^i are lognormally distributed over the stated income level ($\ln(y^i) = \mu + \sigma N^{-1}(u^i) + \varepsilon$) the dependent variable $\ln(y^i) - \mu$ is derived.

Table 11.3 Estimation results of Antonides und Hagenaars

model *(std.error)*	(11.15)	(11.17) male female	(11.16)	(11.14) male female
constant	-3.4723 *(.2164)*	-3.4783 *(.2174)*	-4.0222 *(.3390)*	-4.0131 *(.3055)*
private consumption (δ_1, δ_1^i)	.2574 *(.0195)*	.2632 .2518 *(.0239) (.0252)*		
own share of income (β_1, β_1^i)			.2771 *(.0264)*	.2766 .2769 *(.0353) (.0315)*
other's share of income (β_2, β_2^i)			-.0024 *(.0086)*	.0000 .0213 *(.0478) (.0364)*
public goods $(\delta_1, \delta_1^i, \beta_3, \beta_3^i)$	.1296 *(.0183)*	.1232 .1374 *(.0242) (.0233)*	.1876 *(.0249)*	.1877 .1873 *(.0447) (.0408)*
effects on the husband's share π				
constant (γ_0)			.0733 *(.9499)*	.0755 *(.8846)*
male's age (γ_1)			.0017 *(.1863)*	.0000 *(.1899)*
male's personal income (γ_2)			.0058 *(.0551)*	.0058 *(.0556)*
female's personal income (γ_3)			-.0631 *(.0205)*	-.0674 *(.0247)*
male's working hours (γ_4)			-.0070 *(.0392)*	-.0115 *(.0406)*
female's working hours (γ_5)			-.2875 *(.0751)*	-.2935 *(.1027)*
male's education (γ_6)			-.1620 *(.1160)*	-.1825 *(.1226)*
female's education (γ_7)			-.2897 *(.1201)*	-.3349 *(.1409)*
Number of observations R^2	440 .3958	440 .3952	440 .4108	440 .4052

Source: Antonides/Hagenaars (1990)

11.4 Marriage and divorce: estimates with explicit threat point

The impact of divorce laws on marriage and divorce bahavior is analyzed in the work of Peters (1986). She assumes a bargaining process within the family, from which she derives the conditions for a divorce. Like in the model with uncertainty in chapter 8, Peters supposes a divorce if no marriage gain results in comparison to separated households. Otherwise, the marriage will be continued because a cooperative solution can be reached through redistribution[110].

Above all, Peters analyzes the impact of two different types of divorce laws which exist in several states of the USA. One law allows unilateral divorce, i.e. one spouse can leave the marriage. Therefore, to continue marriage a mutual consent of the spouses is required[111]. Under the other law both spouses have to agree to the divorce.

Even though no sharing rule is defined, Peters concludes from her theoretical model that under the unilateral divorce law the intrafamily distribution depends on the conflict payoffs, whereas it is determined by other factors if mutual agreement on divorce is required. In the latter case the distribution of income in a divorce will be a bargaining result, because the spouse desiring the divorce has to pay a compensation to obtain the other spouse's agreement (ibid., p. 439ff.).

This result is also plausible from the point of view of a cooperative bargaining game. In the case of unilateral divorce law, the utility of the external alternatives results only from the individual's own characteristics independent from the actual bargaining[112]. Therefore, the conflict payoff can always be realized by each of the partners and may be used as a threat in the actual bargaining on intrafamily distribution. This corresponds to the situation as it was assumed in the theoretical model derived in chapter 4 to

---

[110] This will not be true in the case of asymmetrical information which is also analyzed by Peters. But, because she could not find empirical evidence for this case, it will not be described.

[111] This was the assumption for the theoretical models derived in the chapters 4 to 8.

[112] Nevertheless, the conflict payoff is not only determined by exogenous factors, but also by previous bargained decisions.

6. But, if both spouses have to agree to a divorce, the divorce cannot be a credible threat because it cannot be enforced by one partner. Therefore, intrafamily distribution will be determined by other factors. In the case that both spouses can gain from a divorce, this internal distribution will be the threat point of the divorce game from which the conflict payoffs result.

In her empirical analysis based on the data from the 1979 *Current Population Survey* Peters investigates the impact of the divorce law on divorce settlements, probabilities for divorce and remarriage, number of children and labor force participation of women. Because in 1979 about half of the U.S. states have a unilateral divorce law, whereas the others require mutual consent for divorce, there is a sufficient variance of this explanatory variable in the data base. This seems to be a good indicator in modelling the conflict point in a bargaining game. However, this cannot be done with data from many other countries, because there is mostly a uniform divorce law.

The intrafamily distribution is not observed in the data. Therefore, the influence of the conflict point on the internal solution cannot be investigated directly. However, the hypotheses about the division of family resources at divorce are supported by the empirical results. The divorce settlement payments for women are higher if a mutual consent is required for divorce than in the case of a unilateral divorce law. This is also true for child alimony (ibid., p. 449). The same result is also obtained by other studies based on longitudinal data from states in which the divorce law was changed (see Seal 1983 or Dixao/Weitzman 1980). This supports the assumption that in the case of a mutual divorce law the alimony payments result from a bargaining process. But, if negotiations obviously take place under one divorce law, then there is no reason why they should not occur in the other case as well.

This hypothesis is further supported by the estimation results regarding the probability of divorce. Let us assume that in an existing family no bargaining takes place. In this case, the divorce would be more profitable for one of the spouses as compared with the marriage payoff, because no compensation would be offered for persuading the partner to remain married. Then, under a unilateral divorce law, a higher probability for divorce would be expected, because this spouse is more likely to dissolve the marriage. On the other

Table 11.4 Estimation results of Peters

	Divorce Settlement Recieved (t-stat.)	Probability of Divorce (χ^2-stat.)	Labor Force Participation	Number of Children less than 6 (t-stat.)
Intercept	-1423.22 (4.26)	-2.81 (4.91)	71.98 (426.38)	1.91 (25.73)
Unilateral divorce law	-185.65 (2.19)	0.01 (0.00)	2.22 (6.34)	-0.02 (1.23)
Age	22.20 (5.77)	-0.26 (405.05)	-1.92 (2119.43)	-0.04 (22.81)
White	247.72 (1.75)	-0.3 (0.37)	-12.52 (71.21)	-0.11 (3.64)
Urban area	97.86 (1.15)	0.56 (2.87)	-0.1 (.14)	-0.03 (1.98)
Education	59.47 (3.43)	-0.19 (8.95)	3.46 (452.74)	-0.01 (3.23)
Children less than 18	23.16 (0.27)	-1.55 (21.33)	-	-
Children less than 6	-	-	-30.84 (752.80)	-
Children 6-18	-	-	-8.80 (99.30)	-
Children < 18 squared	-1.80 (0.08)	0.07 (0.56)	1.42 (54.94)	-
South	-	1.81 (12.47)	-0.08 (0.00)	-0.02 (0.80)
West	-	3.12 (30.21)	-0.71 (0.28)	0.06 (2.19)
North Central	-	1.91 (13.86)	2.54 (4.98)	0.04 (1.74)
In Labor force 1978	-205.81 (1.86)	-	-	-
Time since Divorce	-65.19 (1.41)	-	-	-
Proportion of time in 1978 eligible to receive payments	321.45 (1.71)	-	-	-
Sample:	divorced women	ever married women	ever married women	women younger 40
Sample Size	1,221	21,214	19,501	8,413

Source: Peters (1986)

hand, if redistribution takes place within the marriage, there should be no difference between the two different divorce law settings. Then, in both cases the conflict will occur, if no gains from marriage result. As we can see in table 11.4, Peters does not find any influence of the divorce law on the probability of divorce, which is consistent with the theoretical results of the bargaining approach.

Regarding employment and fertility behavior of married women, the theoretical bargaining model predicts a high labor force participation and a small number of children for the case of a unilateral divorce law, because then the conflict payoffs are determined, above all, from the individual's own earning capacity. At least with respect to labor supply this hypothesis is supported by Peter's empirical results. The estimated parameter in the equation for the number of children has also the expected negative sign, but it is not statistically significant. But, this may result from an inappropriate fertility indicator, as Peters herself states (ibid., p. 452)[113]. Nevertheless, Peter's empirical results altogether are consistent with the bargaining approach, and cannot easily be explained with traditional models.

---

[113] The divorce law was changed in many states only few years before the data were collected. Therefore, the number of children younger than 6 years may not reflect the optimal decision under the actual law, because the decisions were made before the law was changed.

12 Empirical evidence of the bargaining approach - first findings with German data

Up to now, empirical research based on bargaining models was scarce. Nevertheless, the results given in the few empirical papers presented in the previous chapters indicate the empirical relevance of the bargaining model. These results are consistent with the bargaining model whereas they can hardly be explained with competing approaches. In spite of this, at present, it cannot be decided whether and for which questions a model of the traditional type suffices as a basis for empirical analyses. A strong empirical test of the bargaining approach against traditional models cannot be developed easily, this is due especially to the problems in modelling the conflict payoffs. However, we can state that the advantage of the bargaining approach consists in providing a comprhensive framework for explaining of different family decisions, from which new, supplementary perspectives on many problems result. In this chapter some first estimates based on German data will be presented. Of course, they cannot be seen as a strong test of the bargaining model against the traditional approach. Nevertheless, they confirm the empirical evidence of the bargaining approach, and they demonstrate different types of analysis that are possible with bargaining models.

12.1 Balance of power within marriages

Difficulties in the estimation of bargaining models arise above all from the fact that neither the conflict point nor the intrafamily distribution of welfare is observed. Therefore, corresponding indicator variables such as the earning capacity have to be used as an essential determinant of the conflict payoff or the intrafamily division of consumption or leisure as a measure of the intrafamily welfare distribution. But, often these variables are not observed, either. In most data bases no information about individual consumption of several household members is available. Additionally, information about time allocation is incomplete in many cases, with the exception of time budget studies. But, these surveys do not contain the other interesting variables. Therefore, another way to find empirical evidence on the bargaining approach may be to use indicator variables which can measure the bargaining power directly.

Such an indicator for intrafamily bargaining power is in the data from the housewives' survey of the 'Institut für Wirtschafts- und Sozialforschung' (see Pross 1975)[114]. Among other things, the women in the sample were asked to give their subjective estimates of the balance of power within their marriages. The question runs as follows[115]:

> "Who is in fact the more powerful in your marriage: your husband, yourself, or do you think, you are about equal?"
>
> (1) my husband
> (2) both about equal
> (3) myself
> (4) variably, it is the matter
> (5) I don't know

The answers to this question are used in a simple model for analyzing intrafamily balance of power. This should give some insights on the question whether family decisions depend on individual characteristics, or whether they are made with an a-priori consensus which could be interpreted as a stable household utility function. In principle, such an analysis requires longitudinal data in order to investigate whether changes in individual characteristics result in a changed position within the family or not. Nevertheless, assuming identical utility functions except for the controlled characteristics and a random influence[116], systematic differences between the individuals can also be interpreted in that sense.

---

[114] In this study a sample of 1219 non-working married women between 18 and 54 years old were interviewed. The survey was carried out in 1973, and is therefore not up to date, but no comparable indicator could be found in newer studies.

[115] The original text of the question in German is: "Wer ist eigentlich in Ihrer Ehe der stärkere Teil: Ihr Mann, Sie selber, oder meinen Sie, Sie wären etwa gleich stark?" Items for answer: "(1) mein Mann, (2) beide etwa gleich stark, (3) ich selbst, (4) unterschiedlich, kommt darauf an, (5) weiß nicht".

[116] This assumption is usually in microeconometric estimates based on utility models.

For the empirical analysis an ordered probit model[117] with three outcomes was chosen. Then, the probability for the first value is $prob\{y=1\} = F(c_1 - x'\beta)$, where x is the vector of the independent variables and F the distribution function of the standardized normal distribution (see figure 12.1). The probability for the second value is $prob\{y=2\} = F(c_2 - x'\beta) - F(c_1 - x'\beta)$, and for the third value $prob\{y=3\} = 1 - F(c_2 - x'\beta)$.

Figure 12.1

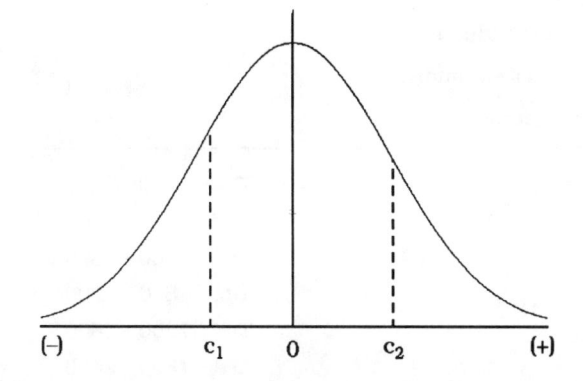

(−) c_1 0 c_2 (+)

The subjective estimation of the wife about who the more powerful spouse is, is used as the dependent variable. In order to reach a well-defined rank of the items, which is necessary for an ordered probit model, the items (2) and (4) were summarized to category (2) "about equal". With this rank, a positive coefficient of an independent variable shows a more powerful position of the wife.

As explanatory variables those individual characteristics of the spouses which can be interpreted as economic resources are used. Furthermore, characteristics of the household were included which can be viewed as indicators for the possibilities of the wife to improve her bargaining position by entering the labor force. In table 12.1 the frequencies of the variables are presented.

---

[117] See for the estimation method e.g. Maddala (1983), p. 46ff. or Amemiya (1985), p. 292ff.

Table 12.1: Frequencies of the variables

more powerful spouse	(1) husband	35.8%
	(2) about equal	54.5%
	(3) wife	9.7%
own house (dummy)		38.5%
children have left home (dummy)		4.6%
higher education of wife (dummy)		4.4%
own income of wife (dummy)		21.5%
husband's income	DM 0 - 400	0.1%
	DM 400 - 600	0.7%
	DM 600 - 800	0.7%
	DM 800 - 1200	26.1%
	DM 1200 - 1800	39.6%
	DM 1800 - 2400	15.6%
	DM 2400 - 3000	10.8%
	DM 3000 +	6.3%
number of cases: 1101		

The estimation results are presented in table 12.2. The parameter estimates for the indicator variables for individual economic resources confirm the expected dependencies. Women with a higher education (college/university) have a more powerful position in marriage than other women. The same is true if the woman has her own income. This is non-wage income or income from temporary employment because only housewives had been sampled. Also, the size of the income is unknown. However, the mere existence of an own income leads to a more powerful position for the wife. On the other hand, the husband is more powerful the higher his income is.

Table 12.2: Balance of power within marriages

ordered probit model for housewives

dependent variable: more powerful part in marriage	(1) husband (2) both about equal (3) wife		
		b	t-value
constant 1		-0.585	-5.861
constant 2		1.101	10.680
own house		-0.169	-2.294
children have left home		0.280	1.646
higher education of wife		0.419	1.956
own income of wife		0.162	1.975
husband's income[*]		-0.127	-2.464
-2* log-lik= 2011.6107			cases: 1101

[*] based on the middle of income brackets

If the couple owns a house, the husband is on the average the more powerful part. On the other hand, if children have already left the parents' home, the position of the wife will be improved. However, this effect is significant only on the 10% level. From the viewpoint of the bargaining model these two variables can be interpreted as indicators for the wife's possibilities to increase her bargaining power. Managing the household in one's own house often requires more time than managing an appartment because mostly there are more rooms and a garden. This reduces the possibilities for housewives to increase their bargaining power through other activitis. On the other hand, as the children grow up and leave the parental household, the necessity of someone staying at home no longer exists, which increases that person's scope for other activities.

These empirical findings show that individual resources are relevant for intrafamily decision making. This implies that at least in some families no contracts concerning intrafamily distributions exist. In this case a disruption of the working life and the specialization on household work implies a significant risk for individual well-being. Therefore, family formation and especially fertility should depend on the distribution of individual resources in the family.

12.2 Fertility decision

Some insights into this relationship can be obtained from a fertility model. In traditional economic fertility models attention is paid, above all, to the opportunity costs of child rearing. The disruption of the working life of one spouse, which is often linked with the decision for a child, results in loss of income, and therefore affects the welfare production of the household. In addition to this effect on the household level, the decision on fertility as was shown in chapter 7 may be like a prisoner's dilemma due to the asymmetrical detorioration of one spouse's bargaining power. Therefore, these two factors - the opportunity costs and the possible prisoner's dilemma situation - should have an essential influence on fertility. We should expect, that the probability for deciding against a child will be higher, the larger the opportunity costs and the higher the probability for a constellation like a prisoner's dilemma is.

Based on the dynamic bargaining approach the couple's fertility decision is modelled as a discrete choice problem. Introducing an additional argument for children in the utility functions and not modelling household production explicitly the following system results:

$$\max_{C^{i1}, K} \quad N = (U^{m1} + U^{m2} - D^m) * (U^{f1} + U^{f2} - D^f) \qquad (12.1)$$

$$\max_{C^{i2}, K} \quad N_2 = (U^{m2} - D^{m2}) * (U^{f1} - D^{f2}) \qquad (12.2)$$

subject to

$$C^{mt} + C^{ft} = Y_t \qquad t = 1,2 \qquad (12.3)$$

where $\quad U^{it} = U^i(C^{it}, K) \qquad i = m, f$
$\quad\quad\quad$ K: number of children.

The couple's optimal choice betweeen the two alternatives 'decision for an (additional) child' and 'decision against a child' is the alternative which maximizes the Nash product.

The total differential of the Nash function is used as an approximation for the difference of both alternative Nash values. It can be written as a function of changes in income, the marginal utilities of a child and the bargaining weights in both periods (see appendix 10):

$$dN = \lambda_1 dY_1 + \lambda_2 dY_2 \qquad (12.4)$$
$$+ s_1^m(U_K^{f1} + g_1 U_K^{m1})dK + s_2^m(U_K^{f2} + g_1 U_K^{m2})dK$$
$$+ (s_1^m - s_2^m)(dU^{f2} + g_1 dU^{m2}) + s_1^m(dU^{m2} - U_K^{m2}dK)(g_2 - g_1)$$

$$= \lambda_1 dY_1 + \lambda_2 dY_2 \qquad (12.5)$$
$$+ h(K)dK$$
$$+ f(g_1, g_2, dK)$$

In the traditional model

$$\max_{C^1, C^2, K} U(C, K) = U^1 + U^2 \qquad (12.6)$$

s. t. $\quad C^t = Y_t \qquad (12.7)$

the total differential results as follows:

$$dU = dU^1 + dU^2 \qquad (12.8)$$
$$= \frac{\partial U^1}{\partial C^1} dC^1 + \frac{\partial U^1}{\partial K} dK + \frac{\partial U^2}{\partial C^2} dC^2 + \frac{\partial U^2}{\partial K} dK$$
$$= \lambda_1 dY_1 + \lambda_2 dY_2 + \frac{\partial U^1}{\partial K} dK + \frac{\partial U^2}{\partial K} dK.$$

Comparing this equation with the total differential of the bargaining model, the terms in the first and the second line in (12.5) can be interpreted as the effect on the household level which can also be described by the household utility function U. Then from (12.5) and (12.8) the following results

$$dN \approx dU + f(g_1, g_2, dK) \tag{12.9}$$

which decomposes the Nash differential into one part resulting from a traditional approach and one resulting from the bargaining effect. The last term is determined by the bargaining weights of the two periods, and it decribes the bargaining effect, i.e. a change in the bargaining power due to the decision for a child. If the weights in both periods are equal, i.e. if the bargaining positions of the spouses do not change, this term disappears and the model collapses into the traditional counterpart[118].

Based on this property a nested model can be derived for the econometric analysis. This can be used to test the bargaining model against the traditional approach. Using a specific household utility function

$$U = \alpha \ln\left(\frac{Y}{n^\theta}\right) + h(K) \tag{12.10}$$

where $Y = Y^i + Y^j$ income of the household
$Y^i = w^i m^i$ income of person i
n number of persons in the household
h(K) utility from the children
K number of children,

the the total differential results:

$$dU = \frac{\alpha}{Y} dY - \frac{\alpha\theta}{n} dn + \frac{\partial h}{\partial K} dK \tag{12.11}$$

The decision for a child implies

$$\Delta n = \Delta K = 1 \tag{12.12}$$

$$\Delta Y = \Delta Y^i = \gamma Y \tag{12.13}$$

where i: index of the spouse with lower income
γ: share of person i's income which is lost by reducing market work.

---

[118] If the bargaining positions do not change, then and $g_1 = g_2 = -\frac{dU^{f2}}{dU^{m2}}$ holds. Then the third line in (12.5) dissapears.

Corresponding to the theoretical results (see chapter 5) it is assumed, that the spouse with the lower income will undertake the additional housework and will reduce or interrupt his or her employment. Then, using equation (12.9) the difference between the Nash gains of the two alternatives is approximately

$$dN = \alpha\gamma\frac{Y^i}{Y} - \frac{\alpha\Theta}{n} + \frac{\partial h}{\partial K} + f(g_1, g_2, dK) \qquad (12.14)$$

Introducing an error term ε, the following specification is obtained:

$$N(K+1) - N(K) = \alpha\gamma\frac{Y^i}{Y} - \frac{\alpha\Theta}{n} + \frac{\partial h}{\partial K} + f(g_1, g_2, dK) + \varepsilon \qquad (12.15)$$

$$= x'\beta + \varepsilon$$

Since the couple will decide on a child if the condition $N(K+1) > N(K)$ is satisfied, the probability for this results as

$$\text{prob}\{K+1\} = \text{prob}\{\,N(K+1) > N(K)\,\} \qquad (12.16)$$

$$= \text{prob}\{\,\varepsilon > x'\beta\,\}$$

which can be estimated by a probit model, if a normal distributed error ε is assumed.

The data used are the first wave (1984) of the panel study 'Generatives Verhalten in Nordrhein-Westfalen' of the 'Institut für Bevölkerungsforschung und Sozialpolitik, Bielefeld' (see Kaufmann and Strohmeier 1987). This survey contains the data of women, 18 to 33 years old, and their partners. The question whether the couple practices birth control or not is used as the dependent variable. This variable has been chosen instead of observed fertility since birth control requires a conscious decision whereas observed fertility also depends on other factors. Events, which do not result from a conscious decision, cannot be explained with an economic model based on rational behavior. Regarding fertility the assumption of a conscious decision is surely fulfilled by practicing birth control, but not for the birth as such. This can be seen also in the data base, where many couples voice the wish for a child in two successive waves, but no birth is observed in the corresponding time interval of two years.

Independent variables of the model are the duration of marriage, a dummy variable for urban regions, the number of children and indicator variables for the opportunity costs of child caring. The dummy variables for the number of children control the size of the household on one hand and measure the marginal utility of an additional child on the other hand. This corresponds to the term $(\frac{\partial h}{\partial K} - \frac{\alpha \Theta}{n})$ in equation (12.15). The relative loss in household income if the spouse with the lower income would leave employment is chosen as an indicator for the opportunity costs of child caring (term $\frac{y^i}{Y}$). This variable has the value zero if one spouse is not employed, and it is included separately for couples with and couples without children younger than 3 years. The opportunity costs should be lower for couples with children in which both spouses work, because these couples have already found an arrangement for child caring that usually can be extended to an additional child.

A second model version contains additional variables representing the bargaining power of the spouses (term $f(g_1, g_2, dK)$). From a theoretical point of view an operationalization of the change in the bargaining positions would be required (see equation (12.4)), but appropriate indicator variables cannot be found easily. However, in discrete choices like the fertility decision, a change in bargaining positions will be relevant only in prisoner's dilemma situations (see chapter 7). Such a prisoner's dilemma will arise mainly in situations with a symmetrical status quo position and a relatively large expected decrease in bargaining power.

For working women an indicator for symmetry in bargaining positions is formed by a function of the spouses' wage ratio

$$\left[\frac{w^i}{w^j} - 1 \right]^2 \qquad \text{with i = index of the spouse with the lower wage rate.}$$

This indicator is zero for couples with equal wages, and its value increases with growing asymmetry. The quadratic approach is motivated by the hypothesis, that the probability for a prisoner's dilemma is high in a symmetrical situation but decreases quickly with increasing asymmetry[119].

---

[119] Given a convex payoff space a change of the conflict payoff has a bigger effect on the individual's cooperative payoff if the starting conflict point is symmetrical than if is asymmetrical. The strength of this decrease depends on the curvature of the Pareto frontier.

Table 12.3 Wage regression

dependent variable: ln(wage)	coeff.	t-value
constant	1.698	45.662
years of schooling - 7	0.099	7.155
(years of schooling - 7)^2	-0.004	-3.052
experience before actual working spell		
years of working fulltime	0.019	4.696
years of working parttime	0.021	2.201
interruption of working life (dummy)	-0.018	-0.700
duration of actual spell	0.046	5.792
(duration of actual spell)^2	-0.002	-3.321
actual part-time working	0.108	4.284
number of cases: 1000		$R^2 = 0.245$

Occupational opportunities for advancement of the wife are chosen as indicator for potential losses in bargaining power.

For a non-working woman a prisoner's dilemma does not arise by interrupting her working life, because losses in earning capacity are already realized. Nevertheless, a situation comparable to that for working women arises, because an additional child would reduce the possibilities for future employment. on the other hand, with a return to the labor market she could increase her bargaining power, especially if her human capital stock is high. In this case, she could expect a fast advancement. However, the possibilities of re-entering the labor force depend, above all, on the age of the children in the household. With older children the time till a possible return is short and the possibilities of increasing one's own bargaining power will increase. Therefore, the potential wage for wives with children over 5 years of age is used as an indicator for the potential increase in their bargaining power. Because the potential wage is not observed for non-working women, a hypothetical wage was imputed based on wage regression for working women (see table 12.3).

Table 12.4   Descriptive Statistics of the Variables

	mean	std.dev.	min	max	n
birth control (dummy)	0.75		0.00	1.00	790
city (dummy)	0.38		0.00	1.00	790
duration of marriage	5.51	2.99	0.00	16.00	790
children in household (dummy variables)					
1 child	0.41		0.00	1.00	790
2 children	0.27		0.00	1.00	790
3 or more children	0.05		0.00	1.00	790
opportunity costs					
couples without children < 3	0.24	0.19	0.00	0.50	439
couples with children < 3	0.07	0.14	0.00	0.49	351
employed women					
occupational opportunities	0.32		0.00	1.00	377
(ratio of wages - 1)^2	0.18	0.12	0.00	0.77	377
non-employed women, youngest child > 5					
hypothetical wage	6.89	0.61	5.8	8.9	36

The descriptive statistics of the variables used is given in table 12.4. Three quarters of the sample practice birth control. Nevertheless, most of the couples have children already. The average opportunity costs, as defined above, are not large for couples with small children (younger than 3 years), because most of the mothers do not work. But, even if the wife is employed, we observe a large range of wage differences between the spouses, as the symmetry indicator shows.

Table 12.5 contains the estimation results of a probit model[120], which show the influences of different characteristics on the probability of practicing birth control.

The probability for practicing birth control is larger for couples living in urban areas and decreases with the duration of the marriage. Both variables could be interpreted from the view point of the bargaining model as

---

[120] See e.g. Maddala (1983), p. 22f. or Amemiya (1983), p.268ff.

opportunity costs respectively trust in long-term contracts[121]. In urban areas living space is not childfriendly and childcaring may be more problematical because often no relatives (e.g. the grandmother) live nearby. Thus, the monetary and immaterial costs of children may be higher and therefore the propensity for a child may be reduced. On the other hand, among the couples with long duration of marriage the share of those with never broken contracts should be high which may increase the trust in making further long-term contracts.

If the couple already has children, the probability for birth control increases and reaches a maximum for two children. This can be interpreted as a decreasing marginal utility from an additional child. That the probability

Table 12.5   Birth control

probit model for couples

	coeff.	t-value	coeff.	t-value
constant	-0.070	-0.338	-0.021	-0.102
urban aerea	0.208	2.006	0.180	1.728
duration of marriage	-0.036	-1.870	-0.046	-2.343
children in household				
1 child	0.781	3.941	0.769	3.856
2 children	1.351	5.611	1.361	5.566
3 or more children	0.985	3.071	1.011	3.101
opportunity costs				
couples without children < 3	1.245	2.590	1.219	2.416
couples with children < 3	-0.194	-0.391	-0.239	-0.443
employed women				
occupational opportunities			0.290	1.876
(ratio of wages - 1)^2			-0.703	-1.393
non-employed women				
hypothetical wage, if youngest child > 5			0.108	2.328
number of cases: 790	log-lik = -424.84		log-lik = -418.71	

---

[121] Nevertheless, other interpretations may also be plausible for the effect of these variables.

decreases if the couple has three or more children may eventually be explained by a faster decrease in marginal costs as compared to the decreasing marginal utility.

The indicators for the opportunity costs show the expected effects. Couples with no children under 3 years of age are more likely to practice birth control if the potential loss in household income becomes larger. For couples with small children no such effect is observed. Because they already have child care arrangements, it is probable that having an additional child will not require a disruption of working and consequently the opportunity costs are lower.

The variables measuring the bargaining power also have the expected effect. The probability for practicing birth control is larger for working women with occupational opportunities and with a symmetrical status quo situation. For non-working women the probability increases with high potential wage rates. The likelihood-ratio test for the two models indicates a significant (on the 10% level) effect of the additional variables. Therefore, the traditional model, at least in the used specification, must be rejected.

Nevertheless, the influence of the used indicator variables cannot be interpreted unambiguously as a bargaining effect. Both, the opportunity costs and the probability for a prisoner's dilemma depend on the same causal factors, the income or the income capacity of the spouses. Moreover, all indicator variables work in the same direction. The higher the wage rate of the spouse who would leave employment, the higher are the opportunity costs and the more symmetrical are the bargaining positions in general. Both will increase the probability against a child. Women with occupational opportunities for advancement would worsen their bargaining position by disrupting their employment, and simultaneously a larger loss in household income would result in the long run. A similar case holds for non-working women. A quick return on the labor market would improve their bargaining position, but also the household income. In spite of using different functional forms, the opportunity costs effect and the bargaining effect of these variables cannot be exactly separated because of problems of multicollinearity.

This is a principle problem of empirical tests of the bargaining approach, as was already discussed in chapter 10. The majority of the explanatory variables affect both the welfare production of the household as well as the conflict point. Thus, for a stronger test, additional variables are required which have an influence on family decision only through the conflict point. But, in spite of these problems in identifying the bargaining effect in empirical analysis, using a bargaining approach in empirical research results in some new insights and gives rise - like in the next example - to some new questions.

12.3 Divorce behavior

As already discussed in chapter 2 models regarding divorce behavior differ from other economic models of family decisions, because approaches with a joint household utility function are not suitable for this question. Therefore, in traditional family economics arguments are also used that focus on the individual interests and assume in principle a bargaining process within the family.

Based on the results of the dynamic bargaining model, the question arises as to how decisions concerning long-term contracts affect the stability of the family. Considering the limited enforcement of such contracts and the high incentives for a later breach, different effects were to be expected over the course of the marriage. Because the probability for a divorce is high for low gains from cooperation (see chapter 9) the development of these marriage gains in the course of the marriage should be modelled in empirical research.

For empirical research on such questions which imply a time dependent perspective the methods of event-history analysis[122] offer appropriate instruments. An exponential hazard model has been used to estimate the risk of divorce. There, a time independent hazard rate is assumed with proportional effects of the covariables:

$$r(t) = r_0 * \exp(b_1 x_1 + ... + b_n x_n).$$

---

[122] Compare e.g. Kalbfleisch/Prentice (1980) or Cox/Oakes (1984).

For dummy variables x_i the antilogs of the estimated parameters, $\exp(b_i)$, can be interpreted as multipliers on the baseline hazard.

For the estimation retrospective data on family and employment biographies questioned in the first wave of the German Socio Economic Panel (see Hanefeld 1984 and Wagner 1991) have been used. To analyze the effect of long-term contracts which are usually made in connection with the decision for a child, the duration of marriages with children was considered from the date of the first birth. In order to eliminate influences from the second world war, only data on women who were first married in 1950 or later have been used. In addition, only first marriages were considered because later marriages may take a different course due to the previous experience. Because divorce behavior is analyzed, only the end of a marriage through a divorce is treated as an event, all other cases are marked as censored either at the date of one spouse's death or at the time of the interview.

Independent variables of the model are different indicators for the welfare gains during the marriage. One of these is the educational level of the woman (coded as a dummy variable for intermediate school and higher), because the gains of specialization turns out to be less with a higher level of education. Appropriately, the level of education of both partners has to be considered. But, because the retrospective data contain only information about the questioned person, the corresponding information for the man is not available if the couple did not live together at the time of interview. Nevertheless, the educational level of the wife might be an appropriate indicator for the welfare gains from specialization, because it is a recent phenomenon that the wife has a higher educational level than the husband in a considerable number of cases. The general reduction of the family welfare gains through recent economic development[123] will be considered through a dummy variable if the wife is born after 1950. Another dummy variable for young married women (younger than 21) could be an indicator for the higher probability of a mismatch of the partners due to less information because of the shorter search period.

---

[123] The reduction of family welfare gains is caused, above all, by better possibilities to substitute household goods by market goods. Another important reason is the loss of insurance function through establishment of insurance markets and social security (see Ott 1989b).

In order to control the development of the welfare gains over time, different time dependent covariables were included[124]. An indicator variable for the degree of specialization and the utilization of production advantages during marriage, is formed by the difference between the duration of the marriage and the duration of the full time employment of the wife (measured in 10 yearly steps). This will be an approriate indicator if the husband is employed throughout the duration of the marriage, a not unrealistic assumption. But, because high welfare gains from specialization will appear especially in times of childcaring, we must expect that these welfare gains change during the course of the marriage. Therefore, the age group of the youngest child and the employment status were controlled for each year. For this, only interruptions of the working life for at least 4 years due to parenthood (child younger than 6) were treated as non-employment. In that case, we should expect considerable losses in the income capacity, which, according to the bargaining model, are only accepted with long-term contracts. Then, an interruption of employment in favor of parenthood can be seen as a part of a long term contract.

Table 12.6 gives the estimation results. As expected, the hazards of divorce are higher for young married women and women born in 1950 or later. The same is true for women with a higher educational level. For these women, the marriage gain is small, because they could also reach a high welfare level outside the family.

The indicator for the degree of specialization and the utilization of productivity advantages also shows the expected effect. The risk of divorce is reduced with longer periods of non-employment in relation to the duration of marriage, because these couples may gain higher profits from specialization. However, it cannot be followed from this, that a traditional intrafamily division of work leads to a reduced risk of divorce in general. Here it is necessary to compare different time intervals in the course of marriage.

The influence of the variables discussed up to now hold for the entire observed duration of the marriage. Because time periods with children younger than 7 years in the household were chosen as reference, further influences

---

[124] Some of them do change every year which leads to a split of episodes into separate yearly spells.

Table 12.6: Divorce behavior of married couples with children, marriage age-groups 1950 and later

Exponential hazard model

	exp(b)	b	b/std(b)
constant	0.004	-5.560	-33.370
born after 1950	1.940	0.663	3.289
young married	1.897	0.640	4.003
higher education	1.536	0.429	2.681
(years of marriage - years of full time work)/10	0.773	-0.258	-2.018
age of the youngest child			
- 6 to 15 years			
- ever working	2.735	1.006	4.959
- non-working	1.244	0.218	0.715
- again working	1.966	0.6760	2.017
-15 years and older			
- ever working	0.593	-0.523	-0.874
- non-working	1.160	0.148	0.234
- again working	2.708	0.996	2.485
Reform of marriage laws 1976/78	0.835	-0.178	-0.801

Log-Lik = -1088.869   Global χ^2 = 70.058
Null-Log-Lik = -1123.898   Prob(χ^2) = 0.000
Cases: 1895   Events: 183

Data base: First wave of the German Socio-economic Panel

must be added to these effects, if the children are older than 6. In part, these additional effects move in opposite directions.

The risk of divorce increases with the increasing age of the children. This can be explained by the fact that the additional welfare gains from children arise, above all, at the very beginning, and after a few years they decrease. During the time in which the youngest child is between 6 and 15 years old, the risk of divorce is 2.7 times higher than in the previous time period. Women who have re-entered the labor force after an interruption also have an increased risk for divorce. Only for wifes still staying at home due to parenthood no significant difference in comparison to the time before are observed. If the children are over 15 years old or have already left the home, a further increase in the risk of divorce is observed for women who are employed again after an interruption. However, in the case of long-term housewives, the risk is again reduced.

Behind these results one may suppose selection effects of such a nature that women with a higher risk of divorce would rather re-enter the labor force in order to better their external alternatives. From the perspective of the bargaining model, an interruption of employment implies a (mostly implicit) contract dealing with internal distribution. If the contracts are fulfilled within the family, Pareto-efficient solutions are possible, and a higher welfare profit results in the family, which leads to a lower risk of divorce. However, if these agreements are broken, and the woman perceives an one-sided deterioration of her welfare situation, it seems plausible that she will re-enter the labor force, in order to improve her bargaining position[125]. But then, in the group of long-term housewives the share of marriages in which no breach of the contracts has occured should be large. If, on the other hand, the contract has been broken, we would expect the women to tend to re-enter the labor force. Both, the breach of contract[126] and the reaction of the wife, reduce the welfare gain in the family which in turn leads to an increasing risk of divorce.

---

[125] In the study of Gaugler et al. (1984, p. 62), a considerable portion of women (ca. 30%) mention as motive for re-entering the labor force the wish to become independent from their husbands.

[126] Here, a not necessarily seldom case may occur in which from the husband's point of view the wife commits a breach of contract by re-entering the labor force. If the agreement was only made implicitly and if the subject of the contract has not been specified explicitly, the expectations of the partners may differ regarding the exchange of the mutual promises. From that, possibly both partners may feel deceived, because from a subjective point of view they assume to have fulfilled their part of the agreement. In these cases as well as in real breaches of contract, the welfare gain of the family decreases, which increases the probability of divorce.

13 Concluding remarks

The aim of this study was to develop a model of household decisions which provides a comprehensive framework for analyzing family behavior. The basic assumption was the economic principle of rationality. The model developed describes the allocation of scarce resources based on the principle of utility maximization. Certainly, there are factors in the family - in particular of an affective nature - which can hardly be explained by rationality, or only in a less fruitful, tautological manner. However, this should not lead us to deny rational behavior in the family as such. If affections do not crowd out all rational behavior, we should observe some systematical reactions which can be described by an economic model.

With this intention in mind, an attempt has been made to develop a model which is appropriate to describe family behavior as systematical reactions to changes in the environment, and which can be applied in empirical research. The empirical results appear auspicious - some findings cannot be explained by other models. However, a strong test of the bargaining approach against the traditional one is still outstanding. Problems arise above all by the fact that the variables used influence the joint production as well as the conflict payoff. Therefore, due to multicollinearity, the two effects, given the available data, cannot be distinguished empirically. But, variables which solely affect the conflict point are usually not available. Thus, further empirical research in this field requires data which contain more individual information about the household members.

Further work on the theoretical level is also necessary, since assumptions which appear rather restrictive have been made:

- The bargaining process itself is not modelled. The axiomatic solution concept supposes an equilibrium in the family. But, because the real bargaining process requires time, and family members act in the meantime, observed behavior might reflect a short-term disequilibrium situation.

- In the dynamic model, only two periods are considered. Although this approach allows us to analyze the results of strategic behavior, the incentives for breaking intrafamily contracts cannot be described adequately. Feedback effects of endogenous conflict probabilities also cannot be analyzed. For both problems, a model containing more periods is required.

- Time allocation in the family household is the only behavior considered in the study. Here, extensions of the model are possible for analyzing other household decisions, for example consumer or saving behavior.

- The model is limited to a two-person decision problem. This appears adequatly for the decisions analyzed in the study. Nevertheless, for investigating other decisions, like consumer behavior, considering intrafamily coalitions, e.g. between children and one parent, may be important.

These points show the limits of the model, but they also indicate questions for further theoretical research.

In spite of all these limitations, the simple model developed in this study already offers an explanation for some observed phenomena in the past. Economic development has reduced the family gains in an essential way. First, market substitutes have been provided for many traditional household goods. Due to this trend and the increase in female wages, household production has become more and more inefficient and, in turn, gains from intrafamily specialization have decreased. Family gains have been reduced further by external insurance markets and the social security system. Also the gains from the joint use of household public goods have lost in importance due to the increased welfare level.

On the other hand, the losses in relative bargaining power resulting from an interruption of employment have increased. Due to increased income and a large supply of market substitutes for household goods, household production is efficient in the single-person household only to a very restricted extent. Thus, being employed provides a large conflict payoff, while interrupting employment reduces it. This means that intrafamily specialization leads to a great change in the bargaining positions resulting from both, the high bargaining power of the spouse specialized in market work and the large loss in the bargaining power of the other. Therefore, today a traditional intrafamily contract appears to be more asymmetrical than it was in the past.

Both, the reduced marriage gains and the increased asymmetry in the traditional contract of intrafamily specialization may give an explanation for the behavior observed in many countries. As discussed in chapter 9, the risk of divorce rises with diminishing marriage gains and, as has been shown in chapter 7, the incentive for breaking the intrafamily contract grows with increasing asymmetry. Then, from the view point of the bargaining model we should expect also rising female labor force participation. Both has been observed in the past. The empirical findings on female labor force participation and divorce risks on the micro level also support this explanation.

Arguments beyond those given by the traditional approach are also provided for the explanation of the relationship between observed female labor force participation and birth rates. Both, the increased opportunity costs for child rearing due to the reduced efficiency of household production as well as the increased probability of a breach of contract may have induced this development. This line of argument is also supported by the empirical results on fertility behavior. The influence of the bargaining power may then explain the distinctions between countries with different institutional settings, from which a more or less asymmetrical situation for the fertility decision result.

All these arguments are of a preliminary character. But they demonstrate the usefulness of the bargaining approach for explaining family decisions. As compared to traditional microeconomics, it provides a comprehensive theoretical setting from which all observed processes can be explained consistently, and it allows the explicit discussion of the effects of institutional settings as well. Thus, further theoretical and empirical research in this field should provide many more interesting insights.

Appendix

Appendix 1: First-order conditions of the simple Nash-household model

The maximization problem

$$\max N = (U^i - D^i) * (U^j - D^j)$$
$$\text{s.t. } (X^i + X^j)' p = Y$$

yield the Lagrangian

$$\mathcal{L} = (U^i - D^i) * (U^j - D^j) + \lambda \{Y - (X^i + X^j)' p\}$$

from which the first order conditions follow:

$$\frac{\partial \mathcal{L}}{\partial x_k^i} = (U^j - D^j) \frac{\partial U^i}{\partial x_k} - \lambda p_k = (U^j - D^j) U_k^i - \lambda p_k = 0$$

$$\frac{\partial \mathcal{L}}{\partial \lambda} = Y - (X^i + X^j)' p = 0$$

From these the following properties of the solution are derived:

$$\frac{U_k^i}{U_l^i} = \frac{p_k}{p_l} = \frac{U^i - D^i}{U^j - D^j} \tag{A1.1}$$

$$\frac{U_k^i}{U_k^j} = \frac{U^i - D^i}{U^j - D^j} \tag{A1.2}$$

$$\frac{U_k^i}{U_l^j} = \frac{U^i - D^i}{U^j - D^j} \frac{p_k}{p_l} \tag{A1.3}$$

Appendix 2: Derivation of the fundamental matrix equation

From the maximization problem

$$\max N = (U^m(X) - D^m) * (U^f(X) - D^f)$$

s.t. $X^t p = Y$

the first order conditions result:

(1) $\quad U_i^m(U^f - D^f) + U_i^f(U^m - D^m) = \lambda p^i \qquad \forall\, i$

$\qquad$ with $\quad U_i^j = \dfrac{\partial U^j}{\partial x^i}$

(2) $\quad \sum_i x^i p^i = Y$

The derivatives of (1) and (2) with respect to p^i yield the uncompensated price effect:

(1') $\quad (U^m - D^m) \sum_j U_{ij}^f \dfrac{\partial x^j}{\partial p^i} + (U^f - D^f) \sum_j U_{ij}^m \dfrac{\partial x^j}{\partial p^i} +$

$\qquad + U_i^m \sum_j U_j^f \dfrac{\partial x^j}{\partial p^i} + U_i^f \sum_j U_j^m \dfrac{\partial x^j}{\partial p^i} - U_i^m \dfrac{\partial D^f}{\partial p^i} - U_i^f \dfrac{\partial D^f}{\partial p^i} =$

$\qquad = \lambda + \dfrac{\partial \lambda}{\partial p^i} p^i \qquad \forall\, i$

(2') $\quad \sum_j \dfrac{\partial x^j}{\partial p^i} p^j + x^i = \dfrac{\partial Y}{\partial p^i} \qquad \forall\, i$

or in matrix notation:

(1") $\quad J X_p - p \lambda_p = \lambda I + U D_p$

$\qquad$ with $J = \left[U_i^m U_j^f + U_i^f U_j^m + U_{ij}^m (U^f - D^f) + U_{ij}^f (U^m - D^m) \right]_{ij}$

(2") $\quad p' X_p = -X + Y_p$

$\qquad$ with $X_p = \left[\dfrac{\partial x^i}{\partial p^i} \right]_{ij}, \quad Y_p = \left[\dfrac{\partial Y}{\partial p^i} \right]_i$

$$\Rightarrow \begin{bmatrix} J & p \\ p' & 0 \end{bmatrix} \begin{bmatrix} X_p \\ -\lambda_p \end{bmatrix} = \begin{bmatrix} \lambda I + UD_p \\ -X + Y_p \end{bmatrix}$$

The fundamental matrix equation results

(I) $$\begin{bmatrix} X_p \\ -\lambda_p \end{bmatrix} = \begin{bmatrix} B & b \\ b' & c \end{bmatrix} \begin{bmatrix} \lambda I + UD_p \\ -X + Y_p \end{bmatrix} \qquad (A2.1)$$

and holding the nominal income and the conflict point constant

$$\frac{\partial Y}{\partial p^i} = 0 \quad \forall\, i, \qquad \frac{\partial D^j}{\partial p^i} = 0 \quad \forall\, i,j$$

the compensated price effect results:

(II) $$\begin{bmatrix} X_p \\ -\lambda_p \end{bmatrix} = \begin{bmatrix} B & b \\ b' & c \end{bmatrix} \begin{bmatrix} \lambda I \\ -X \end{bmatrix} \qquad (A2.2)$$

Subtracting (II) from (I) yields

$$\begin{bmatrix} X_p - X_p^* \\ 0 \end{bmatrix} = \begin{bmatrix} B & b \\ b' & c \end{bmatrix} \begin{bmatrix} UD_p \\ Y_p \end{bmatrix} \qquad (A2.3)$$

$$\Rightarrow X_p = X_p^* + BUD_p + bY_p \qquad (A2.4)$$

Appendix 3: Effects of a wage change

A 3.1 Welfare effect

The welfare effect results as the marginal change of the utility level holding the rate of utility tranfer between the spouses (F' = const.) and the conflict outcomes (D = const.) constant:

$$\left.\frac{dU^i}{dw^i}\right|_{\substack{F'_{fix} \\ D_{fix}}} = \left.\frac{dU^i}{dN}\right|_{F'_{fix}} \left.\frac{dN}{dw^i}\right|_{D_{fix}} \qquad (A3.1)$$

Both terms are derived separately:

a) $F' = \dfrac{U^i - D^i}{U^j - D^j} = k \implies U^j - D^j = \dfrac{U^i - D^i}{k}$

$\implies N = (U^i - D^i) * (U^j - D^j) = \dfrac{(U^i - D^i)^2}{k}$

Differentiation with respect to N yields:

$$1 = \frac{1}{k} 2(U^i - D^i) \frac{dU^i}{dN}$$

$$\implies \left.\frac{dU^i}{dN}\right|_{F'_{fix}} = \frac{k}{2(U^i - D^i)} = \frac{1}{2(U^j - D^j)} \qquad (A3.2)$$

b) Differentiating (5.3) to (5.5) with respect to w^i, holding D constant, yields:

(1) $\dfrac{dN}{dw^i} = (U^i - D^i) \dfrac{dU^j}{dw^i} + (U^j - D^j) \dfrac{dU^i}{dw^i}$

(2) $\dfrac{dC^i}{dw^i} + \dfrac{dC^j}{dw^i} =$

$= Z_H a_i \dfrac{dH^i}{dw^i} + Z_H a_j \dfrac{dH^j}{dw^i} + Z_Y Y_M w^i \dfrac{dM^i}{dw^i} + Z_Y Y_M w^j \dfrac{dM^j}{dw^i} +$

$+ Z_Y Y_M M^i$

(3) $\quad 0 = \dfrac{dH^i}{dw^i} + \dfrac{dM^i}{dw^i} + \dfrac{dL^i}{dw^i}$

(4) $\quad 0 = \dfrac{dH^j}{dw^i} + \dfrac{dM^j}{dw^i} + \dfrac{dL^j}{dw^i}$

Using the first order conditions results in:

(1') $\quad \dfrac{dN}{dw^i} = (U^i - D^i)\left[U^i_C \dfrac{dC^i}{dw^i} + U^i_L \dfrac{dL^i}{dw^i} \right] + (U^j - D^j)\left[U^j_C \dfrac{dC^j}{dw^i} + U^j_L \dfrac{dL^j}{dw^i} \right]$

(2') $\quad \dfrac{dC^i}{dw^i} + \dfrac{dC^j}{dw^i} =$

$= \left[\dfrac{U^i_L}{U^i_C} - \dfrac{v^i}{U^i_C(U^j - D^j)} \right] \dfrac{dH^i}{dw^i} + \left[\dfrac{U^j_L}{U^j_C} - \dfrac{v^j}{U^j_C(U^i - D^i)} \right] \dfrac{dH^j}{dw^i}$

$+ \left[\dfrac{U^i_L}{U^i_C} - \dfrac{\sigma^i}{U^i_C(U^j - D^j)} \right] \dfrac{dM^i}{dw^i} + \left[\dfrac{U^j_L}{U^j_C} - \dfrac{\sigma^j}{U^j_C(U^i - D^i)} \right] \dfrac{dM^j}{dw^i}$

$+ Z_Y Y_M M^i$

with (3) and (4) follows

(2") $\quad \dfrac{dC^i}{dw^i} + \dfrac{dC^j}{dw^i} =$

$= \dfrac{U^i_L}{U^i_C}\left[\dfrac{dH^i}{dw^i} + \dfrac{dM^i}{dw^i} \right] + \dfrac{U^j_L}{U^j_C}\left[\dfrac{dH^j}{dw^i} + \dfrac{dM^j}{dw^i} \right] + Z_Y Y_M M^i$

$= - \dfrac{U^i_L}{U^i_C} \dfrac{dL^i}{dw^i} - \dfrac{U^j_L}{U^j_C} \dfrac{dL^j}{dw^i} + Z_Y Y_M M^i$

$\Rightarrow \dfrac{1}{U^i_C}\left[U^i_C \dfrac{dC^i}{dw^i} + U^i_L \dfrac{dL^i}{dw^i} \right] + \dfrac{1}{U^j_C}\left[U^j_C \dfrac{dC^j}{dw^i} + U^j_L \dfrac{dL^j}{dw^i} \right] = Z_Y Y_M M^i$

multiplication by $\lambda = U^i_C(U^j - D^j) = U^j_C(U^i - D^i)$ gives:

$(U^j - D^j)\left[U^i_C \dfrac{dC^i}{dw^i} + U^i_L \dfrac{dL^i}{dw^i} \right] + (U^i - D^i)\left[U^j_C \dfrac{dC^j}{dw^i} + U^j_L \dfrac{dL^j}{dw^i} \right] =$

$= \boxed{\lambda Z_Y Y_M M^i = \left.\dfrac{dN}{dw^i}\right|_{D_{fix}}}$ (A3.3)

A 3.2 Income induced substitution effect

Holding the conflict outcomes (D = const.), the Nash gain (N = const.) and the ratio of the shadow prices ($\frac{\mu^i}{\lambda}$ = const.) constant, the income induced substitution effect results:

(1) $N = \text{const.}$ $\Rightarrow$ $\frac{dN}{dw^i} = 0 = (U^i - D^i)\frac{dU^j}{dw^i} + (U^j - D^j)\frac{dU^i}{dw^i}$

(2) $\frac{\mu^i}{\lambda} = \text{const.}$ $\Rightarrow$ $\frac{\mu^i}{\mu^j} = \text{const.} = k$

with the first order conditions

$$\frac{U_L^i}{U_L^j} \frac{U^j - D^j}{U^i - D^i} = k \quad \Rightarrow \quad U_L^i(U^j - D^j) = U_L^j(U^i - D^i)k$$

differentiating this equation with respect to w^i

$$\frac{dU_L^i}{dw^i}(U^j - D^j) + U_L^i \frac{dU^j}{dw^i} = \frac{dU_L^j}{dw^i}(U^i - D^i)k + U_L^j \frac{dU^i}{dw^i} k$$

and with (1) and (2) the income induced substitution effect results:

$$\left. \frac{dU^i}{dw^i} \right|_{\substack{N_{fix} \\ P_{fix} \\ D_{fix}}} = \frac{U^i - D^i}{2} \left(\frac{1}{U_L^i} \frac{dU_L^i}{dw^i} - \frac{1}{U_L^j} \frac{dU_L^j}{dw^i} \right) \qquad (A3.4)$$

The income induced substitution effect will be analyzed in detail in the following. For this, the first order conditions

$$U_L^i = U_C^i Z_Y Y_M w^i + \frac{\sigma^i}{U^j - D^j} = U_C^i Z_H a_1 + \frac{v^i}{U^j - D^j}$$

are differentiated with respect to w^i:

$$\frac{dU_L^i}{dw^i} = U_C^i Z_Y Y_M + U_C^i w^i \frac{dZ_Y Y_M}{dw^i} + w^i Z_Y Y_M \frac{dU_C^i}{dw^i} + \frac{\frac{d\sigma^i}{dw^i}}{U^j - D^j} - \frac{\sigma^i \frac{dU^j}{dw^i}}{(U^j - D^j)^2}$$

$$= U_C^i a^i \frac{dZ_H}{dw^i} + a^i Z_H \frac{dU_C^i}{dw^i} + \frac{\frac{dv^i}{dw^i}}{U^j - D^j} - \frac{v^i \frac{dU^j}{dw^i}}{(U^j - D^j)^2}$$

$$\frac{dU_L^j}{dw^i} = U_C^j w^j \frac{dZ_Y Y_M}{dw^i} + w_j Z_Y Y_M \frac{dU_C^j}{dw^i} + \frac{d\sigma^j}{dw^i}{U^i - D^i} - \frac{\sigma^j \frac{dU^i}{dw^i}}{(U^i - D^i)^2}$$

$$= U_C^j a^j \frac{dZ_H}{dw^i} + a^j Z_H \frac{dU_C^j}{dw^i} + \frac{\frac{dv^j}{dw^i}}{U^i - D^i} - \frac{v^j \frac{dU^i}{dw^i}}{(U^i - D^i)^2}$$

Case 1: Person i allocates time to the market as well as to the household
$\Rightarrow v^i = 0, \; \sigma^i = 0$

a) Person j specializes in market work: $\sigma^j = 0, \; v^j > 0$

$$\frac{1}{U_L^i}\frac{dU_L^i}{dw^i} - \frac{1}{U_L^j}\frac{dU_L^j}{dw^i} = \frac{1}{U_C^i}\frac{dU_C^i}{dw^i} - \frac{1}{U_C^j}\frac{dU_C^j}{dw^i} + \frac{1}{w^i} \quad (A3.5)$$

b) Person j specializes in household work: $\sigma^j > 0, \; v^j = 0$

$$\frac{1}{U_L^i}\frac{dU_L^i}{dw^i} - \frac{1}{U_L^j}\frac{dU_L^j}{dw^i} = \frac{1}{U_C^i}\frac{dU_C^i}{dw^i} - \frac{1}{U_C^j}\frac{dU_C^j}{dw^i} \quad (A3.6)$$

Case 2: Person i specializes in market work: $\sigma^i = 0, \; v^i > 0$
Person j works at home and in the market $\sigma^j = 0, \; v^j = 0$

$$\frac{1}{U_L^i}\frac{dU_L^i}{dw^i} - \frac{1}{U_L^j}\frac{dU_L^j}{dw^i} = \frac{1}{w^i} + \frac{1}{U_C^i}\frac{dU_C^i}{dw^i} - \frac{1}{U_C^j}\frac{dU_C^j}{dw^i} \quad (A3.7)$$

Case 3: Person i specializes in household work: $\sigma^i > 0, \; v^i = 0$
Person j works at home and in the market $\sigma^j = 0, \; v^j = 0$

$$\frac{1}{U_L^i}\frac{dU_L^i}{dw^i} - \frac{1}{U_L^j}\frac{dU_L^j}{dw^i} = \underbrace{\frac{1}{U_C^i}\frac{dU_C^i}{dw^i}}_{= 0} - \underbrace{\frac{1}{U_C^j}\frac{dU_C^j}{dw^i}}_{= 0} = 0 \quad (A3.8)$$

if person i does not enter the labor force

A 3.3 Income compensated substitution effect:

Holding the threat point (D = const.), the Nash gain (N = const.) and the ratio of the marginal utilities ($\frac{U_L^i}{U_L^j}$ = const.) constant, the income compensated substitution effect results. (The derivation is analogous to that of the income induced substitution effect).

$$\left. \frac{dU^i}{dw^i} \right|_{\substack{N_{fix} \\ U_{L\,fix} \\ D_{fix}}} = \frac{U^i - D^i}{2} \left(\frac{1}{\mu^j} \frac{d\mu^j}{dw^i} - \frac{1}{\mu^i} \frac{d\mu^i}{dw^i} \right) \qquad (A3.9)$$

Here, also different cases can be distinguished. The first order condition

$$\mu^i = \lambda a^i Z_H + v^i = \lambda Z_Y Y_M w^i + \sigma^i$$

is differentiated with respect to w^i:

$$\frac{d\mu^i}{dw^i} = \lambda a^i \frac{dZ_H}{dw^i} + a^i Z_H \frac{d\lambda}{dw^i} + \frac{dv^i}{dw^i}$$

$$= \lambda Z_Y Y_M + \lambda w^i \frac{dZ_Y Y_M}{dw^i} + w^i Z_Y Y_M \frac{d\lambda}{dw^i} + \frac{d\sigma^i}{dw^i}$$

$$\frac{d\mu^j}{dw^i} = \lambda a^j \frac{dZ_H}{dw^i} + a^j Z_H \frac{d\lambda}{dw^i} + \frac{dv^j}{dw^i}$$

$$= \lambda w^j \frac{dZ_Y Y_M}{dw^i} + w^j Z_Y Y_M \frac{d\lambda}{dw^i} + \frac{d\sigma^j}{dw^i}$$

Case 1: Person i allocates time to the market as well as to the household
$\Rightarrow v^i = 0, \sigma^i = 0$

a) Person j specializes in market work: $\sigma^j = 0, v^j > 0$

$$\frac{1}{\mu^j} \frac{d\mu^j}{dw^i} - \frac{1}{\mu^i} \frac{d\mu^i}{dw^i} = - \frac{Z_Y Y_M}{a^i Z_H} = - \frac{1}{w^i} \qquad (A3.10)$$

b) Person j specializes in household work: $\sigma^j > 0$, $v^j = 0$

$$\frac{1}{\mu^j}\frac{d\mu^j}{dw^i} - \frac{1}{\mu^i}\frac{d\mu^i}{dw^i} = 0 \qquad (A3.11)$$

Case 2: Person i specializes in market work: $\sigma^i = 0$, $v^i > 0$
Person j works at home and in the market $\sigma^j = 0$, $v^j = 0$

$$\frac{1}{\mu^j}\frac{d\mu^j}{dw^i} - \frac{1}{\mu^i}\frac{d\mu^i}{dw^i} = -\frac{1}{w^i} = -\frac{\mu^j}{\mu^i}\frac{Z_Y Y_M}{a^i Z_H} \qquad (A3.12)$$

Case 3: Person i specializes in household work: $\sigma^i > 0$, $v^i = 0$
Person j works at home and in the market $\sigma^j = 0$, $v^j = 0$

$$\frac{1}{\mu^j}\frac{d\mu^j}{dw^i} - \frac{1}{\mu^i}\frac{d\mu^i}{dw^i} = 0 \qquad (A3.13)$$

A 3.4 Bargaining effect:

The bargaining effect results from a change in the conflict outcome while holding the negotiation set constant.

a) First, the reaction of the cooperative outcome on a change in the conflict outcome $\frac{dU^i}{dD^i}$ is derived:

From (4.9) $\frac{U^j - D^j}{U^i - D^i} = -\frac{dU^j}{dU^i}$ result:

$$U^j - D^j = -\frac{dU^j}{dU^i}(U^i - D^i)$$

Differentiation with respect to D^i:

$$\frac{dU^j}{dU^i}\frac{dU^i}{dD^i} = -\frac{dU^j}{dU^i}\left[\frac{dU^i}{dD^i} - 1\right] - (U^i - D^i)\frac{d^2U^j}{dU^{i2}}\frac{dU^i}{dD^i}$$

$$\Rightarrow \frac{dU^i}{dD^i}\left[\frac{dU^j}{dU^i} + \frac{dU^j}{dU^i} + (U^i - D^i)\frac{d^2U^j}{dU^{i2}}\right] = \frac{dU^j}{dU^i}$$

$$\Rightarrow \frac{dU^i}{dD^i} = \frac{-\frac{U^j - D^j}{U^i - D^i}}{-2\frac{U^j - D^j}{U^i - D^i} + (U^i - D^i)\frac{d^2U^j}{dU^{i2}}}$$

$$\boxed{\Rightarrow \quad \frac{dU^i}{dD^i} = \frac{1}{2 - \frac{(U^i - D^i)^2}{U^j - D^j}\frac{d^2U^j}{dU^{i2}}}} \qquad (A3.14)$$

b) In addition, the bargaining effect is also determined by the reaction of the conflict outcome on a wage change $\frac{dD^i}{dw^i}$:

This effect can be derived from the maximization problem in the single-person household:

$$\left.\begin{array}{l}\max_{L,H,M} U(C, L) \\ \text{s.t.} \quad C = Z(aH, Y(wM + I)) \\ \qquad T = M + H + L\end{array}\right\} \Rightarrow D(w, a, I) = U(C, L)$$

The Lagrangian is written as follows:

$$\mathcal{L} = U(C, L) + \lambda[Z(aH, Y(wM)) - C] + \mu(T - H - M - L)$$

$\Rightarrow$ first order conditions:

$$\left.\begin{array}{l}\lambda = U_C \\ \mu = U_L \\ \lambda Z_H a = \mu \\ \lambda Z_Y Y_M w = \mu\end{array}\right\} \Rightarrow U_L = U_C a Z_H = U_C w Y_M Z_Y$$

Differentiation of the system equations in the optimum with respect to w:

(I) $\quad \dfrac{dD}{dw} = U_C \dfrac{dC}{dw} + U_L \dfrac{dL}{dw}$

(II) $\quad \dfrac{dC}{dw} = Z_M a \dfrac{dH}{dw} + Z_Y Y_M w \dfrac{dM}{dw} + Z_Y Y_M M$

(III) $\quad 0 = \dfrac{dH}{dw} + \dfrac{dL}{dw} + \dfrac{dM}{dw}$

with the first order conditions the marginal change in the conflict outcome results:

$$\boxed{\dfrac{dD}{dw} = \lambda Z_Y Y_M M} \qquad (A3.15)$$

Appendix 4: Effects of changes in household productivity

The effects of a change in household productivity are derived analogously to those of a wage change.

(A4.1)

$$\frac{dU^i}{da^i} = \cfrac{1}{2 - \cfrac{(U^i - D^i)^2}{U^j - D^j} \cfrac{d^2 U^j}{dU^{i2}}} \lambda Z_H \mathcal{H}^i \quad \Big\} > 0 \quad \text{bargaining effect}$$

$$+ \frac{1}{2(U^j - D^j)} \lambda Z_H H^i \quad \Big\} \geq 0 \quad \text{welfare effect} \ (0 \text{ for } M^i = 0)$$

$$+ \frac{(U^i - D^i)}{2} \left[\frac{1}{U_L^i} \frac{\partial U_L^i}{\partial a^i} - \frac{1}{U_L^j} \frac{\partial U_L^j}{\partial a^i} \right] \quad \Big\} \begin{matrix} > \\ = \\ < \end{matrix} 0 \quad \begin{matrix}\text{income induced} \\ \text{substitution effect} \\ (0 \text{ for } M^i = 0)\end{matrix}$$

$$+ \frac{(U^i - D^i)}{2} \left[\frac{1}{\mu^j} \frac{\partial \mu^j}{\partial a^i} - \frac{1}{\mu^i} \frac{\partial \mu^i}{\partial a^i} \right] \quad \Big\} \leq 0 \quad \begin{matrix}\text{income compensated} \\ \text{substitution effect} \\ (0 \text{ for } M^i = 0)\end{matrix}$$

For this, the effect on the conflict outcome $\frac{dD^i}{da^i}$ and on the welfare level $\left.\frac{dN}{da^i}\right|_D$ are derived as follows:

a) $\frac{dD^i}{da^i}$ results from the maximization problem in the single-person household:

$$\left.\begin{matrix} \max_{L,H,M} U(C, L) \\ \text{s.t.} \quad C = Z(aH, Y(wM + I)) \\ T = M + H + L \end{matrix}\right\} \quad D(w, a, I) = U(C, L)$$

⇒ first order conditions:

$$\left.\begin{matrix} \lambda = U_C \\ \mu = U_L \\ \lambda Z_H a = \mu \\ \lambda Z_Y Y_M w = \mu \end{matrix}\right\} \quad U_L = U_C a Z_H = U_C w Y_M Z_Y$$

Differentiation with respect to a:

(I) $\quad \dfrac{dD}{da} = U_C \dfrac{dC}{da} + U_L \dfrac{dL}{da}$

(II) $\quad \dfrac{dC}{da} = Z_{\mathcal{H}} a \dfrac{d\mathcal{H}}{da} + Z_Y \mathcal{Y}_M w \dfrac{dM}{da} + Z_{\mathcal{H}} \mathcal{H}$

(III) $\quad 0 = \dfrac{d\mathcal{H}}{da} + \dfrac{dL}{da} + \dfrac{dM}{da}$

with the first order conditions the marginal change in the conflict outcome results:

$$\boxed{\dfrac{dD}{da} = \lambda\, Z_{\mathcal{H}} \mathcal{H}} \qquad (A4.2)$$

b) Differentiating (5.3) to (5.5) with respect to w^i holding D constant:

(1) $\quad \dfrac{dN}{da^i} = (U^i - D^i) \dfrac{dU^j}{da^i} + (U^j - D^j) \dfrac{dU^i}{da^i}$

(2) $\quad \dfrac{dC^i}{da^i} + \dfrac{dC^j}{da^i} =$

$\quad = Z_H a_i \dfrac{dH^i}{da^i} + Z_H a_j \dfrac{dH^j}{da^i} + Z_Y Y_M w^i \dfrac{dM^i}{da^i} + Z_Y Y_M w^j \dfrac{dM^j}{da^i} +$

$\quad + Z_H H^i$

(3) $\quad 0 = \dfrac{dH^i}{da^i} + \dfrac{dM^i}{da^i} + \dfrac{dL^i}{da^i}$

(4) $\quad 0 = \dfrac{dH^j}{da^i} + \dfrac{dM^j}{da^i} + \dfrac{dL^j}{da^i}$

Using the first order conditions result in:

$$\boxed{\lambda Z_H H^i = \left. \dfrac{dN}{da^i} \right|_{D_{fix}}} \qquad (A4.3)$$

Appendix 5: Model with binding contracts for period 2

A 5.1 One-step model

$$\max_{C^{it}, M^{it}, L^{it}} (U^{m1} + U^{m2} - A^m)(U^{f1} + U^{f2} - A^f) = (G^m - A^m)(G^f - A^f)$$

subject to

(I) $C^{mt} + C^{ft} = Z(a^{ft}H^{ft} + a^{mt}H^{mt}, Y(w^{mt}H^{mt} + w^{ft}H^{ft} + I^{mt} + I^{ft}))$ $\qquad t = 1, 2$

(II) $T = H^{it} + M^{it} + L^{it}$ $\qquad t = 1, 2 \quad i = m, f$

(III) $C^{mt} > 0, C^{ft} > 0, L^{mt} > 0, L^{ft} > 0$
$H^{mt} \geq 0, H^{ft} \geq 0, M^{mt} \geq 0, M^{ft} \geq 0$ $\qquad t = 1, 2$

(IV) $a^{i2} = f(a^{i1}, H^{i1})$ $\qquad i = m, f$

(V) $w^{i2} = g(w^{i1}, M^{i1})$ $\qquad i = m, f$

First order conditions:

(1) $U_C^{i1}(G^j - A^j) - \lambda_1 = 0$ $\qquad i, j = m, f, \quad i \neq j$

(2) $U_L^{i1}(G^j - A^j) - \mu_1^i = 0$

(3) $\lambda_1 Z_H a^{i1} - \mu_1^i + \nu_1^i + \lambda_2 Z_H H^{i2} \dfrac{da^{i2}}{dH^{i1}} = 0$

(4) $\lambda_1 Z_Y Y_M w^{i1} - \mu_1^i + \sigma_1^i + \lambda_2 Z_Y Y_M M^{i2} \dfrac{dw^{i2}}{dM^{i2}} = 0$

(5) $U_C^{i2}(G^j - A^j) - \lambda_2 = 0$

(6) $U_L^{i2}(G^j - A^j) - \mu_2^i = 0$

(7) $\lambda_2 Z_H a^{i2} - \mu_2^i + \nu_2^i = 0$

(8) $\lambda_2 Z_Y Y_M w^{i2} - \mu_2^i + \sigma_2^i = 0$

(9) $\sigma_t^i M^{it} = 0$ $\qquad t = 1, 2$

(10) $\nu_t^i H^{it} = 0$

A 5.2 Two-step model:

$$\max_{L^{i1}, H^{i1}, M^{i1}} N = (U^{m1} + U^{m2} - D^m) * (U^{f1} + U^{f2} - D^f)$$

$$\max_{L^{i2}, H^{i2}, M^{i2}} N_2 = (U^{m2} - D^{m2}) * (U^{f2} - D^{f2})$$

subject to (I) - (V)

First order conditions:

(1) $U_C^{i1}(G^j - A^j) - \lambda_1 = 0$ $\qquad$ i, j = m, f, $\quad i \neq j$

(2) $U_L^{i1}(G^j - A^j) - \mu_1^i = 0$

(3) $\dfrac{\partial U^{j2}}{\partial H^{i1}}(G^j - A^j) + \dfrac{\partial U^{j2}}{\partial H^{i1}}(G^i - A^i) +$

$\qquad + \lambda_1 Z_H a^{i1} - \mu_1^i + \nu_1^i + \lambda_2 Z_H H^{i2} \dfrac{da^{i2}}{dH^{i1}} = 0$

(4) $\dfrac{\partial U^{j2}}{\partial M^{i1}}(G^j - A^j) + \dfrac{\partial U^{j2}}{\partial M^{i1}}(G^i - A^i) +$

$\qquad + \lambda_1 Z_Y Y_M w^{i1} - \mu_1^i + \sigma_1^i + \lambda_2 Z_Y Y_M M^{i2} \dfrac{dw^{i2}}{dM^{i2}} = 0$

(5) $U_C^{i2}(U^{j2} - D^{j2}) - \lambda_2 = 0$

(6) $U_L^{i2}(U^{j2} - D^{j2}) - \mu_2^i = 0$

(7) $\lambda_2 Z_H a^{i2} - \mu_2^i + \nu_2^i = 0$

(8) $\lambda_2 Z_Y Y_M w^{i2} - \mu_2^i + \sigma_2^i = 0$

(9) $\sigma_t^i M^{it} = 0$ $\qquad\qquad\qquad\qquad$ t = 1 2

(10) $\nu_t^i H^{it} = 0$

Comparing the first order conditions, both models are equivalent for

$$\dfrac{G^m - A^m}{G^f - A^f} = \dfrac{U^{m2} - D^{m2}}{U^{f2} - D^{f2}} \qquad (A5.1)$$

Appendix 6: Allocation in period 1

The two-period model (6.6) to (6.14) can also be solved recursively. First the maximization problem in period two is solved. This problem is identical to the static model. Because the solution depends on wages and productivities in period 2 which are determined by the decisions in period 1, two indirect utility fuctions V^i result which depends on these endogenous variables. Then, the solution in period 1 can be derived as follows:

$$\max N = (U^{m1} + U^{m2} - A^m)(U^{f1} + U^{f2} - A^f)$$

$$= (U^m + V^m - A^m)(U^f + V^f - A^f)$$

$$= (G^m - A^m)(G^f - A^f)$$

with

$U^i = U^{i1} = U^i(C^{it}, L^{it})$ — Utility function of person i in period 1

$V^i = U^{i2} = V^i(w^{j2}, a^{i2}, w^{j2}, a^{j2}, I^{i2}, I^{j2})$
$\quad = V^i(M^{i1}, M^{j1}, H^{i1}, H^{j1})$ — indirect utility function of person i in period 2

$G^i = U^i + V^i$ — Total utility of person i

subject to[1]

(I) $\quad C^m + C^f = Z(a^f H^f + a^m H^m, Y(w^m H^m + w^f H^f + I^m + I^f))$

(II) $\quad T = H^i + M^i + L^i \qquad\qquad i = m, f$

(III) $\quad C^m > 0, C^f > 0, L^m > 0, L^f > 0$
$\quad\quad\;\; H^m \geq 0, H^f \geq 0, M^m \geq 0, M^f \geq 0$

---

[1] All variables except V^i relate to period 1 and correspond to those of the model (6.6) to (6.14) which have the time index 1. In order to simplify the formulas this index is omitted.

From the Lagrangian

$$\mathcal{L} = (U^m + V^m - A^m)(U^f + V^f - A^f) + \\
+ \lambda \{ Z(a^f H^f + a^m H^m, Y(w^m M^m + w^f M^f + I^m + I^f)) - C^f - C^m \} + \\
+ \mu^f (T - H^f - L^f - M^f) + \mu^m (T - H^m - L^m - M^m) + \\
+ v^f H^f + v^m H^m + \sigma^f M^f + \sigma^m M^m$$

the first order conditions result:

(1) $\quad \dfrac{\partial \mathcal{L}}{\partial C^m} = U_C^m (G^f - A^f) - \lambda = 0$

(2) $\quad \dfrac{\partial \mathcal{L}}{\partial C^f} = U_C^f (G^m - A^m) - \lambda = 0$

(3) $\quad \dfrac{\partial \mathcal{L}}{\partial L^m} = U_L^m (G^f - A^f) - \mu^m = 0$

(4) $\quad \dfrac{\partial \mathcal{L}}{\partial L^f} = U_L^f (G^m - A^m) - \mu^f = 0$

(5) $\quad \dfrac{\partial \mathcal{L}}{\partial H^m} = \dfrac{\partial V^m}{\partial H^m}(G^f - A^f) + (G^m - A^m)\dfrac{\partial V^f}{\partial H^m} + \lambda Z_H a^m - \mu^m + v^m = 0$

(6) $\quad \dfrac{\partial \mathcal{L}}{\partial H^f} = \dfrac{\partial V^f}{\partial H^f}(G^m - A^m) + (G^f - A^f)\dfrac{\partial V^m}{\partial H^f} + \lambda Z_H a^f - \mu^f + v^f = 0$

(7) $\quad \dfrac{\partial \mathcal{L}}{\partial M^m} = \dfrac{\partial V^m}{\partial M^m}(G^f - A^f) + (G^m - A^m)\dfrac{\partial V^f}{\partial M^m} + \lambda Z_Y Y_M w^m - \mu^m + \sigma^m = 0$

(8) $\quad \dfrac{\partial \mathcal{L}}{\partial M^f} = \dfrac{\partial V^m}{\partial M^f}(G^m - A^m) + (G^f - A^f)\dfrac{\partial V^m}{\partial M^f} + \lambda Z_Y Y_M w^f - \mu^f + \sigma^f = 0$

(9) $\quad \dfrac{\partial \mathcal{L}}{\partial \lambda} = Z(a^f H^f + a^m H^m, Y(w^m M^m + w^f M^f + I^m + I^f)) - C^f - C^m = 0$

(10) $\quad \dfrac{\partial \mathcal{L}}{\partial \mu^m} = T - H^m - L^m - M^m = 0$

(11) $\quad \dfrac{\partial \mathcal{L}}{\partial \mu^f} = T - H^f - L^f - M^f = 0$

(12) $\quad \nu^m H^m = 0$

(13) $\quad \nu^f H^f = 0$

(14) $\quad \sigma^m M^m = 0$

(15) $\quad \sigma^f M^f = 0$

(1), (2) $\Rightarrow \quad \lambda = U_C^i (Y^j - A^j) = U_C^j (U^i - A^i) \Rightarrow \dfrac{U_C^i}{U_C^j} = \dfrac{G^i - A^i}{G^j - A^j}$

(3), (4) $\Rightarrow \quad \mu^i = U_L^i (Y^j - A^j)$

(5), (6) $\Rightarrow \quad \nu^i = \mu^i - \lambda Z_H a^i - \dfrac{\partial V^i}{\partial H^i}(G^j - A^j) - \dfrac{\partial V^j}{\partial H^j}(G^i - A^i)$

$\quad\quad\quad\quad\quad = (G^j - A^j)\left[U_L^i - U_C^i Z_H a^i - \dfrac{\partial V^i}{\partial H^i} - \dfrac{U_C^i}{U_C^j}\dfrac{\partial V^j}{\partial H^j} \right]$

(7), (8) $\Rightarrow \quad \sigma^i = \mu^i - \lambda Z_Y Y_m w^i - \dfrac{\partial V^i}{\partial M^i}(G^j - A^j) - \dfrac{\partial V^j}{\partial M^j}(G^i - A^i)$

$\quad\quad\quad\quad\quad = (G^j - A^j)\left[U_L^i - U_C^i Z_Y Y_m w^i - \dfrac{\partial V^i}{\partial M^i} - \dfrac{U_C^i}{U_C^j}\dfrac{\partial V^j}{\partial M^j} \right]$

$$\Rightarrow \boxed{\begin{aligned} \dfrac{U_L^i}{U_C^i} &= Z_Y Y_m w^i + \dfrac{1}{U_C^i}\dfrac{\partial V^i}{\partial M^i} + \dfrac{1}{U_C^j}\dfrac{\partial V^j}{\partial M^j} + \dfrac{\sigma^i}{U_C^i (G^j - A^j)} \\ &= Z_H a^i + \dfrac{1}{U_C^i}\dfrac{\partial V^i}{\partial H^i} + \dfrac{1}{U_C^j}\dfrac{\partial V^j}{\partial H^j} + \dfrac{\nu^i}{U_C^i (G^j - A^j)} \end{aligned}} \quad (A6.1)$$

From this equation, the conditions for different time allocation patterns can be derived:

Case 1: Person i allocates time to the market as well as to the household

$$M^i > 0, \; H^i > 0 \Rightarrow \sigma^i = 0, \; v^i = 0.$$

$\Rightarrow$ (A6.2)

$$\frac{1}{U_C^i}\frac{\partial V^i}{\partial M^i} + \frac{1}{U_C^j}\frac{\partial V^j}{\partial M^i} + Z_Y Y_m w^i = \frac{U_L^i}{U_C^i} = Z_H a^i + \frac{1}{U_C^i}\frac{\partial V^i}{\partial H^i} + \frac{1}{U_C^j}\frac{\partial V^j}{\partial H^j}$$

Case 2: Person i specializes in market work

$$M^i > 0, \ldots H^i = 0 \Rightarrow \sigma^i = 0, \; v^i \geq 0,$$

$\Rightarrow$ (A6.3)

$$\frac{1}{U_C^i}\frac{\partial V^i}{\partial M^i} + \frac{1}{U_C^j}\frac{\partial V^j}{\partial M^i} + Z_Y Y_m w^i \geq \frac{U_L^i}{U_C^i} = Z_H a^i + \frac{1}{U_C^i}\frac{\partial V^i}{\partial H^i} + \frac{1}{U_C^j}\frac{\partial V^j}{\partial H^j}$$

Case 3: Person i specializes in household work

$$M^i = 0, \ldots H^i > 0 \Rightarrow \sigma^i \geq 0, \; v^i = 0,$$

$\Rightarrow$ (A6.4)

$$\frac{1}{U_C^i}\frac{\partial V^i}{\partial M^i} + \frac{1}{U_C^j}\frac{\partial V^j}{\partial M^i} + Z_Y Y_m w^i \leq \frac{U_L^i}{U_C^i} = Z_H a^i + \frac{1}{U_C^i}\frac{\partial V^i}{\partial H^i} + \frac{1}{U_C^j}\frac{\partial V^j}{\partial H^j}$$

Appendix 7: The substitution effect in the two-period model

$$\frac{dU^{i2}}{dw^{i2}}\bigg|_{\substack{D_{fix}\\N_{fix}}}\frac{dw^{i2}}{dM^{i2}} - \frac{dU^{i2}}{da^{i2}}\bigg|_{\substack{D_{fix}\\N_{fix}}}\frac{da^{i2}}{dH^{i2}} =$$

$$= \frac{U^{i2} - D^{i2}}{2}\left[\left(\frac{1}{U_L^i}\frac{\partial U_L^i}{\partial w^{i2}} - \frac{1}{U_L^j}\frac{\partial U_L^j}{\partial w^{i2}}\right) + \left(\frac{1}{\mu^{j2}}\frac{\partial \mu^{j2}}{\partial w^{i2}} - \frac{1}{\mu^{i2}}\frac{\partial \mu^{i2}}{\partial w^{i2}}\right)\right]\frac{dw^{i2}}{dM^{i1}}$$

$$- \frac{U^{i2} - D^{i2}}{2}\left[\left(\frac{1}{U_L^i}\frac{\partial U_L^i}{\partial a^{i2}} - \frac{1}{U_L^j}\frac{\partial U_L^j}{\partial a^{i2}}\right) + \left(\frac{1}{\mu^{j2}}\frac{\partial \mu^{j2}}{\partial a^{i2}} - \frac{1}{\mu^{i2}}\frac{\partial \mu^{i2}}{\partial a^{i2}}\right)\right]\frac{da^{i2}}{dH^{i1}}$$

$$= \frac{U^{i2} - D^{i2}}{2}\left[\left(\frac{1}{U_L^i}\frac{\partial U_L^i}{\partial w^{i2}} - \frac{1}{U_L^j}\frac{\partial U_L^j}{\partial w^{i2}}\right)\frac{dw^{i2}}{dM^{i1}} + \left(\frac{1}{U_L^i}\frac{\partial U_L^i}{\partial a^{i2}} - \frac{1}{U_L^j}\frac{\partial U_L^j}{\partial a^{i2}}\right)\frac{da^{i2}}{dH^{i1}}\right]$$

$$- \frac{U^{i2} - D^{i2}}{2}\left[\left(\frac{1}{\mu^{j2}}\frac{\partial \mu^{j2}}{\partial w^{i2}} - \frac{1}{\mu^{i2}}\frac{\partial \mu^{i2}}{\partial w^{i2}}\right)\frac{dw^{i2}}{dM^{i1}} + \left(\frac{1}{\mu^{j2}}\frac{\partial \mu^{j2}}{\partial a^{i2}} - \frac{1}{\mu^{i2}}\frac{\partial \mu^{i2}}{\partial a^{i2}}\right)\frac{da^{i2}}{dH^{i1}}\right]$$

$$= \frac{U^{i2} - D^{i2}}{2}\left[\left(\frac{1}{U_L^i}\frac{\partial U_L^i}{\partial w^{i2}} - \frac{1}{U_L^j}\frac{\partial U_L^j}{\partial w^{i2}}\right)\frac{dw^{i2}}{dM^{i1}} + \left(\frac{1}{U_L^i}\frac{\partial U_L^i}{\partial a^{i2}} - \frac{1}{U_L^j}\frac{\partial U_L^j}{\partial a^{i2}}\right)\frac{da^{i2}}{dH^{i1}}\right]$$

$$- \frac{U^{i2} - D^{i2}}{2}\left[-\delta_w \frac{1}{w^i}\frac{dw^{i2}}{dM^{i1}} + \delta_a \frac{1}{a^i}\frac{da^{i2}}{dH^{i1}}\right]$$

$$\underbrace{}$$

$$\begin{array}{ll} > 0 & \text{for } M^{i2} = 0, H^{i2} > 0 \\ < 0 & \text{for } M^{i2} = 0, H^{i2} > 0 \\ \frac{\lambda}{\mu^i}\left[Z_H \frac{da^{i2}}{dH^{i1}} - Z_Y Y_M \frac{dw^{i2}}{dM^{i1}}\right] & \text{for } M^{i2} > 0, H^{i2} > 0 \end{array}$$

where

$$\delta_w = \begin{cases} 1 & M^{i2} > 0 \\ 0 & M^{i2} = 0 \end{cases} \qquad \text{(see (A3.10) - (A3.13))}$$

$$\delta_a = \begin{cases} 1 & H^{i2} > 0 \\ 0 & H^{i2} = 0 \end{cases}$$

Appendix 8: Marginal effects in the model with uncertainty

A 8.1   Effects of a wage change

From the model

$$\max N = (U^i - D^i)^\alpha - (U^j - D^j)^{1-\alpha}$$

s.t. (5.4) to (5.7)

the maximum outcome for person i results as the limit of his cooperative payoff when his bargaining power increases up to full dictatorship:

$$\bar{D}^i = \lim_{\alpha \to 1} U^i(\alpha, D^i, D^j) = N + D^i$$

$$\Rightarrow \bar{D}^i - D^i = N$$
and
$$\bar{D}^i(\varepsilon^j) - D_0^i = E(N|\varepsilon^j)$$

The marginal change of the Nash gain can be derived as follows:

$$\frac{dN}{dw^i} = \left[\frac{dU^i}{dw^i} - \frac{dD^i}{dw^i}\right]\alpha\,(U^i - D^i)^{\alpha-1}\,(U^j - D^j)^{1-\alpha}$$

$$+ (U^i - D^i)^\alpha\,(1-\alpha)\,(U^j - D^j)^{-\alpha}\,\frac{dU^j}{dw^i}$$

$$= \left[\frac{dU^i}{dw^i} - \frac{dD^i}{dw^i}\right]\alpha\left[\frac{U^i - D^i}{U^j - D^j}\right]^{1-\alpha} + \frac{dU^j}{dw^i}\,(1-\alpha)\left[\frac{U^i - D^i}{U^j - D^j}\right]^\alpha$$

$$\Rightarrow \frac{dU^i}{dw^i} = \frac{1}{\alpha}\frac{dN}{dw^i}\left[\frac{U^i - D^i}{U^j - D^j}\right]^{\alpha-1} + \frac{dD^i}{dw^i} - \frac{1-\alpha}{\alpha}\frac{U^i - D^i}{U^j - D^j}\frac{dU^j}{dw^i}$$

$$\Rightarrow \frac{d\bar{D}^i}{dw^i} = \lim_{\alpha \to 1}\frac{dU^i}{dw^i} = \frac{dN}{dw^i} + \frac{dD^i}{dw^i}$$

$$\Rightarrow \frac{d\bar{D}^i}{dw^i} - \frac{dD^i}{dw^i} = \frac{dN}{dw^i}$$

and with $D^i = D_0^i + \epsilon^i$

$$\frac{d\bar{D}^i}{dw^i} - \frac{D_0^i}{dw^i} = \frac{dN}{dw^i}$$

The marginal Nash gain can also be written as

$$\frac{dN}{dw^i} = \underbrace{\left.\frac{\partial N}{\partial w^i}\right|_D}_{>0} + \underbrace{\frac{\partial N}{\partial D^i}\frac{dD^i}{dw^i}}_{<0} \qquad (A\ 8.1)$$

On the other hand, from the discussion in chapter 6 on the household production function in the single-person and the multi-person household follows, that in general the relationship will hold:

$$\frac{dD^i}{dw^i} > \left.\frac{\partial N}{\partial w^i}\right|_D \qquad (A\ 8.2)$$

The effect of a change in the conflict payoff on the Nash gain results as

$$\frac{dN}{dD^i} = (U^j - D^j)\left[\frac{dU^i}{dD^i} - 1\right] + (U^j - D^j) + (U^i - D^i)\frac{dU^j}{dD^i} =$$

$$= (U^j - D^j)\frac{dU^i}{dD^i} - (U^j - D^j) + (U^i - D^i)\frac{dU^j}{dU^i}\frac{dU^i}{dD^i} =$$

$$= \frac{dU^i}{dD^i}\left[(U^j - D^j) - (U^i - D^i)\frac{U^j - D^j}{U^i - D^i}\right] - (U^j - D^j) =$$

$$= D^j - U^j < 0$$

The term $\dfrac{dN}{dD^i}$ is the smaller, i.e. $\left|\dfrac{dN}{dD^i}\right|$ is the greater, the greater the gain of the other partner is.

$$\Rightarrow \frac{dN}{dw^i} = \underbrace{\left.\frac{\partial N}{\partial w^i}\right|_D}_{>0} + \underbrace{\frac{\partial N}{\partial D^i}}_{<0}\underbrace{\frac{dD^i}{dw^i}}_{>0} < 0 \text{ if } \left|\frac{dN}{dD^i}\right| \text{ is sufficiently large}$$

⇒ in general

$$\frac{d\bar{D}}{dw^i} - \frac{dD_0^i}{dw^i} = \frac{dN}{dw^i} < 0 \qquad (A\ 8.3)$$

But, if the situation is more asymmetrical in favor of the partner, $U^j - D^j$ is smaller and $\frac{dN}{dw^i} > 0$ is more likely.

A 8.2   Effect of a change in household productivity

$$\frac{dN}{da^i} = \left.\frac{\partial N}{\partial a^i}\right|_D + \frac{\partial N}{\partial D^i}\frac{dD^i}{da^i}$$
$$\phantom{\frac{dN}{da^i} = } > 0 \qquad < 0 \quad > 0$$

in general the effect is larger in a joint household than in separate households:

$$\left.\frac{\partial N}{\partial a^i}\right|_D > \frac{dD^i}{da^i}$$

$$\Rightarrow \frac{dN}{da^i} > 0, \text{ if } \left|\frac{\partial N}{\partial D^i}\right| \text{ sufficiently small.}$$

But, if $\left|\frac{\partial N}{\partial D^i}\right|$ is relatively large, then the following will hold:

$$\frac{dD^i}{da^i} - \frac{dD^{i0}}{da^i} = \frac{dN}{da^i} < 0$$

A 8.3   Comparison of the effects

$$\frac{dN}{da^i} - \frac{dN}{dw^i} = \underbrace{\left(\left.\frac{\partial N}{\partial a^i}\right|_D - \left.\frac{\partial N}{\partial w^i}\right|_D\right)}_{< 0} + \underbrace{\frac{\partial N}{\partial D^i}\left(\frac{dD^i}{da^i} - \frac{dD^i}{dw^i}\right)}_{\substack{< 0 \qquad \ll 0 \\ \gg 0}}$$

Therefore, in general $\frac{dN}{da^i} > \frac{dN}{dw^i}$ will hold.

Appendix 9: The effect of a wage change on the expected outcome

$$V^i(\varepsilon^i, \varepsilon^j) = \delta D^i(\varepsilon^i) + (1-\delta) U^i(D_0^i + \varepsilon^i, D_0^j + \varepsilon^j)$$

where

$$\delta = \begin{cases} 1 & \text{in the case } D^i > \bar{D}^i \\ 0 & \text{otherwise} \end{cases}$$

Then, the expected value results from

$$V_E^i = E(V^i) = \int_{-\infty}^{+\infty} \left[\int_{\bar{D}^i(\varepsilon^j) - D_0^i}^{+\infty} (D_0^i + \varepsilon^i) \, dF(\varepsilon^i) + \int_{-\infty}^{\bar{D}^i(\varepsilon^j) - D_0^i} U^i(D_0^i + \varepsilon^i, D_0^j + \varepsilon^j) \, dF(\varepsilon^i) \right] dF^j(\varepsilon^j).$$

Derivation with respect to w^i yield:

$$\frac{dV_E^i}{dw^{i2}} = -\int_{-\infty}^{+\infty} \left\{ -f(\bar{D}^i(\varepsilon^j) - D_0^i) \, \bar{D}^i(\varepsilon^j) \left[\frac{d\bar{D}^i(\varepsilon^j)}{dw^{i2}} - \frac{dD_0^i}{dw^{i2}} \right] + \int_{\bar{D}^i(\varepsilon^j) - D_0^i}^{+\infty} \frac{dD_0^i}{dw^{i2}} \, dF(\varepsilon^i) \right.$$

$$\left. + f(\bar{D}^i(\varepsilon^j) - D_0^i) \, U^i(\bar{D}^i(\varepsilon^j), D_0^j + \varepsilon^j) \left[\frac{d\bar{D}^i(\varepsilon^j)}{dw^{i2}} - \frac{dD_0^i}{dw^{i2}} \right] + \int_{-\infty}^{\bar{D}^i(\varepsilon^j) - D_0^i} \frac{dU^i(\varepsilon^i, \varepsilon^j)}{dw^{i2}} \, dF(\varepsilon^i) \right\} dF^j(\varepsilon^j)$$

$$= \int_{-\infty}^{+\infty} \left[\int_{\bar{D}^i(\varepsilon^j) - D_0^i}^{+\infty} \frac{dD_0^i}{dw^{i2}} \, dF(\varepsilon^i) + \int_{-\infty}^{\bar{D}^i(\varepsilon^j) - D_0^i} \frac{dU^i(\varepsilon^i, \varepsilon^j)}{dw^{i2}} \, dF(\varepsilon^i) \right] dF^j(\varepsilon^j)$$

$$= q * \frac{dD_0^i}{dw^{i2}} + (1 - q) * E\left[\frac{dU^{i2}}{dw^{i2}} \bigg|_{D^i < \bar{D}^i} \right]$$

Appendix 10:

The maximization problem

$$\max_{C^{i1},K} \quad N = (U^{m1} + U^{m2} - D^m) * (U^{f1} + U^{f2} - D^f)$$

$$\max_{C^{i2},K} \quad N_2 = (U^{m2} - D^{m2}) * (U^{f1} - D^{f2})$$

subject to

$$C^{mt} + C^{ft} = Y_t \qquad\qquad t = 1,2$$

yield the following first order conditions for period 1:

$$\lambda_1 = \frac{\partial U^{f1}}{\partial C^{f1}}(U^{m1} + U^{m2} - D^m) = \frac{\partial U^{m1}}{\partial C^{m1}}(U^{f1} + U^{f2} - D^f)$$

which is used in transforming the total differential of the Nash function:

$$\begin{aligned}
dN &= (U^{m1} + U^{m2} - D^m)(dU^{f1} + dU^{f2}) + (U^{f1} + U^{f2} - D^f)(dU^{m1} + dU^{m2}) \\
&= (U^{m1} + U^{m2} - D^m)\left[\frac{\partial U^{f1}}{\partial C^{f1}}dC^{f1} + \frac{\partial U^{f1}}{\partial K}dK + dU^{f2}\right] + \\
&\quad + (U^{f1} + U^{f2} - D^f)\left[\frac{\partial U^{m1}}{\partial C^{m1}}dC^{m1} + \frac{\partial U^{m1}}{\partial K}dK + dU^{m2}\right] \\
&= \lambda_1 dY_1 + \qquad\qquad\qquad\qquad\qquad\qquad\qquad\qquad (A10.1) \\
&\quad + (U^{m1} + U^{m2} - D^m)\left[\frac{\partial U^{f1}}{\partial K}dK + dU^{f2}\right] + \\
&\quad + (U^{f1} + U^{f2} - D^f)\left[\frac{\partial U^{m1}}{\partial K}dK + dU^{m2}\right]
\end{aligned}$$

The total differential for period 2 is derived analogously:

$$\lambda_2 = \frac{\partial U^{f2}}{\partial C^{f2}}(U^{m2} - D^{m2}) = \frac{\partial U^{m2}}{\partial C^{m2}}(U^{f2} - D^{f2})$$

$$dN_2 = (U^{m2} - D^{m2})(dU^{f2} - dD^{f2}) + (U^{f2} - D^{f2})(dU^{m2} + dD^{m2})$$

$$= (U^{m2} - D^{m2})\left[\frac{\partial U^{f2}}{\partial C^{f2}}dC^{f2} + \frac{\partial U^{f1}}{\partial K}dK - dD^{f2}\right] +$$
$$+ (U^{f2} - D^{f2})\left[\frac{\partial U^{m2}}{\partial C^{m2}}dC^{m2} + \frac{\partial U^{m2}}{\partial K}dK - dD^{m2}\right]$$

$$= \lambda_2 dY_2 +$$
$$+ (U^{m2} - D^{m2})\left[\frac{\partial U^{f2}}{\partial K}dK - dD^{f2}\right] +$$
$$+ (U^{f2} - D^{f2})\left[\frac{\partial U^{m2}}{\partial K}dK - dD^{m2}\right]$$

This gives:

(A10.2)
$$U^{m2}dU^{f2} + U^{f2}dU^{m2} = \lambda_2 dY_2 + D^{m2}dU^{f2} + D^{f2}dU^{m2} +$$
$$+ (U^{m2} - D^{m2})\frac{\partial U^{f2}}{\partial K}dK + (U^{f2} - D^{f2})\frac{\partial U^{m2}}{\partial K}dK$$

Using (A10.1) and (A10.2) the total differential can be written as

$$dN = \lambda_1 dY_1 + \lambda_2 dY_2$$
$$+ \left[(U^{m1} + U^{m2} - D^m)\frac{\partial U^{f1}}{\partial K} + (U^{m2} - D^{m2})\frac{\partial U^{f2}}{\partial K}\right]dK$$
$$+ \left[(U^{f1} + U^{f2} - D^f)\frac{\partial U^{m1}}{\partial K} + (U^{f2} - D^{f2})\frac{\partial U^{m2}}{\partial K}\right]dK$$
$$+ [U^{m1} - (D^m - D^{m2})]dU^{f2} + [U^{f1} - (D^f - D^{f2})]dU^{m2}$$

$$= \lambda_1 dY_1 + \lambda_2 dY_2$$
$$+ (s_1^m U_K^{f1} + s_1^f U_K^{m1})dK + (s_2^m U_K^{f2} + s_2^f U_K^{m2})dK$$
$$+ (s_1^m - s_2^m)dU^{f2} + (s_1^f - s_2^f)dU^{m2}$$

Using

$$g_t = \frac{s_t^f}{s_t^m}$$

as a measure of the bargaining power, the total differential of the Nash function can be written as follows

$$dN = \lambda_1 dY_1 + \lambda_2 dY_2$$
$$+ s_1^m(U_K^{f1} + g_1 U_K^{m1})dK + s_2^m(U_K^{f2} + g_2 U_K^{m2})dK$$
$$+ (s_1^m - s_2^m)dU^{f2} + (s_1^m g_1 + s_2^m g_2)dU^{m2}$$

In order to compare the bargaining approach with the traditional one which implies unchanged bargaining positions, this expression is extended and decomposed into a part with time constant weights of the individual marginal utilities with respect to an addititonal child and a part with changing individual influences:

$$dN = \lambda_1 dY_1 + \lambda_2 dY_2$$
$$+ s_1^m(U_K^{f1} + g_1 U_K^{m1})dK + s_2^m(U_K^{f2} + g_1 U_K^{m2})dK$$
$$+ s_2^m(g_2 - g_1)U_K^{m2}dK$$
$$+ (s_1^m - s_2^m)dU^{f2} + g_1(s_1^m - s_2^m)dU^{m2}$$
$$+ s_2^m(g_1 - g_2)dU^{m2}$$

$$= \lambda_1 dY_1 + \lambda_2 dY_2 \qquad (A10.3)$$
$$+ s_1^m(U_K^{f1} + g_1 U_K^{m1})dK + s_2^m(U_K^{f2} + g_1 U_K^{m2})dK$$
$$+ (s_1^m - s_2^m)(dU^{f2} + g_1 dU^{m2}) + s_2^m(dU^{m2} - U_K^{m2}dK)(g_1 - g_2)$$

$$= \lambda_1 dY_1 + \lambda_2 dY_2$$
$$+ h(K)dK$$
$$+ f(g_1, g_2, .dK)$$

The second line of this expression can be interpreted as the marginal evaluation of a child by the household as a whole, given a time independent household utility function. The third line represents the effect which results from a change in the bargaining power. This line disappears when the bargaining positions are identical in both periods, which is the necessary assumption in interpreting the traditional model as a special bargaining model. If the bargaining positions remain unchanged, then

$$g_1 = g_2 \quad \text{holds, and with (4.9)} \quad g_1 = g_2 = -\frac{dU^{f2}}{dU^{m2}}.$$

Then, both terms in the third line in (A10.3) dissapear.

In the traditional model

$$\max_{C^1, C^2, K} U(C, K) = U^1 + U^2$$

s. t. $\quad C^t = Y_t$

the total differential results as follows:

$$\begin{aligned}
dU &= dU^1 + dU^2 \\
&= \frac{\partial U^1}{\partial C^1} dC^1 + \frac{\partial U^1}{\partial K} dK + \frac{\partial U^2}{\partial C^2} dC^2 + \frac{\partial U^2}{\partial K} dK \\
&= \lambda_1 dY_1 + \lambda_2 dY_2 + \frac{\partial U^1}{\partial K} dK + \frac{\partial U^2}{\partial K} dK.
\end{aligned} \qquad (A10.4)$$

Comparing (A10.3) and (A10.4) the traditional model can be seen as a special case of the bargaining model. Interpreting the two terms in the second line of (A10.3) as the evaluation on the household level and using the sum of the marginal household utilities in both periods as a linear approximation for the function h we get the following nested model:

$$\begin{aligned}
dN &= \lambda_1 dY_1 + \lambda_2 dY_2 + h(K) dK + f(g_1, g_2, dK) \\
&\approx \lambda_1 dY_1 + \lambda_2 dY_2 + \frac{\partial U^1}{\partial K} dK + \frac{\partial U^2}{\partial K} dK + f(g_1, g_2, dK) \\
&= dU + f(g_1, g_2, dK)
\end{aligned}$$

Bibliography

Amemiya, T. (1985), Advanced Econometrics, Oxford: Blackwell.

Anbar, D., Kalai, E. (1978), A One-Shot Bargaining Problem. *International Journal of Game Theory*. 13-18.

Antonides, G., Hagenaars, A. J. M. (1990), The Distribution of Welfare in the Household. Papers on Economic Psychology, 81. Erasmus University Rotterdam.

Ashenfelter, O. (1979), Comment. In: Lloyd C.B., Andrews E.S., Gilroy C.L. (ed.), *Women in the Labor Market*. New York: Columbia University Press.

Ashenfelter, O., Heckman, J. (1974), The Estimation of Income and Substitution Effects in a Model of Family Labor Supply. *Econometrica*, 42, 73-85.

Ashworth, J..S., Ulph, D..T. (1981), Household Models. In: Brown C.V. (ed.), *Taxation and Labor Supply*, London: Allen & Unwin

Aumann, R. J. (1974), Subjectivity and Correlations in Randomized Strategies. *Journal of Mathematical Economics*, 1, 67-96.

Axelrod, R. (1986), An Evolutionary Approach to Norms. *American Political Science Review*, 80(4), 1095-1111.

Azariadis, C. (1981), Implicit Contracts and Related Topics: A Survey. In: Hornstein Z., Grice J., Webb A. (eds.), *The Economic of the Labour Market*, London: Her Majesty's Stationary Office, 221-248.

Barnes, R., Gillingham, R. (1984), Demographic Effects in Demand Analysis: Estimation of the quadratic Expenditure System using Microdata. *Review of Economics and Statistics*, 66, 591-602.

Barten, A. P. (1967), Evidence on the Slutsky Conditions for Demand Equations. *Review of Economics and Statistics*, Vol. 49, S. 77-84.

Barten, A. P. (1969), Maximum Likelihood Esimation of a complete System of Demand Equations. *European Economic Review*, 1, 7-73.

Becker, G. S. (1960), An Economic Analysis of Fertility. In: *Demographic and Economic Change in Developed Countries*. National Bureau Committee for Economic Research. Princeton: Princeton University Press.

Becker, G. S. (1962), Investment in Human Capital. *Journal of Political Economy*, 70, Suppl., 9-49.

Becker, G. S. (1964), Human Capital. New York:Columbia University Press.

Becker, G. S. (1965), A Theory of the Allocation of Time. *Economic Journal*, 75, 493-517.

Becker, G. S. (1973), A Theory of Marriage: Part I. *Journal of Political Economy*, 81, 813-846.

Becker, G. S. (1974), A Theory of Marriage: Part II. *Journal of Political Economy*, 82, 813-846.

Becker, G. S. (1976), The Economic Approach to Human Behavior. Chicago: University of Chicago Press.

Becker, G. S. (1981), A Treatise on the Family. Cambridge: Harvard University Press.

Becker, G. S. (1985), Human Capital, Effort, and the Sexual Division of Labor. *Journal of Labor Economics*, 3, S33-S58.

Becker, G. S., Landes, E. M., Michael, R. T. (1977), An Economic Analysis of Marital Instability. *Journal of Political Economy*, 85(69), 1141-1187.

Becker, G. S., Lewis, H. G. (1973), Interaction between Quantity and Quality of Children. *Journal of Political Economy*, 81, 279-288.

Belsley, D. A., Kuh, E., Welsch, R. (1976), Regression Diagnostics: Identifying Influential Data and Sources of Collinearity. New York: Wiley.

Benham, L. (1974), Benefits of Women's Education within Marriage. In: Schultz, T. W. (eds.), *Economics of the Family*, Chicago: University of Chicago Press.

Ben-Porath, Y. (1980), The F-Connection: Families, Friends and Firms and the Organisation of Exchange. *Population and Development Review*, 6, 1-30.

Berger-Schmitt, R. (1986), Innerfamiliale Arbeitsteilung und ihre Determinanten. In: Glatzer W., Berger-Schmitt R. (eds.), *Haushaltsproduktion und Netzwerkhilfe*. Frankfurt: Campus.

Bergstrom, Th. C., Varian, H. L. (1985), When Do Market Games Have Transferable Utility? *Journal of Economic Theory*, 35, 222-233.

Berk, R. A., Berk, S. F. (1983), Supply-Side Sociology of The Family: The Challenge of the New Home Economics. *Annual Review of Sociology*, 9, 375-395.

Binmore, K., Rubinstein, A., Wolinsky, A. (1986), The Nash bargaining solution in economic modelling. *Rand Journal of Economics*, 17, 176-188.

Bolton, P. (1990), Renegotiation and the dynamics of contract design. *European Economic Review*, 34, 303-310.

Borenstein, S., Courant, P. N. (1989), How to Carve a Medical Degree: Human Capital Assets in Divorce Settlements. *Amercan Economic Review*, 79(5), 992-1009.

Boulier, B. L., Rosenzweig, M. R. (1984), Schooling, Search, and Spouse Selection: Testing Economic Theories of Marriage and Household Behavior. *Journal of Political Economy*, 92, 712-732.

Bowen, W. G., Finegan, T. A. (1969), The Economics of Labor Force Participation. Princeton: Princeton University Press.

Bull, C. (1983), Implicit Contracts in the Absence of Enforcement and Risk Aversion. *American Economic Review*, 75, 658-671.

Bull, C. (1987), The Existence of Self-enforcing Implicit Contracts. *The Quarterly Journal of Economics*, 102, 147-159.

Bumpass, L. L., Sweet, J. A. (1972), Differentials in Marital Instability. *American Sociological Review*, Vol. 37, S. 754-766.

Cameron, S. (1985), Towards a Synthesis of Economic and Sociological Theories of Family Labour Supply, *The Journal of Interdisciplinary Economics*, 1, 43-57.

Carmichael, H. L. (1989), Self-Enforcing Contracts, Shirking, and Life Cycle Incentives. *Journal of Economic Perspectives*, 3, 65-83.

Carlin, P. St. (1985), The Importance of Bargaining Phenomena in the Economics Marriage and the Household Decision-Making: Theoretical and Empirical Explorations. Ph.D. Dissertation, University of Pittsburgh.

Chatterjee, K., Samuelson, W. F. (1983), Bargaining under Incomplete Information. *Operations Research*, 31, 835-851.

Cheadle, E. A. (1981), The Development of Sharing Principles in Common Law Marital Property States. *UCLA Law Review*, 28, 1269-1313.

Cherlin, A. I. (1977), The effect of children on marital dissolution. *Demography*, 14, 265-272.

Chiappori, P.-A. (1988a), Nash-Bargained Household Decisions: A Comment. *International Economic Review*, 29, 791-797.

Chiappori, P.-A. (1988b), Rational Household Labor Supply. *Econometrica*, 56, 63-89.

Chun, Y., Thomson, W. (1987), Bargaining Problems with Uncertain Disagreement Points. Working Paper No. 77, Department of Economics, Southern Illinois University.

Cigno, A. (1988), The Economics of Household Formation and Marriage. Paper presented at the ESPE-Congress, June 23-25, Mannheim.

Coase, R. H. (1960), The Problem of Social Cost, *Journal of Law and Economics*, 3, 1-44.

Corcoran, M., Duncan, G (1979), Work History, Labor Force Attachment, and Earnings Differences Between Races and Sexes, *Journal of Human Resources*, 14, 3-20.

Corcoran, M., Duncan, G., Ronza, M. (1983), A Longitudinal Analysis of white women's wages, *Journal of Human Resources*, 18, 497-520.

Cox, D. R., Oakes D. (1984), *Analysis of Survival Data*. London: Chapman and Hall.

Crawford, V. P. (1987), A Theory of Disagreement in Bargaining. In: Binmore K., Dasgupta P. (eds.), *The Economics of Bargaining*. Oxford: Basil Blackwell.

D'Amicio, R. (1983), Status Maintenance or Status Competition? Wife's Relative Wages as a Determinant of Labor Supply and Marital Instability. *Social Forces*, 61, 1186-1205.

Damme, E. Van (1987), Stability and perfection of Nash Equilibria. Berlin: Springer.

Diekmann, A. (1987), Determinanten des Heiratsalters und Scheidungsrisikos. Eine Analyse soziodemographischer Umfragedaten mit Modellen und statistischen Schätzmethoden der Verlaufsdatenanalyse. Habilitationsschrift, München.

Diewert, W.E. (1973), Afriat and Revealed Preference Theory. *Review of Economic Studies*, 40, 419-426.

Dixao, R. B., Weitzman, L. J. (1980), Evaluating the Impact of No-Fault Divorce in California. *Family Relations*, 33, 321-327.

Edlefsen, L. E. (1981), The Comparative Statics of Hedonic Price Functions and other Nonlinear Constraints. *Econometrica*, 49, 1501-1520.

Elster, J. (1989), Social Norm and Economic Theory. *Journal of Economic Perspectives*, 3(4), 99-117

Ermish, J. (1986), The Economics of the Family: Applications to Divorce and Remarriage. Discussion Paper No. 140, Centre for Economic Policy Research. London.

Fethke, C. C. (1984), An Economic Model of Asset Division in the Dissolution of Marriage. *American Economic Review*, Papers and Proceedings, 74(2), 265-270.

Freiden, A. (1974), The U.S. Marriage Market. In: Schultz T. W. (ed.), *Economics of the Family*, Chicago: University of Chicago Press.

Galler, H. P. (1979), Schulische Bildung und Heiratsverhalten. *Zeitschrift für Bevölkerungswissenschaft*, 5, 199-213.

Galler, H. P. (1988), Familiale Lebenslagen und Familienlastenausgleich - Zu den Opportunitätskosten familialer Entscheidungen. In: Felderer B. (ed.), *Familienlastenausgleich und demographische Entwicklung*, Berlin: Duncker & Humblot.

Galler, H. P. (1991), Zu den Oportunitätskosten der Familienbildung. In: Silva Gräbe: (ed.), *Der private Haushalt - erkannte, verkannte und unbekannte Dimensionen*, Frankfurt: Campus.

Gaugler, E., Schach, E., Vollmer, M. (1984), *Wiedereingliederung von Frauen in qualifizierte Berufstätigkeit nach längerer Berufsunterbrechung*. Mannheim: Forschungsstelle für Betriebswirtschaft und Sozialpolitik.

Gelles, R. J. (1979), Violence in the Family: A Review of Research in the seventies. *Journal of Marriage and the Family*, 4, 873-885.

Gelles, R.J.; Straus, M. A. (1979), Determinants of Violence in the Family: Toward a Theoretical Integration. In : Burr, W. R.; Hill, R.; Nye, F. I.; Reiss, J. L. (eds.): *Contemporary Theories about the Family*. Vol. 1, 549-581. New York, London.

Graham, J. W., Green, C. A. (1984), Estimating the Parameter of a Household Production Function with Joint Products. *Review of Economics and Statistics*, 66(2), 277-282.

Griliches, Zvi (1974), Comment. In: Schultz T. W. (ed.), *Economics of the Family*, Chicago: University of Chicago Press.

Gronau, R. (1973), The Intrafamily Allocation of Time: The Value of the Housewives' Time. *American Economic Review*, 63, 634-651.

Gronau, R. (1977), Leisure, Home Production and Work - The Theory of the Allocation of Time Revisited. *Journal of Political Economy*, 85, 1099-1123.

Gronau, R. (1986), Home Production - A Survey. In: Ashenfelter, O., Layard, R. (eds.), *Handbook of Labor Economics*, Vol. I, 273-304. North-Holland: Elsevier Science Publishers B.V.

Güth, W. (1978), Zur Theorie kollektiver Lohnverhandlungen. Baden-Baden: Nomos.

Güth, W.; Ockenfels, P.; Wendel, M. (1991), Efficiencay by Thrust in Fairness? - Multiperiod Ultimatum Bargaining Experiments with an Increasing Cake. Discussion Paper, University Frankfurt.

Gustafsson, S., Ott, N. (1987), Demographic Change, Labor Force Participation of Married Women and the Effect of Separate versus Joint Taxation of Earnings in West Germany and Sweden. Sfb3-Working Paper 241. Frankfurt.

Hahn, A. (1983), Konsensfiktion in Kleingruppen. *Kölner Zeitschrift für Soziologie und Sozialpsychologie*, 35, 210-232.

Hanefeld, U. (1984), The German Socio-economic Panel. In: American Statistical Association, Proceedings of the Social Statistical Section. Washington D.C., 117-124.

Harsanyi, J. C. (1956), Approaches To the Bargaining Problem Before and After the Theory of Games: A Critical Discussion of Zeuthen's, Hick's, and Nash's Theorie. *Econometrica*, 24, 144-157.

Harsanyi, J. C. (1977), Rational Behavior and Bargaining Equilibrium in Games and Social Situations, Cambridge: Cambridge University Press.

Harsanyi, J. C. (1979), A new general solution concept for both cooperative and noncooperative games. Rheinisch-Westfälische Akademie der Wissenschaften, Natur-, Ingenieur- und Wirtschaftswissenschaften, Vorträge N 287. Opladen.

Harsanyi, J. C.; Selten, R. (1988), A General theory of Equilibrium selection in Games. Cambridge: MIT-Press.

Hart, O., Moore, J. (1988), Incomplete Contracts and renegotiation. *Econometrica*, 56(4), 755-785.

Havens, E. M. (1973), Women, work and wedlock: a note on female marital patterns in the United States. *American Journal of Sociology*, 78, 975-981.

Heckman, J. J. (1976), The Common Structure of Statistical Models of Truncation, Sample Selection and Limited Dependent Variables and a Simple Estimator for such Models. *Annals of Economic and Social Measurement*, 5, 475-492.

Henrich, D. (1986), Unterhalt nach der Scheidung. Betrag - Dauer - Billigkeit. In: Weyers H.-G. (ed.), *Unterhalt nach Ehescheidung. Betrag, Dauer, Billigkeit.* Frankfurt: Metzner.

Hirschmann, A. O. (1970), *Exit, Voice and Loyalty*. Cambridge: University Press.

Hirshleifer, J. (1977), Shakespeare vs. Becker on Altruism: The Importance of Having the Last Word. *Journal of Economic Literature*, 15, 500-502.

Höhn, Ch. (1980), Rechtliche und demographische Einflüsse auf die Entwicklung der Ehescheidungen seit 1946. *Zeitschrift für Bevölkerungswissenschaft*, 6, 335-371.

Horney, M. J., McElroy, M. B. (1988), The Household Allocation Problem: Empirical Results from a Bargaining Model. *Research in Population Economics*, 6, 15-38.

Houseknecht, S. K., Voughan, S., Macke, A. S. (1984), Marital Disruption among professional women: the timing of career and family events. *Social Problems*, 31, 273-284.

Huber, J., Spitze, G. (1980), Considering Divorce: An Expansion of Becker's Theory of Marital Instability. *American Journal of Sociology*, 86, 75-89.

Hutchens, R. M. (1979), Welfare, Remarriage, and Marital Search, *American Economic Review*, 69, 369-379.

Kalbfleisch, J. D., Prentice, R. L. (1980), *The Statistical Analysis of Failure Time Data*. New York; Wiley.

Kaneko, M. (1976), Note on Transferable Utility, *International Journal of Game Theory*, 5, 183-185.

Kaufmann, F. X., Strohmeier, K. P. (1987), Partnerbeziehungen und Familienentwicklung in Nordrhein-Westfalen. Generatives Verhalten im sozialen und regionalen Kontext. Abschlußbericht über das Forschungsprojekt "Generatives Verhalten in Nordrhein-Westfalen". Schriftenreihe des Ministerpräsidenten des Landes Nordrhein-Westfalen, No. 50. Düsseldorf.

Keely, M. C. (1977), The Economics of Family Formation, *Economic Inquiry*, 15, 238-250.

Kenny, L. W. (1983), The Accumulation of Human Capital during Marriage by Males. *Economic Inquiry*, 21, 223-231.

Killingsworth, M. R. (1983), *Labor Supply*. Cambridge: Cambridge University Press.

Killingsworth, M. R., Heckman, J. J.(1986), Female Labor Supply: A Survey. In: Ashenfelter O., Layard R. (eds.), *Handbook of Labor Economics*, I, 103-204.North-Holland: Elsevier Science Publishers B.V.

Kirchler, E. (1988), Household Economic Decision Making. In: Van Raaij, W. F., van Veldhofen, G. M., Wärneryd, K. E. (eds.), *Handbook of Economic Psychology*, 258-292, Dordrecht: Kluwer.

Klein, B. (1985), Self-Enforcing Contracts. *Journal of Institutional and Theoretical Economics*, 141, 594-600.

Klein, B., Leffler, K. B. (1981), The Role of Market Forces in Assuring Contractual Performance. *Journal of Political Economy*, 89, 615-641.

Kooreman, P. (1988), Household Labor Force Participation as a Cooperative Game; an Empirical Model. Research Memorandum FEW 323, Department of Economics, Tilburg University.

Kooreman, P., Kapteyn, A. (1985), Estimation of a Game Theoretical Model of Household Labor Supply. Research Memorandum FEW 180, Department of Economics, Tilburg University.

Kooreman, P., Kapteyn, A. (1987), On the Identifiability of Household Production Functions with Joint Products: a Comment. Research Memorandum FEW 254, Department of Economics, Tilburg University.

Krelle, W. (1976), Preistheorie, Teil I und II, 2. Auflage, Tübingen: J.C.B. Mohr.

Lam, D. (1988), Marriage Markets and Assortative Mating with Household Public Goods. *Journal of Human Resources*, 23, 462-487.

Lancaster, K. (1966), A New Approach to Consumer Theory, *Journal of Political Economy*, 74, 132-157.

Lehrer, E., Nerlove, M. (1981), The Labor Supply and Fertility Behavior of Married Women. *Research in Population Economics*, 3, 123-145.

Leuthold, J. H. (1968), An empirical Study of Formula Income Transfers and the Work Decision of the Poor. *Journal of Human Resources*, 3, 312-323.

Lommerud, K. E. (1989), Marital Division of Labor with Risk of Divorce: The Role of "Voice" Enforcement of Contracts, *Journal of Labor Economics*, 7, 113-127.

Lundberg, S. (1988), Labor Supply of Husbands and Wives: A Simultaneous Equation Approach. *The Review of Economics and Statistics*, XLL, 2, S. 224-235.

Maddala, G.S. (1983), Limited-dependent and qualitative variables in econometrics. Cambridge: Cambridge University Press.

Manser, M., Brown, M. (1979), Bargaining Analysis of Household Decisions. In: Lloyd C.B., Andrews E.S., Golroy C.L. (eds.), *Women in the Labor Market*. New York: Columbia University Press.

Manser, M., Brown, M. (1980), Marriage and Household Decision-Making: A Bargaining Analysis. *International Economic Review*, 21(1), 31-44.

Marrewijk, Ch. van; Bergeijk, P. A. G. van (1990), Trade uncertainty and specialization. Social versus private planning. *De Economist*, 138(1), 15-32.

McDonald, M.M., Rindfuss, R.R. (1981), Earnings, relative income and family formation. *Demography*, 18, 123-136.

McElroy, M. B., (1990), The empirical Content of Nash-Bargained Household Behavior. *Journal of Human Resources*, XXV(4), 559-583

McElroy, M. B., Horney, M. Jean (1981), Nash-Bargained Household Decisions: Towards a Generalisation of the Theory of Demand. *International Economic Review*, 22(2), 333-349

McElroy, M. B., Horney, M. J. (1990), Nash-Bargained Household Decisions: Reply. *International Economic Review*, 31(1), 237-242

Michael, R. M. (1979), Determinants of Divorce. In: Levy-Garboua L. (ed.), Sociological Economics, 223-254, London: Sage.

Mincer, J., Polachek, S. (1974), Family Investments in Human Capital: Earnings of Women. *Journal of Political Economy*, 82, S76-S108.

Mincer, J., Ofek, H. (1982), Interrupted Work Carreers: Deprecation and Restoration of Human Capital. *Journal of Human Resources*, 17, 3-24.

Montgomery, M., Trussell, J. (1986), Models of Marital Status and Childbearing. In: Ashenfelter O., Layard R. (eds.), *Handbook of Labor Economics*, Vol. I, 205-271. North-Holland: Elsevier Science Publishers B.V.

Moreh, J. (1986), Women, Men and Society. *Kyklos*, 39, 209-229.

Mott, F. L., Moore, S. F. (1979), The Causes of Marital Disruption Among Young American Women: An Interdisciplinary Perspective. *Journal of Marriage and the Family*, 41, 355-365.

Muth, R. F. (1966), Household Production and Consumer Demand, *Econometrica*, 34, 699-708.

Nash, J. (1950), The Bargaining Problem, *Econometrica*, 18, 155-162.

Nash, J. (1953), Two-Person Cooperative Games, *Econometrica*, 21, 128-140.

Nerlove, M. (1974), Toward a new Theory of Population and Economic Growth. In: Schultz T.W. (ed.), *Economics of the Family*, Chicago: University of Chicago Press.

Ott, N. (1989a), Haushaltsökonomie und innerfamiliäre Arbeitsteilung: eine spieltheoretische Analyse familialer Entscheidungen. Dissertation, Bielefeld.

Ott, N. (1989b), Familienbildung und familiale Entscheidungsfindung aus verhandlungstheoretischer Sicht. In: Wagner, G.; Ott, N.; Hoffmann-Nowotny, H.-J. (ed.): *Familienbildung und Erwerbstätigkeit im demographischen Wandel*. Berlin: Springer.

Ott, N., Rolf, G. (1987), Zur Entwicklung von Frauenerwerbstätigkeit und Geburtenhäufigkeit. Sfb3-Arbeitspapier Nr. 244. Frankfurt.

Ouchi, W. G. (1980), Markets, Bureaucracies, and Clans. *Administrative Science Quarterly*, 25, 129-147.

Parker, J. E., Shaw, L. B. (1968), Labor Force Participation in Metropolitan Areas. *Southern Economic Journal*, 34, 538-547.

Parsons, D. O. (1986), The Employment Relationship: Job Attachment, Work Effort, and the Nature of Contracts. In: Ashenfelter O., Layard R. (eds.), *Handbook of Labor Economics*, Vol. II, 789-848, North-Holland: Elsevier Science Publishers B.V.

Pen, J. (1952), A Genral Theory of Bargaining. *American Economic Review*, 42, 24-42.

Perles, M.A., Maschler, M. (1981), The Super-Additive Solution for the NASH Bargaining Game. *International Journal of Game Theory*, 10(3/4), 163-193.

Peters, E. (1986), Marriage and Divorce: Informational Constraints and Private Contracting. *American Economic Review*, 76, 437-454.

Phlips, L. (1974), *Applied Consumption Analysis*, Amsterdam: North-Holland.

Pollak, R. A.: (1977), Price Dependent Preferences. *American Economic Review*, 767, 64-75.

Pollak, R. A.: (1985), A Transaction Cost Approach to Families and Households. *Journal of Economic Literature*, XXIII, S. 581-608.

Pollak, R. A., Wales, T. J. (1981), Demographic Variables in Demand Analysis. *Econometrica*, 49, 1533-1551.

Preston, S.J., Richards, A.Th. (1975), The Influence of women's work opportunities on marriage rates. *Demography*, 12, 202-222.

Pross, H. (1975), *Die Wirklichkeit der Hausfrau*. Reinbeck: Rowohlt

Rogerson, W. P. (1984), Efficient reliance and damage measures for breach of contract. *The Rand Journal of Economics*, 15, 39-53.

Rosen, S. (1985), Implicit Contracts: A Survey. *Journal of Economic Literature*, XXIII, 1144-1175.

Ross, C. E. (1987), The Division of Labor at Home. *Social Forces*, 65, 816-833.

Roth, A. E. (1979), Axiomatic Models of Bargaining. Berlin: Springer.

Rubinstein, A. (1982), Perfect Equilibrium in a Bargaining Model, *Econometrica*, 50, 97-111

Samuelson, P. A. (1956), Social Indifference Curves. *Quartely Journal of Economics*, 10(1), 1-22.

Sander, W. (1985), Women, Work and Divorce. *American Economic Review*, 75, 519-523.

Scanzoni, J., Polonko, K. (1980), A Conceptual Approach to Explicit Marital Negotiation. *Journal of Marriage and the Family*, 42, 31-44.

Schelling, Th. C. (1960), The Strategy of Conflict. London: Oxford University Press.

Schilp, M.-L. (1984), "Ökonomik der Familie" - Reichweite und Begrenzungen des ökonomischen Ansatzes zur Erklärung familialen Verhaltens. Karlsruhe: M+M

Schotter, A. (1981), *The Economic Theory of Social Institutions*. Cambridge: Cambridge University Press.

Schotter, A., Schwödiauer, G. (1980), Economics and the Theory of Games: A Survey. *Journal of Economic Literature*, 18, 479-527.

Schultz, Th. W. (1959), Investment in Man: An Economist's View, *The Social Service Review*, 33, 109-117.

Seal, K. (1983), A Decade of No-Fault Divorce: What it Has Meant Financially for Women in California. *Family Advocate*, 1, 10-15.

Selten, R. (1975), Reexamination of the Perfectness Concept for Equilibrium Points in Extensive Games. *International Journal of Game Theory*, 4(1), 25-55.

Selten, R., Güth, W. (1981), Game Theoretic Analysis of Wage Bargaining in a Simple Business Cycle Model. *Journal of Mathematical Economics*, 10, 177-195.

Sen, A. K. (1985), Women, Technology and Sexual Divisions. *Trade and Development*, (UNCTAD), 6, 195-223.

Sen, A. K. (1987), Gender and Cooperatvie Conflicts. Discussion Paper No. 1342. Harvard Institute of Economic Research, Harvard University, Cambridge.

Shogren, J. F. (1989), Fairness in Bargaining Requires a Context. An experimental examination of loyality. *Economic Letters*, 31, 319-323.

Shubik, M. (1984a), Game Theory in the Social Sciences. Concept and Solutions. Cambridge: MIT Press

Shubik, M. (1984b), A Game-Theoretic Approach to Political Economy. Volume 2 of Game Theory in the Social Sciences. Cambridge: MIT Pressints in Extensive Games. *International Journal of Game Theory*, 4(1), 25-55.

Simm, R. (1989), Partnerschaft und Familienentwicklung. In: Wagner, G., Ott, N., Hoffmann-Nowotny, H.-J. (eds.), *Familienbildung und Erwerbstätigkeit im demographischen Wandel*. Berlin: Springer

Smith, A. W., Meitz, J. E. G. (1983a), Life course effects on marital disruption. *Social Indicators Research*, 13, 395-417

Smith, A. W., Meitz, J. E. G. (1983b), Cohorts, education, and the decline in undisrupted marriages. *Journal of Marriage and the Family*, 45, 613-622.

South, S. J., Spitze, G. (1986), Determinants of Divorce over the Marital Life Course. *American Sociological Review*, 51, 583-590.

Spiegel, U., Templeman, J. (1985), Interdependent Utility and cooperative Behavior. *Journal of Comparative Economics*, 9(3), 314-328.

Stark, O. (1984), Bargaining, Altruism and Demographic Phenomena. Discussion Paper No. 1109. Harvard Institute of Economic Research, Harvard University, Cambridge, Massachusetts.

Telser, L. G. (1980), A Theory of Self-Enforcing Agreements. *Journal of Business*, 53, 27-44.

Thomson, W. (1987), Monotonicity of Bargaining Solutions with Respect to the Disagreement Point. *Journal of Economic Theory*, 42, 50-58.

Thornton, A. (1977), Children and marital stability. *Journal of Marriage and the Family*, 39, 531-540.

Tölke, A. (1985), Zentrale Lebensereignisse von Frauen. Veränderungen im Lebensverlaufsmuster in den letzten 30 Jahren. Sfb3-Arbeitspapier Nr. 166, Frankfurt.

Ullmann-Margalit, E. (1977), *The Emergence of Norms*. New York: Oxford University Press.

Ulph, D. (1989), A General Non-Cooperative Nash Model of Household Consumption Behavior. Sfb3-Arbeitspapier Nr. 286. Frankfurt.

Vanberg, V. (1984), "Unsichtbare-Hand Erklärung" und soziale Normen. In: Todt H. (ed.), *Normengeleitetes Verhalten in den Sozialwissenschaften*, Berlin: Duncker & Humblot.

Varian, H. R. (1978), *Microeconomic Analysis*. New York: Norton & Company.

Varian, H. R. (1982), The Nonparametric Approach to Demand Analysis. *Econometrica*, 50, 945-973.

Varian, H. R. (1983), Non-parametric Test of Consumer Behaviour. *Review of Economic Studies*, 50, 99-110.

Wagner, G (1991), Socio Economic Panel for Germany, ESF Working Paper, Network "Household Panel Studies", Essex.

Weiss, Y., Willis, R. J. (1985), Children as Collective Goods and Divorce Settlements. *Journal of Labor Economics*, 3, 268-292.

White, H. (1980), Using Least Squares to Approximate Unknown Regression Function. *International Economic Review*, 21, 149-170.

Williamson, O. E. (1986), Economic Organisation: Firms, Markets and policy control. Brighton: Wheatsheaf.

Wilson, R. (1985), Reputations in games and markets. In: Roth A. E. (ed.), *Game theoretic models of bargaining*, 27-62. Cambridge: Cambridge University Press.

Witt, U. (1986), Evolution and Stability of Cooperation without Enforcable Contracts. *Kyklos*, 39, 245-266.

Woolley, F. (1988), A Non-cooperative Model of Family Decision Making. Working paper No. TIDI 125, London School of Economics and Political Science.

Zamek-Glyscinski, W. von (1985), Neoklassische Bevölkerungsökonomik. München: Florentz

Zeuthen, F. (1930), Problems of Monopoly and Economic Welfare. London: Routledge.

Zimmermann, K. F. (1985), *Familienökonomie*. Berlin: Springer.

Index

agreement, 19;25;98
    and binding force, 77;86;98;110
    ex-ante negotiation, 133
    ex-post negotiation, 135
    implicit assumption in non-cooperative games, 26-27
    on divorce, 173
    on future distribution, 104

altruism, 7
    altruistic behavior, 21
    altruistic head, 7;14
    test of Pareto efficiency, 157

axiomatic
    model, 28;127
    solution concept, 28

balance intrafamily, 119
    of power, 177-182

bargaining
    in the case of divorce, 173
    outcome, 28;33
    position
        changes in, 42;80;83;88;92;95;96;103;106;136;179;191;196
        in period 2, 75;77;78;84;85
        symmetry, 63;65;186;191
    power, 29;37;119;161;162;165;171;178;186;187;191
        and earning capacity, 88
        and specialization, 69-72;99
        changes in, 74;84;99;102;111;121;125;126
    process, 27;33;79;101;108;127;133;169;173;174

bargaining effect, 44;56;57;63-64;83;84;86-89;92-95;96;155;184;191

battle of sexes, 25

behavior
    cooperative, 19;27;105;165
    non-cooperative, 21;22;30;106;113;114;115;119

beliefs, 115

binding force, 73;75;98-103;110-126

birth
- control, 185-191
- rate, 13

breach of contract, 73;107;189;196
- costs, 74;112;111-125
- incentive, 74;104;110
- risk, 105
- sanctions, 111

budget constraint, 8;24;34;41;47;48;78;157

capital, 66;70;86;89;155

child care, 12;13;39;105;106;126;156;186;189;190;194

communication, 25;26;27;113;123;124

composition of household, 14;70;71;163

conflict, 20;30;127
- outcome, 27;30;36;38;39;48;169;177
  - and specialization, 69-72
  - and wage changes, 56-57
  - in period 2, 73;74;76;79;86;87
  - political interventions, 122
- point, 27;34;35;78;100;104;115;144;145;155;156;177;191

consumption, 6;7;8;9;21;24;33;34;40;46;47;73;91;100;152;157;170;177
- joint, 23;110

contract
- binding, 26;73;84
- explicit, 110
- gains from, 20
- implicit, 110;196
- long-term, 19;23;74;104;194
- self-enforcing, 110;111-120
- short-term, 73
- third-party enforcement, 111;120-125

cooperation, 117;120;132;169
- gains from, 20;33;36;37;38;113;115;124;137;192
- non-cooperation, 105

coordination, 25;123;124;125

discrete choice, 103-105;164;165-170;182;186

disequilibrium, 25;196

disruption of employment, 39;103;106;112;113;126;181;182;191;194;195;197

division of work, 8;9;10;11;13;15;19;46;53;56;96-97;125;130;141;168;194

divorce, 16;25;28;127;130
- empirical model, 173-176;192-196
- in traditional models, 15-16
- law, 121-123

earning capacity, 39;68;69;71;74;88;90;91;101;103;105;106;141;168;176;177;187;191;194
emotional
  attachments, 117
  exchange, 119
  relationship, 21;118
  security, 15;21
enforceability, 27;80;93;98;101;102;103;105;108;110
equilibrium, 22;23;25;33;123;160;196
  non-cooperative, 30
  prisoner's dilemma, 105;107
  renegotiation proof, 113;114
  subgame perfect, 111;114;127
  threat game, 32;114
exchange, 20;46;118;120
  market for, 20;69;70;71;85;87
  organization, 19-22
expectations, 33;75;76;124;128
external alternatives, 15;18;26;32;42;56;68;69;71;75;127;131;156;173;196
family gains, 26;197
fertility, 13;12-14;105-109;125;126;182-191
government, 120;124
hazard
  moral, 122;124
  rate model, 192
heterogeneity, 154;164
household production, 6;7;9;10;20;46;47;62;65;69;70;78;87;88;89;93;125;126;197
human capital
  accumulation, 9;69;71;72;77;79;84;85;91;93;103;143
  and specialization, 69-72
  household specific, 69;70;71;103
  investment, 20;68;69;70;72;122;123;125;129
  marketable, 68;71;85;103
immaterial goods, 12;121
incomplete information, 15;20;25;108;115;117;131;132;177
insurance, 20;110;124;197
leisure, 8;9;11;12;29;37;46;47;91;156;162;177
losses
  bargaining power, 125;187
  future cooperation gains, 113;116
  human capital, 39;69;71;101;103;105;168;187;194
  income, 71;93;182;186;190;191
  reputation, 113
love, 117;118

market
    goods, 9;47;70;71
    restricted labor market, 103
    substitutes for household production, 197
    work, 8;9;46;69

marriage, 15;16;17;21;30;75;122;130;192
    contract, 120
    gain, 15;19;34;125;132;198

Nash
    gain, 60;65;89;104;108;141;185
    solution, 29;33;40;73;76;98;100;102;128;133;135

norms, 22;75;111;118;123-125

Pareto
    efficiency, 25;28;31;34;36;39;98-109;157-160
    frontier, 31;134

partnership, 15;16;21;75;111;112;114;115;119;127;128

prisoner's dilemma, 104;105;106;182;187
    generalized, 124
    repeated, 123

private goods, 24;29;121;145;170;171

productivity, 9;69;70;71;77;82;85;87;90;91;92;93;95;129;140;194

public goods, 24;29;34;113;145;170;171;197

redistribution, 21;112;119;121;122;125;173;176

remarriage, 16;174

reservation wage, 82;93;94;95

sanctions, 74;75;111;118;124;126

skills
    household, 55;69;70;71;86;90;103
    market, 68;103

Slutsky decomposition, 5;58;59;146;155

specialization, 9;13;54;69;81;122;125
    gains from, 15;17;55;70;193
    in household production, 57;69;70;72;81;90;95;101;126;141;181
    in market work, 69;70;81

substitution effect, 41;44;59;66;83;84;85;90-92;95;145
    income compensated, 59;62
    income induced, 61-62;65

sunk costs, 103

taxation, 52;53;55

threat, 30;110
   credible, 38;115;116;127
   game, 30
   non-cooperation, 113-115
   threat point, 27;29;79;98
   with dissolution, 31-32;169

time
   allocation, 6;23;96
      and divorce probability, 130;141-143
      dynamic bargaining model, 80
      effects on bargaining power, 95
      non-cooperative models, 23-24
      single-person household, 57;86
      static bargaining model, 56
      traditional models, 7-12
   constraint, 8;48;78
   household work, 8;9;50;52
   input factor, 7;9;11;12;47
   leisure, 8
   market work, 8;50;52;156
   opportunity costs, 12
   time intensive technology, 12;70;89
   time saving technology, 70;87
   types of use, 7;10;11;46;81;162

transaction costs, 20;46;70;89

transferable
   goods, 12;46
   utility, 28

trust, 21;118;124;189

welfare effect, 59-61;65;66;83;84;89-90;92;96

The author acknowledges with deep appreciation the help given so willingly by Mrs. Martin Luther King, Jr., during the many months this book was in preparation. Her kindness in welcoming the author to her home and in providing her with firsthand material has made the writing of this book a memorable experience.

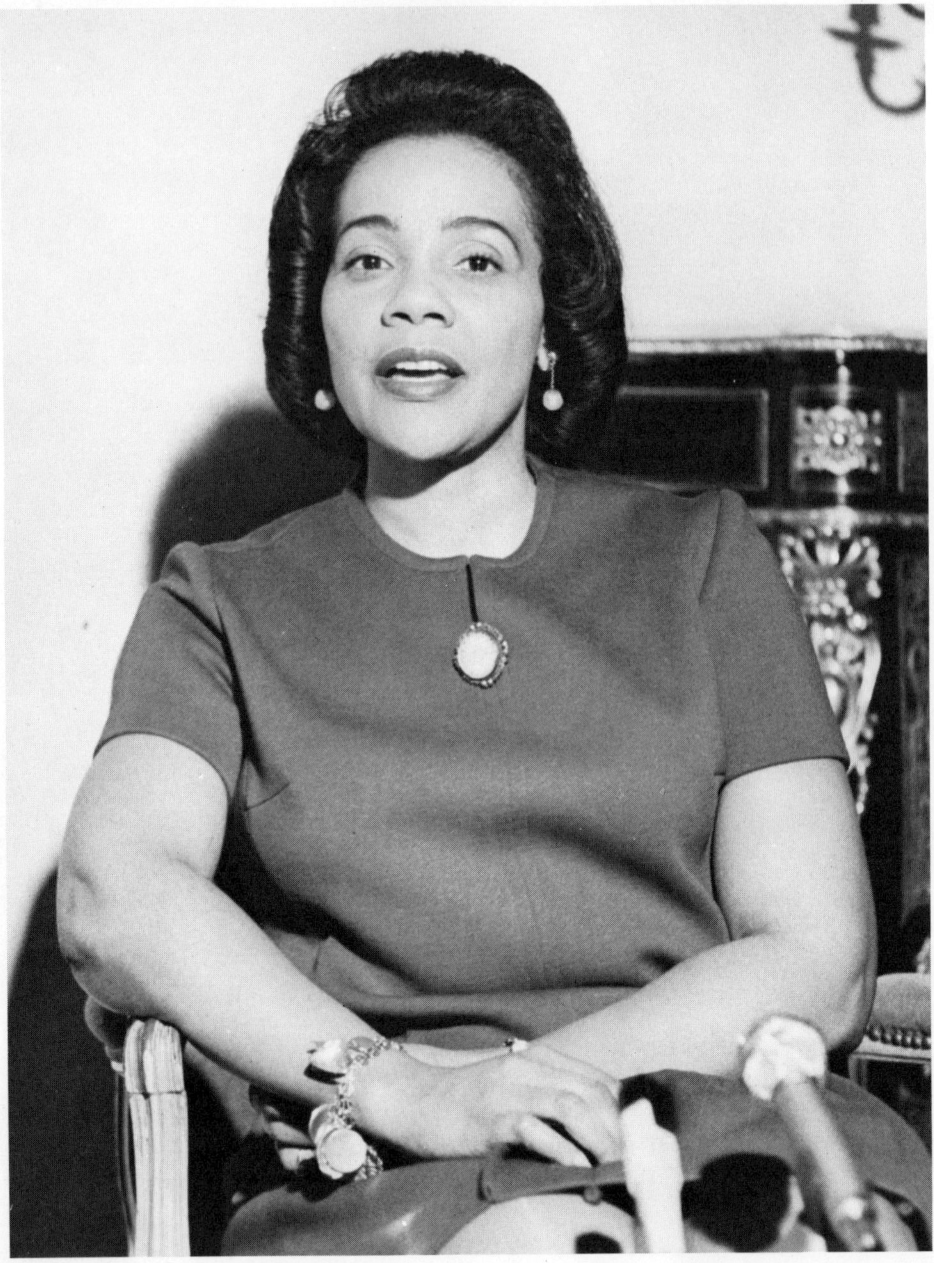

Coretta Scott King

by Lillie Patterson

GARRARD PUBLISHING COMPANY
CHAMPAIGN, ILLINOIS

For Coretta's parents, Bernice and Obie Scott, and all the brave black people who are "keeping the dream alive"

Picture Credits:

Harry Benson from Black Star: p. 75
Dennis Brack from Black Star: p. 76
Robert Cohen from Black Star: p. 2
Ebony Magazine. Courtesy of Mrs. Martin Luther King, Jr.: p. 39, 87 (bottom)
Bob Fitch from Black Star: p. 81 (bottom right)
Food and Agriculture Organization, United Nations: p. 83
Mrs. Martin Luther King, Jr.: p. 5
Leviton-Atlanta from Black Star: p. 53 (bottom)
New Lady Magazine. Courtesy of Mrs. Martin Luther King, Jr.: pp. 25, 31
Paris Match from Pictorial Parade: p. 53 (top)
Photoreporters: p. 67
T.S. Satyan from Black Star: p. 80 (top)
Steve Schapiro from Black Star: p. 62
Moneta Sleet, Jr. *Ebony* Magazine: pp. 87 (middle), 91
Betty Statler. *Time* Magazine © Time, Inc.: p. 81 (bottom left)
London *Times* from Pictorial Parade: p. 80 (bottom)
United Press International. Courtesy of Mrs. Martin Luther King, Jr.: p. 28
United Press International: pp. 70
Grey Villet. Time-Life Picture Agency © Time, Inc.: p. 44
Steve Wall from Black Star: p. 87 (top)
Wide World: p. 81 (top)

Cover photograph by Fletcher Drake of Freelance Photographers Guild

Library of Congress Cataloging in Publication Data

Patterson, Lillie.
   Coretta Scott King.

   (Americans all)
   Includes index
   SUMMARY: A biography of the wife of the slain civil rights leader, Martin Luther King, Jr.
     1. King, Coretta Scott, 1927 -   —Juvenile literature. [1. King, Coretta Scott, 1927- 2. Afro-Americans—Biography] I. Title.
E185.97.K47P37   323.4'092'4 [B]   76-19077
ISBN 0-8116-4585-1

Copyright © 1977 by Lillie Patterson
All rights reserved. Manufactured in the U.S.A.

Contents

1. Signs and Singing 7
2. Church and School 13
3. Miss Olive Williams and Music . . 21
4. College and Career 27
5. Martin! 34
6. Walking Tall Together 41
7. Courage and Nonviolence 48
8. Dangers and Dreams 55
9. Teaching the Children to Understand 65
10. "We Must Carry On!" 77
11. "Keeping the Dream Alive" 84
    Index 95

1. Signs and Singing

As Coretta Scott sang, the sweet notes rose on the soft May air. The chop-chopping of her hoe kept time to the tune. "This little light of mine, I'm going to let it shine."

"Let it shine, shine, shine." Her sister Edythe sang along as the two girls hoed weeds in their cornfield.

They made a pretty picture, framed by the late-spring greening. Seven-year-old Coretta was chubby, with strong arms and legs. Edythe, ten, was taller and slimmer.

Both girls had peach-tan skin and long black hair that glinted in the sunlight.

Then the picture changed. Their mother, Bernice McMurry Scott, joined them in the field. She had high cheekbones and hair that hung in two braids over her shoulders.

The Scott family lived in Heiberger, in Perry County, Alabama. On their farm they raised corn, peas, potatoes, and garden vegetables. The year was 1934. Times were hard, especially for black families like the Scotts.

Coretta, Edythe, and their mother worked in the field until late afternoon. Tired and hungry, they came home to more work. Coretta helped to milk the cows, feed the hogs and chickens, and gather eggs. After that she brought buckets of water from the backyard well.

Coretta heard the chugging of a truck and ran to meet her father and young brother as they rode into the yard. Obie Scott had taken his youngest child with him on the truck that day. Coretta's father hauled lumber for a white sawmill owner.

Obie Leonard, talking all the time, jumped from the truck. "I saw the big logs at the sawmill, and daddy let me—"

"Oh, hush!" Coretta put a hand over her brother's mouth.

"Don't hush me!" With both hands Obie gave her a push.

Coretta's large eyes flashed in anger. She caught Obie and sent him tumbling head over heels.

"Enough!" Their father held Coretta with one hand, Obie with the other. "No fighting in this family. Young lady, you must watch that temper of yours. I keep telling you that."

Coretta's anger left as quickly as it came. Hand in hand with Obie and her father, she went inside the frame house. This was home, where Coretta was born on April 27, 1927. The house had only two rooms, with bare pine floors. In the kitchen stood a big wood-burning stove, on which their mother was cooking supper. In the other room were two double beds and a wide fireplace.

After supper the family sat on the front porch. "Let's hear some music," Coretta said. She went into the bedroom and turned the handle of the Victrola to get it started. Snapping her fingers and tapping her toes, she began singing with the music. Soon everyone on the porch was singing with her.

Next morning the children were up with the sun. It was Saturday, and their father was taking them to town. The family piled into the truck for the twelve-mile drive to Marion, the county seat. They found the town bustling with farm folk who were buying and selling. Little Obie went shopping with his father. Coretta and Edythe went with their mother to buy cloth for dresses. Coretta chose blue, Edythe yellow, and their mother white.

After that the girls walked to a store to buy ice-cream cones. A big sign at the front door stopped them. "Whites Only," it read. Another sign on a side door said "Colored Entrance." Coretta and Edythe had to wait until all the whites in the store were served. Then the clerk handed them their ice cream at the side door.

Such signs and customs were familiar to children growing up in the South. The signs kept the races apart, or segregated. Many whites looked down on black people and felt they were not their equals. According to laws and rules, the two races could not sit, eat, go to school, or have any kind of social life together.

On the way home Coretta and her

11

family stopped to leave the dress material with Mrs. Scott's mother. Grandma Mollie McMurry made most of their dresses. They found her working in her flower garden.

Grandpa Martin McMurry was part Indian. He was a proud man and walked straight and tall. Coretta always enjoyed visiting him and reading some of the many books he owned.

"I went to school only a few days in my life," Grandpa McMurry often said. "But I taught myself to read well by studying the Bible. And I worked hard so I could buy my own land."

In spite of hardships and harsh laws, black people were doing many things to make their lives better. Coretta Scott learned this early. She had big dreams for herself and the future. Happily, she led the whole family in singing on the way home.

2. Church and School

It was Sunday and Children's Day at church. Coretta put on her new blue dress. Then her mother tied blue ribbons in her hair.

The Scotts drove to church in the truck. They passed other families, riding in farm wagons. Some of them were walking. Most of the walkers wore old shoes or were barefoot, for they carried their good shoes. Before they entered the church, they wiped the dust from their feet and put on their "Sunday" shoes.

The Mount Tabor Church was small.

Paint peeled from the boards. The benches were homemade. Oil-burning lamps hung from the ceiling, and a wood-burning stove stood in the middle of the floor. In Coretta's eyes, it was a grand church.

The people made it so. Most of the members were kinfolk. Coretta's other grandfather, Jeff Scott, was Sunday School superintendent and also the leading church officer. The black people of the community looked up to him as their foremost leader. He and his wife, Cora, had worked, saved, and bought a 300-acre farm. Grandma Cora had died before Coretta was born.

In honor of Children's Day, the young people of the church gave a program. Coretta sang a solo, and then she and Edythe sang together. "Coretta acts just like her Grandma Cora," some of the old folks said. Grandma Cora had been a strong woman, with an iron will and a lovely singing voice. Coretta was named for her.

The church had a preacher only two Sundays a month. Other Sundays Grandpa Scott led the services, and Grandpa McMurray led the singing. Coretta's mother and several of her aunts and uncles sang in the choir.

For the Scott children, that summer was filled with work, singing, and fun. They had many cousins and friends to play with. Coretta could outclimb, outrace, outbox, and outfight any boy or girl her age, and many who were older.

"Try to act more like a young lady," her mother would say.

"I'll try," Coretta promised. But by the next day, her quick temper would get her in a fight with one of her playmates.

Autumn came and with it harvest time and schooldays. Grandma McMurry made Edythe and Coretta new dresses for the opening of school. Early one morning the three Scott children started out to walk the four and one-half miles to the Crossroads School.

They had walked half the way when a school bus for whites only drove past. The big wheels rolled through a puddle and splashed mud all over the children's new clothes. Inside the bus the students talked and laughed happily.

Coretta stamped her feet in anger and brushed the mud from her new dress. This was a part of the children's segregated way of life. White students rode to a neat brick school. Coretta and other black students walked to a one-room frame building.

The schoolhouse was crude, both inside and out. Part of one wall was painted black and was used in place of a blackboard. The seats were rough wooden benches. The toilets were outdoors.

There were only two teachers for all grades, one through six. That afternoon Coretta's teacher handed her a book of poetry.

"Oh, thank you," Coretta said, hugging the book to her chest. "You remembered that I like poems." She began to learn "Paul Revere's Ride" for a program.

As the months passed there was a lot of learning and a lot of singing in that building. The two teachers brought Coretta songbooks as well as poetry books. Soon she could help lead the other students in singing.

Coretta's father encouraged her. "Keep on singing. Daddy will see that his little girl has music lessons one day."

Though times were hard, the Scotts bought storybooks and records for their children. "You must learn all you can," Coretta's mother and father said. "Get a good education and try to be somebody."

The summer that Coretta was ten, she and Edythe went to work for a white cotton farmer. First they helped to hoe the long rows in the cotton fields. Then when the white puffs were ready, they worked as cotton pickers. In this way they earned money for school clothes and books.

They knew how hard their father was working on extra jobs. He had taught himself to be a barber, and he cut men's hair on weekends. He also hauled logs at night. These jobs paid little, and most of the money went to pay for the truck. Besides, he saved a small amount each month to buy a better house.

About this time Coretta learned that her father's life was in danger. She overheard what farmers said when they came to get their hair cut.

"Some white men think you're getting too uppity," the farmers told Mr. Scott. "You get hauling jobs that might have gone to them." No other black person in the neighborhood owned a truck.

A few nights later Coretta's father was very late coming home. "What happened?" his family asked anxiously.

"Trouble." His voice showed how tired he was. He explained that a crowd of white men, carrying sticks and guns, had stopped his truck. "Stay in your place, Obie," they warned. "If you don't, folks will fish you from the swamps one day."

"Were you scared, daddy?" Coretta held his hands.

"No, baby," he said gently. "I just looked them straight in the eyes. No use running scared all your life."

So Coretta Scott learned early to live with danger. Each day her father left for work, the family never knew if he would return that night. Still, he kept his head high, paid for his truck, and saved toward a house.

The happy day came when they moved. Coretta and Edythe now had a bedroom all to themselves. There was a large living room and a neat bright kitchen. Their father bought new furniture too.

Coretta was proud of the new house. And her parents were proud of her when she finished the sixth grade at the top of her class. "We will help you go as far as you can," they told her.

Coretta fairly sang her answer. "I plan to go far."

3. Miss Olive Williams and Music

As a seventh grader Coretta entered Lincoln High in Marion. The school had been started by the American Missionary Association in the 1860s. Many of the teachers were from the North. For the first time Coretta saw black and white teachers working together.

The Scotts had a hard time finding money to send both Edythe and Coretta to Lincoln. Students had to pay to go there. The Scotts also had to pay for their daughters to live with a family in

Marion. The nine miles each way was much too far to walk. A school bus took students daily to the all-white high school in Marion. But there was no bus for black high-school students.

It was at Lincoln that Coretta and her sister met Miss Olive J. Williams, a gifted black music teacher. Miss Williams opened the door to a world of music the girls had never dreamed of.

The young teacher took a special interest in the Scott sisters. "I'll work with you to develop your voice," she told Coretta. She also taught Coretta to play the piano and other instruments. Mrs. Frances Thomas, the school secretary, taught her to play the trumpet. Coretta was talented in music, and soon she could play these instruments for school programs. She often sang solos with the school chorus.

When Coretta was fifteen she was busy

with her music both at school and at church. The county was now giving some money to transport black students to and from Marion. Coretta's father got the contract. Since there was no bus available, he converted a truck, and Coretta's mother drove it. Coretta was happy that she could once again live at home.

At church Coretta played the piano and took charge of the choir. She also trained a chorus of young people. For Christmas, Easter, and other holidays, Coretta wrote musical programs and often took the leading part. She enjoyed teaching music to others and even gave piano lessons to her mother and an aunt.

The year 1942, that had started so happily for the Scotts, ended in sadness. On Thanksgiving night their home burned down. Their clothes, their furniture, everything went up in flames. The whole family moved in with Grandpa McMurry.

Grandma McMurry had died a short time before.

Now Coretta's father worked even harder than before. In time he saved enough to buy an old sawmill. In only two weeks he put it into working order. He made it bigger so it would produce more lumber. A white man saw the changes that had been made and asked to buy it.

"Sorry," Mr. Scott said. "I didn't build it to sell. I am going to work it."

"Well," the man answered, "it won't do you any good."

Soon after that the mill burned to the ground. No one knew how these fires started. Perhaps they were set by mean white men who were jealous, some people said.

Coretta was heartbroken for her father. Now the family had no home, no business, and little money.

A day to remember: Coretta Scott's graduation from Lincoln High School in 1945

Obie Scott refused to feel sorry for himself. "Things will get better," he told his family. "I am going to open another sawmill and build another house." His strong will and drive made a lasting impression upon his children.

Edythe's good news helped to make up for some of the family's troubles. She won a scholarship to Antioch College in Yellow Springs, Ohio. In 1943 she became the first full-time black student to live on the Antioch campus.

Edythe wrote back to her sister, "Oh, you'd just love it here, Coretta."

So Coretta made up her mind to win a scholarship to Antioch too. By the time she was a senior, Coretta had grown into a well-mannered young lady, with honey-clear skin, large dark eyes, and a sparkling smile. She still had her quick temper, though, and her will was strong as steel.

The students who went to Lincoln were taught to use their education to help others. Coretta began thinking about all that must be done before the "Colored" and "Whites Only" signs could be brought down. She knew that education would help in the struggle for equal rights.

Coretta Scott won a scholarship to Antioch. Like so many black students of her day, she had to leave the South for greater opportunities.

4. College and Career

"The people at Antioch are very friendly." Coretta's weekly letters gave her parents a picture of her college life. "My roommates are both white. There are six black students here, but only three were on campus during the fall semester. I am the first of my race to study elementary education, so I am eager to make good grades."

Coretta was taking part in Antioch's work-study plan. Under this plan the students studied half of the year and worked the other half. It took longer to earn a degree, but the plan enabled poor students to earn money toward their schooling.

Though she was studying education, Coretta took all the music courses she could. She studied the violin, as well as voice and piano. Dr. Walter Anderson, the only black teacher, was head of the music department. Like Olive Williams, he spent extra hours giving Coretta lessons. He encouraged her to sing in the college chorus

Coretta Scott and some of her classmates at Antioch College in spring, 1947

and in musicals. She also sang solos with the choir of a large church.

The work-study program gave Coretta a chance to meet many kinds of people. She worked in the music library and as a waitress in the college dining hall. She held jobs as a nursery-school teacher, a social worker, and a camp counselor. While working Coretta learned to watch people closely. She would listen as they talked about their problems. More and more she became interested in helping others.

One year she went home and worked with her father. She helped him to set up bookkeeping records for the store he had opened. Her brother Obie helped her plan a big recital at Lincoln School. Her family and friends were thrilled to hear how well she could sing.

Coretta found her studies as interesting as her work. When the time came for her practice teaching, however, she faced problems. The public schools in Yellow Springs had never had black teachers. So the Board of Education would not let Coretta be a student teacher. She was told to work in the all-black school in a nearby town. Angry and hurt, Coretta went to see the college president.

"Corrie, there is nothing we can do," the president said sadly.

"Well, there is something I can do," Coretta said. She refused to teach in the segregated school. Instead she did all of her practice teaching in the private school on the college campus. "I'm not going to let this get me down," she said. "I'll have to accept it, but I don't accept it as being right."

In 1948 Dr. Anderson helped Coretta get ready for her first big public concert. She gave it in nearby Springfield, Ohio. The people who came cheered her as her

Coretta Scott (fourth from right) singing in an operetta at Antioch

soprano voice filled the church. Later, Coretta sang in another concert in Harrisburg, Pennsylvania, the hometown of Olive Williams.

Each concert made Coretta more sure that she wanted a career in music. Once again she set a goal for herself: "I will become a concert singer."

Dr. Anderson and other teachers helped her in applying to the best music schools in the United States. To Coretta's delight, she was accepted by the New England Conservatory of Music in Boston, Massachusetts. It would cost a lot of money to go there, Coretta knew. So she sent more letters, asking for scholarships.

Coretta graduated from Antioch in 1951 and went home to visit her family.

That year her father had built the new house he always wanted for his family. His store was doing well, and he owned three trucks for hauling.

"We will help you go to music school," Coretta's father and mother told her.

Coretta lifted her chin. "You have helped me enough. You need to rest now."

"What are you going to do if you don't get that scholarship?" her father asked.

"I'll get a job," Coretta said. "I'll work and go to school part time until I'm able to go full time."

That fall she left for Boston. An Antioch teacher found a room for her with a wealthy white woman who lived on Beacon Hill. Coretta helped with the cleaning to pay for her room and breakfast. She received a scholarship grant, which paid for her school fees. But there was little left for food. For a time Coretta lived on crackers, peanut butter, and fruit for lunch and dinner.

Things looked brighter after the Urban League helped her to find a part-time job. Later she began to receive money from the state of Alabama. Since Southern states would not allow black students to attend their all-white colleges, they started giving aid to these students to study elsewhere.

In Boston Coretta studied voice with a former Metropolitan Opera singer. She sang with her school chorus and also with the choir of the Old South Church. She looked forward to years of hard work training for her musical career.

5. Martin!

One cold evening in Boston, Coretta answered the telephone. "Hello?"

The deep voice on the other end sounded friendly. "This is M.L. King, Jr."

"Oh!" Coretta had heard of Martin Luther King, Jr. Mary Powell, another music student, had talked about the young man known as M.L. They had grown up together in Atlanta. Coretta let Mary know that she was not interested in meeting young men—not yet. She was too busy with her music. Still, she found herself talking easily with the stranger.

"I'd like to meet you and talk some more," he said. "Perhaps we could have lunch together tomorrow."

"Fine." By this time Coretta was curious. She wanted to see this M.L. who sounded so sure of himself.

The next day she waited for him outside the music school. Soon a green car pulled up, and a smiling young man jumped out. "You're prettier than I thought," M.L. said as he helped her into the car. "Mary said I would like you."

The friendship got off to a good start. Coretta felt Martin's eyes studying her as she ate. She was wearing her best outfit, a pretty blue suit. Her long hair curled in bangs on her forehead and hung in soft waves to her shoulders.

She studied Martin too. She liked his ready smile and the way his slanting eyes crinkled when he laughed. "He *is* different," Coretta told herself.

They learned more about each other. Martin King had graduated from Morehouse College in Atlanta, and Crozer, a college for ministers in Pennsylvania. Now he was studying for a doctor of philosophy degree at Boston University.

On the way home Martin let Coretta know that he liked her very much. He called her the next day, and the next. That Saturday night she invited him to a party. To her surprise, he knew all the latest dance steps. She noticed how the other girls crowded around him.

That winter the two busy students found time to go to concerts, movies, and dances. Martin liked music too, Coretta discovered. He had sung in his college choir. The two spent long hours talking about their careers and about the future. They shared the same dream. Both wanted to use their educations to help others, especially the poor.

Summer came, and vacation. "Come to Atlanta," Martin invited. "Meet my family."

Coretta went to meet the Kings. The Reverend Martin Luther King, Sr., was pastor of Ebenezer, one of Atlanta's largest churches. His wife, Alberta, played the church organ and directed the choir. Like Coretta, young Martin had an older sister and a younger brother. His sister, Christine, was a reading teacher. She was also musical and sang beautifully. His brother, Alfred Daniel, worked as a businessman and later studied to be a minister. Coretta liked them all, and she liked Atlanta.

After a visit with her family in Alabama, she returned to Boston. The next school year she faced a great decision. Martin King asked her to be his wife. "A preacher's wife?" she asked herself. "No! I want to be a concert artist."

But in the end her answer was yes. On

June 18, 1953, they were married in the garden of her parents' home. Martin's father married them. Coretta wore a long blue dress trimmed with lace.

Coretta and Martin moved into a four-room apartment in Boston. Martin continued to study for his doctorate. Coretta changed her program at the conservatory to music education, with a major in voice. "I will try to be a good minister's wife," she said.

The following year Coretta graduated, and her husband finished most of his studies. Job offers came to him from churches and colleges in both the North and South. Life would have been easier for them in the North, but Coretta and Martin decided to return South. "That is where I am needed," Martin said. He became minister of Dexter Avenue Baptist Church in Montgomery, Alabama.

Montgomery was only 80 miles from

Coretta Scott and Martin Luther King, Jr., on their wedding day, June 18, 1953

Coretta's home, so she saw her parents often. The Scotts were proud of their children. Edythe had started to teach. Obie was studying to be a minister.

Coretta and her husband lived in a frame house which the church had provided for the minister's family. They bought a piano so Coretta could practice singing every day. On Sundays she sang solos with the church choir.

She was also Martin's secretary. He spent part of each day writing the thesis for his Ph.D. Coretta typed the first copies of this long paper.

In June 1955 Coretta traveled to Boston to see her husband receive his doctor of philosophy degree. The following November their first baby, Yolanda Denise, was born. They called her Yoki.

Coretta King was happy. Each day seemed to bring more joy than the one before.

6. Walking Tall Together

Coretta's quiet life changed in late 1955. All that year Dr. King had worked hard with a group of civic leaders. They were trying to end the unfair laws which made life so hard for the black people of Montgomery.

One big problem was the segregation on city buses. By law, black riders sat on back seats. If a bus became crowded, they were expected to stand and give their seats to whites. Anyone who complained was in danger of being beaten or jailed.

On the first of December, 1955, a gentle black woman named Rosa Parks got on a bus after work. When the white riders crowded on, the driver ordered her to give up her seat. Rosa Parks refused, and she was thrown into jail.

News of the arrest spread fast. Angry citizens called for action. Dr. King met with black leaders in his church. By Saturday they had settled on a plan of protest. "Boycott the buses!" They sent the word out all over the city. "Don't ride the bus on Monday, December 5."

That weekend Coretta saw little of her husband as he worked to plan the protest. Yoki was only two weeks old, so Coretta had to stay home. She helped, though. Each day she answered the phone, typed notices, took messages, and gave out information.

Sunday night Coretta and Martin King worried together. The boycott could only work if people stayed off the buses. Would black people be willing to walk?

Monday morning Coretta got up before six. Anxiously, she watched from a window for the first bus to roll past. Soon she saw headlights coming down the dark street. Coretta held her breath as the lights moved closer, closer. *Empty!*

"Martin, Martin, come quickly," she called out. "Darling, it's empty."

Holding hands, they watched in amazement. The second bus was empty, the third, and those that followed. The Montgomery Movement had begun.

The leaders of the boycott formed the Montgomery Improvement Association to keep the protest going. Dr. King was chosen president. One person who worked side by side with him was Ralph Abernathy, another young black minister. Abernathy and his wife were close friends of the Kings.

Coretta well knew the danger Dr. King faced in leading the protest. She believed that white people would become enraged. Blacks had never before tried such a bold move in the South. Still, Coretta smiled and gave her husband support. "You know that whatever you do, you have my backing," she told him.

Dr. King was a brave leader. He was a good speaker, and thousands of people came to church meetings to hear him.

Dr. King speaks at a bus boycott meeting in Montgomery as Mrs. King listens intently.

"We must protest," Dr. King taught, "but the protest must be peaceful. We must never harm or destroy anyone or anything. Instead, we must work to change laws that are unfair or unjust."

Through the cold and the rain of that winter, 50,000 black people walked peacefully. Those who had cars drove others to work and school. At first the boycott leaders asked for equal treatment on buses. Bus owners and city officials refused to listen. So the leaders asked the courts to put an end to all segregation on city buses. "We will walk for equality," the people promised.

Stories of the protest made headlines all over the country. Every day people read about it and watched the action on television. Citizens, black and white, sent money to help.

Almost overnight Dr. King's face became well known throughout America. He was only 27. The news pictures often included his wife and baby daughter.

With the sudden fame came danger, as Coretta had known it would. One day she answered her telephone. The voice at the other end was filled with hate. "You'd better tell your husband to get out of this city while he can. We're going to get him for sure."

Coretta sat in a chair, holding her baby. She tried to think calmly. Their lives were at a crossroads. She could help her husband with his work. On the other hand, she could ask him to leave the city. Coretta made her choice. "I must stand beside my husband. We will stay."

The hate calls kept coming. Letters brought more threats. And city officials warned that they would get tough with the boycott leaders. The bus company, the businessmen, the city, all were losing money because of the boycott.

One day a church member hurried to Coretta's home, calling out as she ran. "Mrs. King, they got him," she cried, tears running down her face. "They arrested Dr. King."

Coretta took the news quietly. Soon church members began to telephone that they would help. In a short time a crowd of people gathered at the jail. The jailer became frightened and quickly let Dr. King leave.

When her husband got home, Coretta greeted him with a kiss. That night they had a long talk. They both knew that the weary walkers took courage from Dr. King's courage. If he and his wife could remain fearless in the face of danger, so could the walkers.

Coretta King knew there was no turning back. The peaceful struggle for civil rights must go on. Her husband must lead the Movement.

7. Courage and Nonviolence

Coretta sat in her living room, talking with a good friend, Mary Lucy Williams. Dr. King was preaching at a church rally. The January night in 1956 was chilly, so Coretta put on a woolen robe. She tucked a blanket around Yoki, who was sleeping in a back bedroom.

Whump! Suddenly something hit the porch. The loud noise brought the friends to their feet. "Run to the back," Coretta cried, moving fast. "It sounds as if someone has hit the house."

Just as they left the living room, a blast shook the house.

Windows broke and glass covered the floor. Smoke filled the rooms.

Mary Lucy started screaming. Coretta, her heart pounding, ran to find her baby. "Thank goodness," she breathed, "Yoki is safe." With shaking hands she reached for the telephone to call for help.

The doorbell started ringing as friends ran from all directions. The news spread over the city: *Dr. King's house has been bombed!* The mayor, the police, and other city officials hurried over. Coretta went from one person to another to let everyone know that she and Yoki were unhurt.

Dr. King rushed home. "Thank God you and the baby are all right," he said, hugging Coretta. Together they stood on the shattered porch. By then a crowd of people had gathered. "Dr. King's wife and child could have been killed," many cried.

Coretta watched her husband, his face serious, hold up his hands to quiet the people. If he showed hate or anger, the crowd might well start a race riot.

He showed no hate. The man whose family had narrowly escaped injury spoke of peace and love. "Go home. We must meet violence with nonviolence. Meet hate with love."

Coretta's face showed her pride and relief. Her husband spoke of his belief that peace and love would outlast hate and violence. "I'll stay strong," Coretta promised herself, "no matter what happens."

Both "Daddy" King and Obie Scott rushed to Montgomery that night. "Come away," the worried fathers pleaded. "Stay with us until it is safe here."

Coretta's answer was no. "My place is with Martin." She later told a newspaper reporter, "When I am away, I feel depressed and helpless." She knew how much her husband needed her beside him.

Dr. King often spoke of his wife's courage. "When I needed to talk things out, she was ready to listen, or to offer suggestions. . . . Afraid for me at times, she never allowed her fears to worry me or impede my work in the protest."

Other bombings followed during the next months. The homes of the Reverend Abernathy and several other boycott leaders were hit. So were many churches. Still the black children, women, and men held their heads high and walked.

Their courage won the attention and the goodwill of people around the world. Newsmen and visitors from far and near came to talk with Dr. King. Coretta welcomed them all. She talked with them until her busy husband had time to answer their questions.

Sometimes when Dr. King came home,

he brought more company. Often, too, important meetings about the boycott were held in the Kings' home. There were days when Coretta did not know if she would have three for dinner, or perhaps a dozen. "I can always whip up a good meal in a hurry," she told friends.

Coretta had taught herself not to get angry when things did not go as she expected. She learned to control her quick temper. Once, however, she lost it. Late one night she received 40 hate calls, one after the other. Finally, she took the telephone off the hook so her family could get some sleep. She put it back early next morning.

It rang at once—with another hate call. "My boys told me you took the phone off the hook last night—"

Tired and sleepy, Coretta shouted back in an angry voice. "It's my phone, and I'll do what I like with it."

There was always time for Yoki! She is seen here with her parents in front of their home in Montgomery and sharing lunch (below) with her mother.

"Oh, darling, don't talk like that," said Dr. King, taking her hands gently. "Be kind. Be nonviolent."

"I will," Coretta promised herself. Her husband had taught the world the power of peaceful action.

She began to use her singing talent to help the movement. On December 5, 1956, she gave a big concert in New York City. It celebrated one full year of the bus boycott. The concert brought in a lot of money to keep the boycott going.

Later that month a ruling from the Supreme Court ordered Montgomery to end segregation on its buses. At last the boycott ended. Black and white citizens began to ride the buses as equals. The weary walkers had won their case.

Coretta sang her joy. "Oh, Martin," she cried, "how happy I am to be living in Montgomery, with you, at this moment in history."

8. Dangers and Dreams

In 1957 Coretta and Martin King went to Africa for the celebration of Ghana's independence. From Africa they traveled to Europe for a short vacation. Wherever they went, Coretta noted, people knew Martin Luther King, Jr. Many knew Coretta King too.

They came home to continue their busy lives. Dr. King was in great demand as a speaker in all parts of the country. In October of that year Martin Luther King III was born. With two babies, Coretta still found time to help her husband.

She helped him in the writing of a book about the bus boycott. He called the book *Stride Toward Freedom* and dedicated it "To Coretta, my beloved wife and co-worker."

In September 1958, Dr. King toured several cities to tell people about his book. Large crowds came to buy copies and to have Dr. King autograph them.

While he was gone, Coretta's brother visited her. The day Dr. King was expected home, the two of them talked happily together.

Then the telephone rang. A minister from New York City was calling. "I have some bad news for you, Mrs. King."

Coretta braced herself. *What now?* A plane crash? An accident? Assassination?

"Dr. King was stabbed as he was autographing a copy of his book," the minister said. "He is alive, but it is serious, very serious."

big protest in Birmingham, the richest city in Alabama. The leaders of SCLC wanted to show the country that segregation everywhere had to end. Before he left home Dr. King kissed Coretta and the children. "If I am arrested, I will call you," he said. Whenever he was jailed, he always called to tell her not to worry.

He was arrested, as the newspapers reported. Coretta stayed close by the telephone, but he did not call. Officers at the jail refused to say what had happened to him. It was the Easter weekend, and Coretta waited from Good Friday until Easter Sunday, not knowing whether her husband was dead or alive. She could not leave home because of her young baby.

At last she called the one person who could help—the president of the United States. President John F. Kennedy called back and talked with her. "We checked on your husband, and he's all right," the

Striding toward freedom! Coretta King took part, with Dr. King, in many of the protest marches of the Civil Rights Movement.

president said. "I want you to know we are doing all we can."

A few minutes later Dr. King called Coretta. He was unharmed. Soon he was out of jail and leading thousands of people in protest marches. Finally, the men who ran the city promised to end segregation in Birmingham. This great success gave hope to black people elsewhere. All that summer of 1963, they marched and sang for equal rights and integration.

Civil rights leaders were inspired to plan a great march on Washington, D.C. The march would demonstrate that black people were determined to gain the rights due all citizens. Americans of all races and creeds were asked to march together and show support for new laws to give equal rights to everyone.

Coretta and her husband arrived in Washington early. Dr. King had been asked to be one of the main speakers.

The night before the march she helped him work on this important speech.

"How does this sound, Corrie?" he would ask, reading aloud a word or a sentence. Dr. King often tried out his speeches and sermons on his wife. This time, as always, she listened and gave ideas for changes.

On August 28, 1963, Martin Luther King, Jr., gave the speech at the close of the biggest rally in American history. More than 250,000 people of all races were there to hear him. Tears filled Coretta's eyes as her husband's voice rang out like the tones of an organ. She knew the speech was one the world would long remember.

Dr. King spoke his hopes for his race, for his country, "I have a dream today—"

"Dream on," the crowd cheered.

9. Teaching the Children to Understand

"Corrie, I just heard that President Kennedy has been shot."

In horror, Coretta ran upstairs to join her husband. Together they watched the news on television. The president had been assassinated. The date was November 22, 1963.

"We have lost a friend," Coretta said sadly.

Dr. King's face had a thoughtful look. "This is what is going to happen to me also," he said.

Coretta moved closer and held his hand in her own. She knew he could be right.

A few months later, Dr. King went abroad to preach in Germany and Italy. He came home tired and thin.

"You need a checkup and a rest," Coretta told him. He agreed to go to a hospital.

Next morning a newsman telephoned. "Mrs. King, we have just received word from Norway that your husband has been awarded the Nobel Peace Prize for 1964."

Coretta felt great joy and excitement, but her voice stayed calm. "I'll get in touch with my husband." This was like Coretta. If she cried, she cried alone. When she was angry or excited, her voice seldom showed it.

After she hung up, Coretta called her husband. "How is the Nobel Peace Prize Winner for 1964 feeling this morning?"

"What's that?" Dr. King asked.

Coretta hurried to the hospital to celebrate with him. Photographers came to take their pictures. Dr. King had won a most important international award, given to the person who has best promoted world peace. He won it because he had used peaceful ways to bring about social change. The Peace Prize also included a large sum of money—$54,600 for 1964!

A party of family and friends flew to Norway to see Dr. King accept the award.

Dr. King accepts the Nobel Peace Prize.

Coretta watched proudly as he was honored. She later said, "Somehow I saw in that experience a purpose, as though everything was taking place according to a plan. . . . It helped me and it strengthened me." She agreed with her husband that he should give the prize money to civil rights groups.

During that exciting year Coretta gave her first official "freedom concert." It was held in New York City's Town Hall. Coretta wrote the program to tell the story of the Civil Rights Movement. She talked about events, recited poetry, and sang spirituals and freedom songs. Her high soprano voice sang of the black American's struggle for freedom, "Lord, I can't turn back."

Over the next few years, Coretta gave more than 30 freedom concerts all over America, and in Europe. She used the $50,000 from these concerts to help SCLC.

By the middle 1960s, Dr. King was traveling much of the time. When he was home, it was time for fun. Yoki, Marty, Dexter, and Bunny were proud of their father and loved him dearly. They enjoyed playing ball games and swimming with him, because he liked all kinds of sports. Dr. King found music relaxing too, and he often gathered the family around the piano to sing. Coretta saw to it that her children grew up with music, for she remembered the joy it brought to her early life. Each child learned to play at least two instruments.

When it was time to say good-bye again, the children were sad. Coretta explained in simple words why their father was in jail so often, and why he led protest marches. "There are many people who don't have food, or warm clothing, or nice homes to live in," she told them. "Daddy is trying to help these people."

Making music together: Yoki, Bunny, Dexter, and Marty, with their mother

She also told them about segregation. "Why can't we go to Funtown?" Yoki wanted to know. Funtown was an amusement park in Atlanta.

Gently, Coretta let Yoki know what the "Whites Only" signs meant. "Your daddy is trying to make it possible for you to go to Funtown and any other place you want to go."

The children grew up learning to share

Dr. King with the world. "You are helping too," Coretta told them, "by being willing to share him." She encouraged them when they showed thoughtfulness. "You are such wonderful and understanding children, and mummy is so proud of you."

The King children learned to share in many other ways. One year they learned firsthand that Christmas is a season for loving and giving. Instead of receiving many gifts, each child picked only one. Marty and Yoki chose skates. Dexter picked a fire truck. Bunny got a toy bunny rabbit. The other gifts the children would have received went to poor children. Their best present was a whole day with their father at home. It was one of the happiest holidays the family ever spent.

In 1966 the King children learned about a new movement their father was leading. He began a "war against poverty," an effort to get better housing and jobs for all poor people, white as well as black. Coretta went with him to Chicago, where they lived in a rundown building in the slums. They did this to dramatize how millions of poor people had to live in big cities.

That summer Coretta brought her children to live in the slums. Yoki, Marty, and Dexter were allowed to join in some of the protest marches. Even Bunny marched once, but she became tired and had to be carried on someone's shoulders.

Coretta and the children heard Dr. King speak out against wrong wherever he saw it. He spoke out against the war which the United States was fighting in Vietnam. In 1968 he made plans with SCLC leaders for a bold Poor People's March, to bring the poor of the nation to Washington, D.C. Laws must be passed to help them, he said.

March 1968 was a busy month for the Kings. Ten-year-old Marty and seven-year-old Dexter went with their father on a trip through Georgia to talk with poor people. Later that month Coretta went to Washington to a peace conference.

On April 3rd, Dr. King's war against poverty took him to Memphis, Tennessee. Black garbage collectors were asking for better wages. Dr. King went to help them protest.

The next afternoon, Coretta took Yoki shopping. Dr. King had promised to call them that night.

When the call came, it was from the Reverend Jesse Jackson, who worked with Dr. King. "Mrs. King, Doc just got shot—"

"I'll check the next flight." Coretta had prepared herself for this moment, hoping it would never come. Already her children were listening with wide-eyed attention to the news flashing on television.

Dexter ran to take her hand. "Mummy, when will daddy be back?"

"Dexter, I'll call you from Memphis and let you know."

"I'll help you pack, mummy." Yoki tried not to cry.

Coretta kissed each child. By then the mayor of Atlanta had come to take her to the airport. It was there that she got the sad news. Dr. King was dead.

Coretta hid her grief and remembered the things that had been important to her husband: love, justice, peace, faith. She went home to her beloved children and helped them accept the loss without anger. "Your daddy wouldn't want you to hate." She received people, the poor and the famous, who poured into Atlanta to show their love and respect for the great leader.

The day before her husband's funeral, Coretta King went to Memphis. "I think

Coretta thought she should go to jail too, like other women who were taking part in the struggle. Her husband talked her out of it. Their three children needed one of them at home.

Dr. King encouraged her to help in the struggle for equal rights in countless other ways. And he supported her in her work with peace groups. Ever since her college days, Coretta had been interested in the movement for world peace. In Atlanta she joined the Women's International League for Peace and Freedom. As a member, she went to Switzerland in 1962 for a big meeting. "The women of the world can become a most powerful force for peace," she said.

A year later Coretta's fourth baby was born. She was named Bernice Albertine, for her two grandmothers, but everyone called her Bunny.

At this time Dr. King was leading a

From Atlanta, Dr. King called upon people everywhere to join him in the fight for equal rights. Thousands answered his call. Students led "sit-ins." Day after day black students sat at "white" lunch counters and asked for service. They kept on sitting until they were either served or put out by force.

Black and white citizens took "freedom rides" to integrate trains and buses in the South. They sat together on seats marked "Whites Only." These brave freedom fighters never used any weapon—except that of love. They were beaten and jailed. Many were killed. But they still carried out Dr. King's teachings of peaceful, or nonviolent, protest.

Dr. King was jailed time and time again. Once when Coretta saw him being led to jail, she started to cry. He turned and spoke softly. "Corrie, dear, you have to be strong. You have to be strong for me."

leading new crusades. He had joined with other ministers to form the Southern Christian Leadership Conference, called SCLC. This group promised to push for equal rights until segregation disappeared. Dr. King was elected president, and the SCLC offices were set up in Atlanta.

Dr. King resigned from Dexter Church and moved his family to Atlanta. He led the SCLC and served as copastor with his father at Ebenezer Church. Coretta was as sad as her husband to leave the church and people they loved in Alabama. They named their second son Dexter Scott, for the church and for Coretta's family.

At Ebenezer, Coretta helped out with church clubs and planned church meetings. She sang in the choir, along with Dr. King's sister, Christine King Farris. Some Sundays both Coretta and Christine sang solos. Both were talented women, and they were as close as sisters.

For once Coretta broke down and cried. Even so, her mind and hands raced ahead to things she had to do. Call the airport! Call Daddy King! Get someone to stay with the children! Pack some clothes—

Coretta rushed to New York. Dr. King had been taken to Harlem Hospital, where doctors removed the knife from his chest. A woman who seemed mentally ill had stabbed him.

Coretta stayed close beside her husband. In the hospital, offices were set up for her on the first floor. From there, by mail and by phone, she tried to carry on her husband's work for civil rights.

When Dr. King was well enough to go home, she still helped with his work so he could rest. She went to Washington, D.C., where she led a march for him and gave his speech.

By 1959 Dr. King was well once again. He devoted more time to directing and

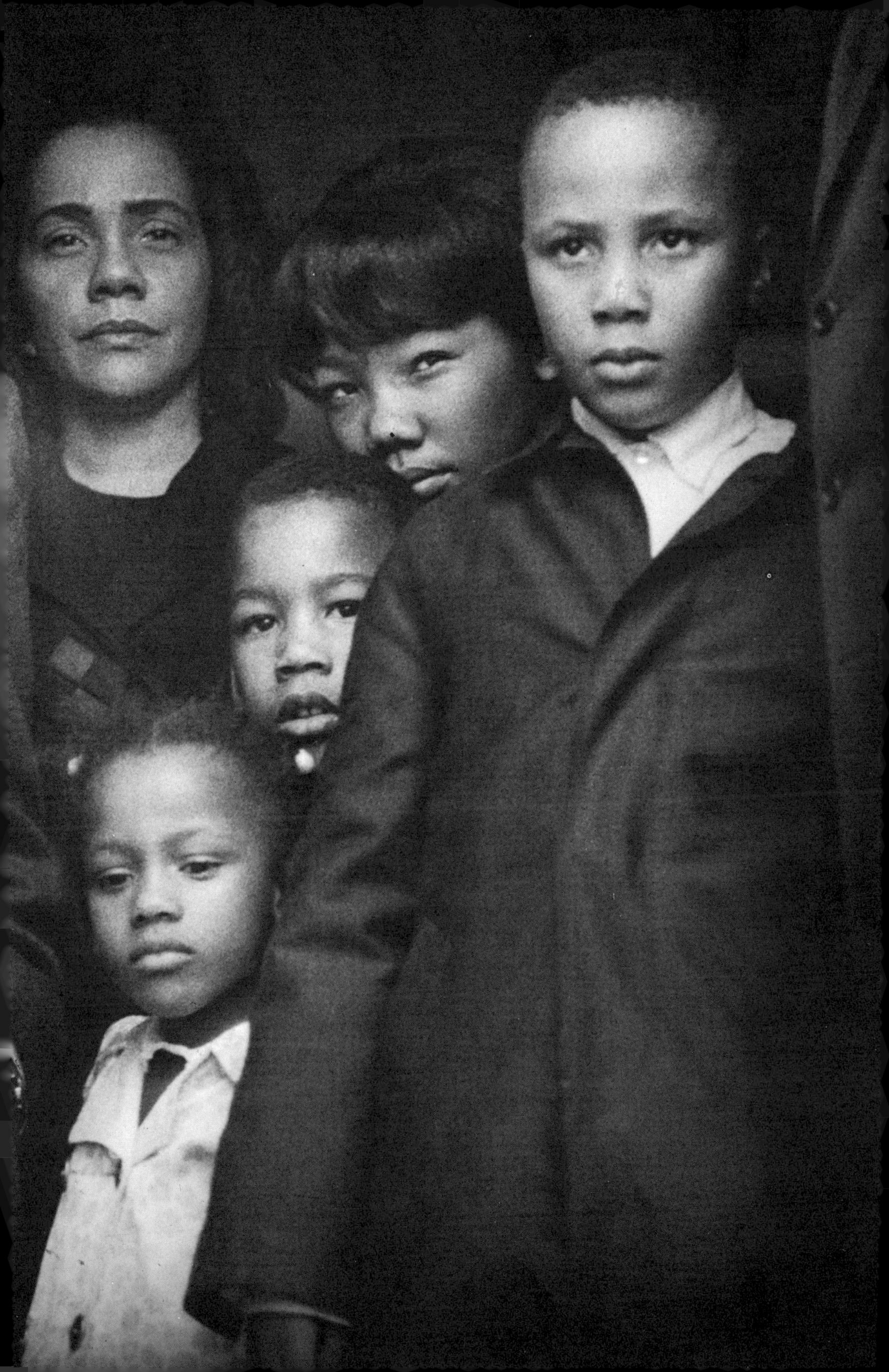

Martin would want me to go," she said. Holding her head high, she led the garbagemen in the peaceful march her husband had planned. Yoki, Marty, and Dexter marched beside their mother.

After that, Mrs. King and her children came home to put the Peaceful Warrior to rest.

Marching in Memphis in Dr. King's place

10. "We Must Carry On!"

Coretta, Marty, and Yolanda sat aboard a jet bound for England. It was Friday, March 14, 1969. Coretta was tired. She had given three major speeches in the past three days. She was worried about the hundreds of speeches and appearances she had turned down. People all over the world admired the dignity and courage she showed when her husband was assassinated. They took comfort from hearing her talk about Dr. King and about his ideas.

When the airplane landed in London, newsmen and television cameramen waited. Coretta hid her weariness behind a smile. She shook hands, posed for pictures, and answered questions. After a year she had grown used to the publicity.

On Sunday, the evening service at St. Paul's Cathedral made history. Coretta King became the first woman ever to speak from its pulpit during a scheduled service. Not even the great English queens had ever done so. Millions of people watched the service on television.

On Monday, Coretta gave a speech in Westminster Abbey. The chairman of the meeting said, "Coretta has taken upon herself the burden of proving to the world that Martin Luther King's death was not the end of his life's work."

He was right. Coretta called upon people everywhere to help. "We are going to continue his work to make all people truly free and to make every person feel that he is a human being."

Coretta became one of the directors of SCLC and helped to keep the Civil Rights Movement going. Whenever poor black workers fought for better pay and working conditions, she went to help them. The poor people did go to Washington for the protest march Dr. King had wanted. Coretta led the march and gave a speech as Dr. King would have given. Whenever peace groups met or marched, she went or gave her support.

Coretta chose to stay in the red-brick home in Atlanta. She added a full basement to make office space and to house Dr. King's papers and belongings. "This way I can work and still be near the children," she decided. Coretta always said, "My children come first."

In 1969 her autobiography, *My Life with Martin Luther King, Jr.*, was

**Coretta Scott King:
Carrying On Dr. King's Work**

Welcomed by Indian women in New Delhi (above) and speaking from the pulpit of St. Paul's in London

Taking Dr. King's place at Harvard's Class Day

Greeting a member of the congregation at Ebenezer Church

Making a speech at the Poor People's March in Washington, D.C.

published. The best seller was printed in at least 20 foreign languages. The story appeared in paperback and in magazines and newspapers. Coretta dedicated the book to the memory of her husband and to her four children, "who may live to see the realization of The Dream."

Coretta King became one of the best-known women in the world. Her picture appeared on covers of leading magazines. American college students named her "Most Admired Woman" in 1968, and again in 1969. Also in 1968 she won the "Woman of the Year Award" given by the National Association of Radio and Television Announcers. And she became the first woman to give the Class Day Address at Harvard University.

More than fifteen colleges and universities have awarded Mrs. King doctorates.

Coretta has been honored by foreign countries as well. In 1968 Italy gave her a "Universal Love Award," and she traveled to Rome to receive it.

One day in 1974 Coretta and her children shared exciting news. Their pictures were on a Ceres Medal! These medals, named for the Roman goddess of agriculture, are awarded by the United Nations. They honor leaders who work to see that all people have enough food.

The King children were even more thrilled when they saw the Ceres Medal, which honored their mother. Coretta's picture was on one side. On the other side were the pictures of the four children, representing future generations. The words were from a sermon preached by Dr. King shortly before his death: "Tell them I did try to feed the hungry."

11. "Keeping the Dream Alive"

The telephone woke Coretta King early one fall Friday in 1975.

"Hello, mummy." It was Yolanda, calling from Smith College in Massachusetts. She was a senior there and wanted to know her mother's thoughts about a school for graduate studies. Yolanda had acted in several plays and was planning a career in the theater.

Coretta listened and gave her advice. "Fine," she ended. "We are all coming up in two weeks to see you in the new play."

Coretta, now wide awake, moved about her bedroom. One side of her oversized bed was always covered with letters to be answered, papers to be read, speeches to be written.

Dexter, fourteen, and Bunny, twelve, began to get ready for school. Bunny planted a kiss on her mother's cheek. "Remember to buy the things I need for my camping trip—for a whole week."

Dexter showed his good-natured grin. "Can you get some film for my camera?"

"Yes, Dexter, and do your homework today if you want to go to the football game tomorrow." Coretta turned to Bunny. "Practice your violin and piano lessons when you get home."

After the children left, Coretta stood looking around the living room. Photographs that covered the walls here and throughout the house told the story of her life. There were pictures of her parents,

Dr. King, her children, President Kennedy, civil rights workers, protest marches, freedom concerts—

A secretary buzzed from a downstairs office. "A congressman wants to speak with Mrs. King." Meanwhile, two more calls were waiting for her on other lines.

After she had finished talking, Coretta started to read through a stack of mail. A typical day for Coretta King had begun.

In late afternoon Marty, a freshman at Morehouse College, came by as he did every day. The four King children have always been very protective of their mother. They have understood her work and shared her with the world, as they shared their father.

"You came just in time," Coretta told Marty, smiling. She had promised to meet a writer that day, but had not found the time, she explained. Now she telephoned

Coretta King and her growing family: with Yolanda backstage; helping Bunny practice the violin; with (left to right) Dexter, Yolanda Marty, and Bunny in Atlanta

the writer. "My son will come to get you. We would like for you to have dinner with us."

Although she was deeply involved with work, Coretta still found time to be thoughtful to guests. At dinner, Dexter and Bunny showed the same friendliness.

It was near midnight when Coretta and the writer had the interview. "Mrs. King, how can you handle so many things at once?" the writer asked. "One minute you are discussing a problem of national importance. The next you are helping the children with their worries. Yet you stay so calm, and you look so young and pretty."

Coretta smiled. "My husband and I lived with one crisis after another. I learned to deal with them as they came."

Early the next morning the telephone and Bunny awakened Coretta. "I play in two soccer games today," Bunny announced. She had always tried to do the things the older children did, and to do them better. All the King children excelled in sports.

Dexter and his cousin Isaac were already up and developing pictures. Coretta had given them a basement area for a darkroom. Dexter had already taken the pictures for the Kings' passports, and now the two boys were developing them. Coretta planned to take her children on a trip to Africa.

Coretta checked her day's schedule. At noon Atlanta's first black mayor, Maynard Jackson, was coming for lunch. At five Coretta was a guest at a reception in Ebenezer Church. After that she had a press conference. The following morning Flip Wilson, the famous entertainer, was flying to Atlanta to talk with her. And on Monday Coretta was due in Detroit.

Coretta King devoted her days to her

children, her church work, and carrying on her husband's work for peace and human rights. "I do not separate these in my mind," she often said. "They make up my world."

The King family has faced one tragedy after another. Dr. King's only brother, Alfred Daniel, drowned one year after Dr. King's death. Then on a Sunday in June 1974, Dr. King's mother was playing "The Lord's Prayer" during church services. Suddenly a shot rang out. Mrs. King, Sr., fell dead, killed by a young visitor who had a sick mind.

"Our deep religious faith keeps us going," Coretta explained. She agreed that there have been times when she has grown lonely and discouraged. Many people cannot understand her strong wish to carry on her husband's work. Some say that nonviolence can no longer be used to settle problems.

Working to keep the dream alive

Always tough-minded, Coretta has never let fault-finding stop her. She has been willing to work eighteen hours a day to see that her husband's name and ideas will be remembered. She has helped with the making of films and filmstrips which dramatize Dr. King's life. Two of the films have won top awards.

Like many other people, Coretta has worked to make Dr. King's birthday, January 15, a national holiday. "It's not for Martin Luther King, Jr.," she said. "He does not need it. The nation needs it."

On January 15, 1975, the home where Dr. King was born was opened to the public as one of America's historic places. Also, ground was broken for the building of the Martin Luther King, Jr., Center for Social Change.

Coretta's face lights up when she talks about the center. "Keeping the Dream Alive" is its motto. She sees the center as a permanent, living memorial to Dr. King.

The main building, Freedom Hall, has been planned with meeting rooms, offices, a theater, exhibition space, and a library. Here, people of all races and backgrounds may meet and learn. Books, tapes, films, pictures, and programs will tell about Dr.

King and about Afro-American history. There will be teaching programs for children as well as for adults.

Coretta King, president of the center, has worked hard to raise millions of dollars to build the project. Part of the money will come from the state of Georgia.

Mrs. King has inspired many people, from all races, to help. One of these has been Congressman Andrew Young of Atlanta. He was a close assistant to Dr. King in SCLC, and became the first black Congressman from the state of Georgia since 1871.

Many artists have used their talents to help raise money for the center. Coretta has used her singing. "I only wish I had more time for music," she has often said wistfully. As a Bicentennial event in Worcester, Massachusetts, she presented one of her freedom concerts in 1975.

Martin Luther King III joined his mother on the stage and led the freedom song, "We Shall Overcome." The audience stood hand in hand as they sang.

Afterward, a little black boy and a little white girl presented Coretta with a big bouquet of red roses. Coretta kissed each child. The evening seemed to symbolize what she and her husband had worked for through the years. There was still much to be done, but the "Colored" and "Whites Only" signs had been brought down. The black and white races were getting to know each other better.

In a speech celebrating Dr. King's birthday, Coretta King once told children of the best birthday present they could give him.

"Keep caring and keep trying to love one another," she said. "Martin Luther King had a dream that you would do this, and we all want to make his dream come true."

Index

Abernathy, Ralph, 43, 51
Anderson, Walter, 28, 30, 31
Antioch College, 25, 26, 27, 28-30, 32

Civil Rights Movement, 68, 79
  freedom concerts, 68
  freedom rides, 59
  protest marches, 69
  sit-ins, 59

Dexter Avenue Baptist Church, 38, 58

Ebenezer Church, 37, 58, 89

Farris, Christine King, 37, 58

Kennedy, John F., 61, 63, 65
King, Alberta, 37, 90
King, Alfred Daniel, 37, 90
King, Bernice Albertine, "Bunny" (daughter), 60, 69, 70 (pic), 71, 72, 74, 75 (pic), 76, 85, 87 (pic), 88, 89
King, Coretta Scott (Mrs. Martin Luther King, Jr.)
  and Antioch College, 26, 27, 28 (pic), 30, 31 (pic), 32
  and autobiography, 79-80
  awards and honors, 82, 83 (pic)
  childhood, 7-12, 13-20
  and children, 40-49, 53 (pics), 55, 58, 60, 69, 70 (pic), 71, 72, 73, 74, 75 (pic), 76 (pic), 83-85, 87 (pics), 88-89
  and Civil Rights Movement, 47, 57, 59-60, 62 (pic), 63-64, 68, 72, 76, 79
  and freedom concerts, 68
  and Lincoln High, 21-22, 25 (pic), 26
  and marriage to Martin Luther King, Jr., 37-38, 39 (pic)
  and Martin Luther King, Jr., Center for Social Change, 92-93
  and Montgomery bus boycott, 41-54
  and New England Conservatory of Music, 32-37, 38
  and Southern Christian Leadership Conference, 68, 79
  and trips abroad, 55, 67, 68, 77, 78, 80 (pics), 82, 83, 89
King, Dexter Scott (son), 58, 69, 71, 72, 73, 74, 76, 85, 87 (pic), 89
King, Martin Luther, Sr., 37, 38, 50, 57
King, Martin Luther, Jr. (husband),
  assassination of, 73, 74, 76
  and children, 69-71
  and Civil Rights Movement, 58-61, 62 (pic), 63-64, 69, 71, 72, 73
  and Dexter Avenue Baptist Church, 38, 58
  and Ebenezer Church, 58
  education of, 36
  and family, 37

95

and marriage to Coretta Scott, 37-38, 39 (pic)
and Montgomery bus boycott, 41-54
and Nobel Prize, 66, 67 (pic), 68
and Southern Christian Leadership Conference, 58, 61, 68, 72
and *Stride Toward Freedom*, 56
and "war against poverty," 71, 72, 73
King, Martin Luther III (son), 55, 69, 70 (pic), 71, 72, 73, 75 (pic), 77, 87 (pic), 88, 94
King, Yolanda Denise, "Yoki" (daughter), 40, 42, 46, 48, 49, 53 (pics), 69, 70, 71, 72, 73, 74, 75 (pic), 76, 77, 84, 87 (pic)

Lincoln High School, 21, 22, 23, 26, 29

McMurry, Martin (grandfather), 12, 15, 23, 24
McMurry, Mollie (grandmother), 12, 15
March on Washington, 63
Martin Luther King, Jr., Center for Social Change, 92-93
Memphis garbagemen's strike, 73, 76 (pic)
Montgomery bus boycott, 41-43, 44 (pic), 45-54

Montgomery Movement, 43, 47
My Life with Martin Luther King, Jr., 79, 82

New England Conservatory of Music, 32, 33, 38
Nobel Peace Prize, 66, 67 (pic), 68

Parks, Rosa, 42
Poor People's March, 72, 79, 81 (pic)

Saint Paul's Cathedral, 77
Scott, Bernice McMurry (mother), 8, 10, 11, 15, 17, 20, 21, 23
Scott, Cora (grandmother), 14
Scott, Edythe (sister), 7, 8, 11, 14, 15, 18, 20, 25, 26, 40
Scott, Jeff (grandfather), 14
Scott, Obie (father), 8, 9, 10, 11, 17, 18, 19, 20, 23, 24, 25, 29, 32, 40, 50
Scott, Obie Leonard (brother), 9, 11, 29
Segregation, 11, 16, 23, 26, 70, 94
Southern Christian Leadership Conference (SCLC), 58, 61, 68, 72, 79
Stride Toward Freedom, 56

Williams, Olive J., 22, 28, 31